Settling to learn

Louise Michelle Bombèr qualified as both a teacher and a therapist. She works with pupils, classes, whole school settings, teachers and support staff across primary and secondary phases. She provides consultations and training for education, social services, health and is a clinical supervisor for counsellors/therapists working in schools. She currently works as an Adoption Support Teacher for Brighton & Hove in an advisory capacity, and, in a freelance capacity, as an Attachment Support Teacher Therapist for The Yellow Kite Attachment Support Service to School which offers a range of services supporting children in care and adopted. She has developed a 7 day course to enable education staff to become Attachment Leads in their own schools (for this and and other courses for INSET days, Key note/workshops and conferences visit www.theyellowkite.co.uk or email admin@theyellowkite.co.uk). Using the developmental trauma framework, her work draws on attachment theory and intersubjectivity, integrating the principles of PACE and Theraplay. Louise is the author of *Inside I'm Hurting* (2007), of *What About Me?* (2011), and a contributor to *Teenagers and Attachment* (2009).

Dan Hughes Ph.D is a clinical psychologist working near Philadelphia. He has specialised in the treatment of children who have experienced abuse and neglect and demonstrate ongoing problems related to attachment and trauma. This treatment occurs in a family setting, and has expanded to become a general model of family treatment. He has conducted seminars, workshops, and spoken at conferences throughout the US, Europe, Canada, and Australia for the past 15 years. He provides extensive training for therapists in his treatment model, and consultation to various agencies and professionals. His professional practice involves teaching, training, consultations, and supervisions, while continuing to see families for treatment. Dan is the author of many books and articles. These include *Building the Bonds of Attachment (2nd Ed.)* 2006, *Attachment-Focused Parenting* (2009), *Attachment-Focused Family Therapy Workbook* (2011) *Brain-Based Parenting* (2012) and *It Was That One Moment* (2012), a book of his poetry and reflections on 30 years' practice. Dan is the father of 3 wonderful daughters, now adults, and 1 granddaughter. Visit www.danielhughes.org or email dhughes202@comcast.net

Settling to learn

SETTLING TROUBLED PUPILS TO LEARN: WHY RELATIONSHIPS MATTER IN SCHOOL

Louise Michelle Bombèr
and Daniel A. Hughes

Worth Publishing

www.worthpublishing.com

First published 2013 by Worth Publishing Ltd, London UK
www.worthpublishing.com

Printed and bound in Great Britain by Berfort's Information Press Ltd

British Library Cataloguing in Publication Data
A catalogue record for this book is available from the British Library

ISBN   9781903269220

Cover and text design by Anna Murphy
Illustration p.217 by Molly Murphy

Acknowledgements

LOUISE: I am so grateful to Dr. Kim Golding for her insight, wisdom and attuned expertise. I have really enjoyed working with her in so many varied contexts. My sincere thanks also to Dr. Tina Rae, Dr. Nikki Luke and Dr. Belinda Harris for sharing their findings and for working so diligently to ensure that we all have a better understanding of troubled pupils' needs in schools.

I'm so glad that I bumped into Karen Milton who is now not only a valued Occupational Health colleague, but a trusted friend, who has joined me on the next part of the journey towards true adaption and recovery, by ensuring we get the right kinds and doses of sensory input to free up our troubled pupils to settle to learn. Thanks for all the smiles, laughter and encouragement! I continue to be inspired by Clare Langhorne, an Assistant Head who was one of the first to facilitate Attachment aware practices and policies within her school in Brighton & Hove, Sussex. I am deeply moved by her continued sensitive care of individual pupils who have suffered greatly, despite the 'busy-ness' of schools nowadays and her senior role and responsibilities. For every child still matters.

I am so grateful that I have the most experienced and skilled clinical supervisor Penny Auton, who has nurtured and challenged me so well over the last 13 years. She may be in the background, but her influence on me and my practice has been considerable and I owe much of what I have learned to her.

It has been a great privilege for me to work alongside Dr. Dan Hughes whom I had followed avidly over the years since my days on the Attachment Team in Brighton & Hove. His down-to-earth and animated, playful approach motivated me back then in 2000 and continues even now. Because of Dan I am convinced that each one of us can make a difference in the lives of troubled pupils - whatever our role and responsibility.

Thanks to Martin Wood of Worth Publishing for his tireless work behind the scenes to ensure that this much needed subject is published, and published well. And to my insightful and incisive Editor, Andrea Perry, whose fundamental values around personhood resonate through every interaction and text she contributes to. It is a pleasure to work together.

Finally, I so appreciate the patience and support of my husband Jonathan Fordham, who constantly encourages me to extend myself out of my comfort zone to facilitate inclusion on every level! Thankyou. I couldn't have written this without you.

DAN: Before writing anything else, I would like to first acknowledge the delight and inspiration that has come from writing this work with Louise Bombèr. I am not an expert on the life of teachers and students in schools, but she is. As I know well the therapist's office, Louise knows well the classroom, the teacher's needs for training and support and the tremendous challenges and opportunities that are present in schools everywhere. What I might know about the psychology of adults, children, and relationships, Louise knows about how they play out in the day-to-day life of the school. To the degree that this work improves the ability of schools to meet the needs of troubled children, we all need to thank Louise.

In previous works I have acknowledged my great indebtedness to my parents, siblings, children and granddaughter. Also my teachers and mentors and colleagues and friends. Each had added so much to my life, to my understandings about people and relationships and how to help those who have been traumatised to heal, integrate, and thrive.

Now I would like to acknowledge my students and clients - adults and children. They too have greatly added to my understandings and also to the meanings of my life. They have greatly influenced me and my development and their influence has become greater when I learned how to allow them to have an impact on me, to touch me. The more that I understand and use PACE (playfulness, acceptance, curiosity, and empathy) which is mentioned throughout this book, the more that I develop alongside the person with whom I am engaged. If I am not open to being influenced by my students and clients, then I am less able to have an influence on their lives as well.

An example: A former student of mine, David, has been volunteering for quite some time in an orphanage in northern Uganda which has been ravished by war for years, and where a rebel army has forced many children - after killing their parents - to become child soldiers. That army has finally been driven from the area. A brave young man, Richard Akana, who also witnessed the murder of his parents, founded an orphanage for the many children in need there and it is here that David came. He has provided great support and training for Richard and his staff and the children in his care now have a better life than thought possible. During an activity with David and some of the children, Richard was asked to describe something that makes him happy. Richard replied: "PACE!" He believes that PACE has made a great difference in the quality of care that he is able to provide for the children.

How have Richard and David influenced me? They have reminded me to never forget and to never underestimate what we bring to a relationship with someone when we come with an attitude of PACE. They have filled me with gratitude and awe over the good that individuals can do for others. They have made me aware again that our greatest gift to another is simply our open engagement in his or her life. Such engagement, for me, is greatly enhanced when I am present with PACE. I am indebted to Richard and David for helping me to know this truth more deeply than before.

Preface

I began my career with vulnerable children some 30 years ago, working in women's refuges, child protection units and then going on to found two children's charities; Place 2 Be which offers counselling to children in schools, and Kids Company, which as I write supports some 36,000 children, young people and families annually. In 30 years, sadly, the statistics have not changed. One in four children in inner city classrooms is experiencing significant psycho-social challenges.

With the constant exposure to toxic stress and the relentless fear, childhood becomes about survival. Recent research carried out by UCL (2013) demonstrated that one in five of the children who accessed Kids Company's educational facility, the Urban Academy, had been shot at and/or stabbed, and 50% of the children overall had witnessed shootings and stabbings in the last year. Sometimes survival is about life and death, at other times it's about maintaining dignity in the face of abuse. Any child who has to prioritise survival will experience difficulties in accessing education. There isn't enough stillness of spirit: sometimes the self feels scattered, and despair prohibits the belief that step by step achievement is possible. Whilst struggling with a decimated sense of self and devastating dysregulated emotional states, attachment to a caring adult becomes a lifeline.

Rarely do our political leaders comprehend the importance of loving care in the classroom. Like military generals, they believe through sanctions and rewards children can be driven towards attainment. For those who have organised brains and stable emotions, the march to achievement is possible. But sadly, for one in four children, no matter how much they are punished, it doesn't lead to learning; it just destroys another layer of self-esteem.

So this book is a gift to teachers and support staff who deep down understand the potency of love, and who just need permission to work with it to reach children who are yearning for attachment. Only when a child feels understood and sustained by another's love do they go on to see the value of learning.

It's an unpretentious, practical, yet visionary read, and we've all been waiting for it.

Camila Batmanghelidjh
London, July 2013

EDITOR'S NOTE

In many co-authored books, the writers find a way to combine their voices into one, and we don't really know who wrote what, though we may guess. Here, in honour of the relational approach the authors of *Settling to Learn* advocate between adults and troubled pupils in schools, the process of Louise and Dan's exchanges has been kept transparent. We hope you'll feel an essential part of the conversation between these two professionals as they share their experience and insight, mistakes and successes, with you and with each other. Each of their perspectives, drawing on their rich and extensive backgrounds and understanding, has a unique but complementary strength; and the whole is so much greater than the sum of the parts, as is true for us all.

NOTES ABOUT THE BOOK

* **Key Adult** An adult who is allocated to a pupil in the school context to take on the role of an additional attachment figure for that pupil. This adult is usually employed within the nurture facilities or special needs/inclusion department of the school - usually someone with an individual teaching assistant, individual support teacher or mentor background. Please note that it is not recommended that this role is given to class teachers or senior managers as these members of staff need their roles to be boundaried: their responsibility is to the whole class or whole school, not to an individual pupil.
* **Troubled pupil** For the purposes of this book we are referring to a child or young person who has experienced significant relational traumas and losses (such as abuse/neglect/violence and so on) in their early years within their family/home context. See *Inside I'm Hurting* (Bombèr 2007) for a more detailed list of the possible risk factors for these pupils that might now make them 'troubled' within the school context.
* To protect the confidentiality of individuals, carers or professionals, names and autobiographical details have been altered in every case quoted. Any case examples written are composite and drawn from a number of similar examples known to the authors from their experiences over many years of working with children and adolescents.
* To simplify the text, in case examples where specific gender issues are not involved, a single gender is used on occasion to represent the pupil who has experienced trauma, and a single gender to represent educational staff. No prejudice or gender bias is intended by this.
* To simplify the text, the terms 'child' and 'pupil' have been used on occasion to represent both children and young people. The strategies described are relevant to both primary and secondary phases, unless stated otherwise.
* To simplify the text, the term 'educator' has been used throughout the book to include everyone involved in a pupil's education throughout the extended school system.

Contents

(continues ...)

Contents (continued)

Settling to learn

Our joint statement

Louise and Dan write: *For such a time as this* ... We are acutely aware that we are writing this book at a very significant time within education, when important judgments are being made about what is 'best' for learning. We would like the opportunity here at the beginning of writing together to clearly summarise the foundation of what we will be communicating throughout our book, for the purpose of clarifying our position for everyone involved in education and for policy makers in the UK and further afield.

We do not believe that 'bad teachers' are the reason why many pupils do not settle to learn or reach their potential in schools. We believe that we have many traumatised pupils in our school communities that any adult - however skilled and experienced - would find challenging. None of us need any further criticism. We need to assist the many committed and skilled teachers out there within our communities to develop and maintain relationships with those pupils who actively reject such relationships, no matter how desperately our pupils need them.

We need to apply the knowledge that we now have - extensive and comprehensive knowledge - about how children and adults develop their emotional, cognitive, sensory, behavioural, and psychological abilities. This knowledge includes the thousands of research studies that have emerged from attachment theory and interpersonal neurobiology.

Those genuinely interested in researching the value of relational interventions offered by school support staff (to date mainly teaching assistants trained up in this model of support), need to ensure they use recent data, as schools have not had access to these findings till more recently. Surely the contribution made by teaching assistants needs to be evaluated in the appropriate context, as at the moment there is not a distinction between their different roles, and there should be. We believe we can be bold enough to state that teaching assistants trained up as Key Adults to work in this relational model make a significant difference to their pupils. Past research does not seem to distinguish between those who have been focusing on behaviourist interventions, and those trained up in the fully relational approach Dan and I advocate. We invite researchers to look into this.

The overriding conclusion that we have come to understand through this new knowledge is that pupils need relationships with important adults, if they are to be influenced by these adults to develop satisfying and productive lives. We have therefore got to get relationships back on the map in our schools.

THIS WILL MEAN

- ensuring that attachment theory and interpersonal neurobiology are core curriculum for all education providers
- increasing the number of support staff employed to be alongside teaching staff
- allowing time within the school day for relationship building
- developing creative and alternative ways of relating and providing activity for troubled pupils, informed by therapeutic practice
- increasing staff care so that their own care-giving capacities can be maximised

Too often, behaviour management does not facilitate the development of these relationships. So, rather than merely relying and insisting on traditional methods in our schools to deal with every pupil, we need whole school policies to be adapted *now* to include provision for individual needs and developmental vulnerabilities. This will mean that individual development planning will be necessary for troubled pupils within any educational setting. For too long we have thought that vulnerable students could 'do it if they wanted to', when, in fact, they can only 'do it' *within a relationship with a trusted adult*. For too long we have stressed the need for students to 'respect authority' without realising that such 'respect' needs to be based on their ability to 'trust authority'.

And we adults also need relationships with other adults if we are to provide relationships for vulnerable and troubled pupils who are frightened by them, feel that they do not deserve them, and so resist entering into them. We need quality, reflective time, built into the school day, to meet up with those colleagues who can be our Key Adults for our own support, so that we can then be freed up to be Key Adults for the pupils in our care. All human beings are designed for interdependence. To overlook this truth is to deny what it is to be human.

So, let's begin together to apply what we know to be true. Only then will we see traumatised pupils 'switching on' … to all they were intended to be - capable of making their unique contribution and a positive impact on their local communities, country and the world.

All children need relationships to thrive; traumatised children need relationships to heal.   Golding & Hughes, 2012

Introduction

If relationships are where things developmental can go wrong, then relationships are where they are most likely to be put right.

(Howe 2005, p.278)

Exclusion

Louise writes: In recent years, there have been, on average, 380,000 fixed term exclusions and 8,000 permanent exclusions per year (The Guardian 22/1/10) in the UK. It is widely recognised that the majority of these pupils will have experienced or are experiencing significant relational traumas and losses in their own homes. Relational traumas and losses are what a child might experience either through intentional or unintentional harm when he or she has to survive extraordinary levels of stress, often in a toxic familial context. Such factors can include emotional abuse, sexual abuse, neglect, physical abuse, witnessing domestic violence ... they can include being burned, beaten, starved, locked up and treated in other unbelievably cruel ways. Many of these children and young people, who are pupils in our care in our school, have already experienced countless experiences of being blamed, accused, manipulated, controlled, groomed, resented and looked upon as an inconvenience back at home.

The consequences of exclusion from their school for these particular pupils is therefore severe; yet another rejection and failure. Exclusion colludes with what Taransaud (2011) has called the pupil's existing 'internal survival kit' - increasing the pupil's already high levels of shame and fear, increasing his internalised sense of isolation.

This is a dangerous combination for the well-being and welfare of our pupils, for ourselves, for our economy and our communities. In fact, Dr. Bruce Perry warns that additional impermanency (for example that created by the loss and rupture of the relationships that the pupil had formed in the school that has now excluded him), can often have far worse consequences than the original traumatic experiences (Conference, UK: 24/5/11). He states that these children and young people need the experience of permanency in order to have the best opportunity to adapt and recover. The University of East Anglia and TACT Fostering and Adoption produced an executive summary about reducing risk and promoting resilience in looked after children in January 2012. Amongst their many recommendations, the need for stability and longer term relationships is highlighted (UEA/TACT 2012, p.11).

Some of the consequences of exclusion will be apparent within the criminal justice and mental health systems. Of the children held in custody, between a quarter and a half have been looked after (HM Inspectorate of Prisons/YJB, 2009). It is estimated that amongst adult prisoners, 27% have been looked after at some point (Social Exclusion Unit 2002, *Reducing re-offending by ex-prisoners*).

But we know that no-one is born 'evil'. It is far more likely that the excluded pupil or young offender was denied a positive and loving relationship in his early life and was deprived of the emotional care and attention necessary for his basic needs. Left unattended and repeatedly frustrated, thwarted needs can all too easily be expressed through aggression, to self or others. Abuse and neglect have a dangerous legacy, imprisoning the wounded child beneath the high and deep wall of adaptive defences he had to create to survive (Taransaud 2011). As long as this wounded child remains trapped, the more ingrained his negative view of himself, others and the world at large becomes, and the further apart from our shared reality and our common values the pupil becomes. The more cut off the pupil becomes, the more severe the possibilities. A shocking 60% of looked after children have some level of mental health problem (NICE) and, in addition, are often the most marginalised in our society (Young Minds, 2012) .

So the impact of relational trauma and loss is now well documented. We know we cannot continue on in our schools 'regardless'. We all need to explore new ways of being and relating in our schools in order to interrupt this toxic cycle.

Fortunately, the impact of providing sensitive, attuned care is beginning to be recognised. Our book expresses our understanding of the importance of relationships in schools, our profound hope that they will become a practical reality for every troubled pupil in education now and into the future, and our approach to enabling this to happen.

Resilience

Dan writes: In contrast to the young offender and excluded child is the young person who, while having had a very difficult youth, is now, as an adult, a quite content and productive member of the community. This person is considered to be resilient, having withstood significant hardships and yet still thrived as he developed. Resilient youth have been studied by Alan Sroufe and colleagues (2005). They found that in every history of the young adults they reviewed they were able to identify *at least one significant relationship with an adult.* Such findings have led to resilience itself now being seen as *secondary* to having had a meaningful relationship with an adult, rather than as an innate constitutional factor, and Louise and I agree with this view.

Many of the pupils who are excluded are also looked after in foster care. Their entire lives are impermanent: home, school, and their community. Having been failed by their parents, they are now failed by their educators, social workers, and government. We all need to stop for a minute to reflect on what the experience must be like for a pupil to always live with strangers, go to school with strangers, while walking down strange streets. These pupils don't even see familiar trees under which they might dream. They have no roots, and with no roots, they will not grow.

The relationship

Louise writes: Over time our society has become increasingly individualistic. Psychotherapist Sue Gerdhaldt, author of *Why Love Matters* (2004), has written prolifically about *The Selfish Society* (2010): a society that prefers to exclude rather than engage with difference and diversity. A society that still chooses to segregate the vulnerable, rather than include them. That being said, it was encouraging to observe the success of the Paralympics in 2012. The Games created hope for those of us who work alongside troubled pupils who present with emotional and social difference, rather than physical difference. However, we still have some distance to go within education to enable the possibilities and opportunities that difference, together with hope, allows.

Our society has become so preoccupied with speed that many casualties have been left behind. The pupils for whom success comes easily and who find relationships enjoyable are welcome into our schools. The children who struggle to achieve any success, and who are mistrustful of relationships, tend to receive fewer greetings. Our society wants fast turnover, and wants it now, overlooking the significance and value of reflection, and long-term planning. In our communities, highly sensitive individuals who have also experienced significant relational trauma and loss are most at risk.

By now, many of us are aware that we need to be urgently engaging more closely with the pupils in our care who have experienced significant relational traumas and losses - but the key question is, how do we do this? For a very long time now, we have been bombarded with a huge number of changes in our school activities, policies and education agendas. To survive as teachers, our focus has been taken up with the 'stuff' of school, rather than the relationship between teachers and pupils. And yet it's this core relationship that has the power to enable pupils to reach further and to achieve more - to settle into their learning at every level. We have neglected the very tool that is the most powerful of all - ourselves!

Too often we realise that many pupils are not reaching their potential. Too often we realise that they need something more than a perfectly delivered lesson or a good ticking off. All the research points us towards the significance of the direct correlation between emotional growth and learning. We know that developing safe and meaningful relationships with a few Key Adults is central to emotional growth. The same is true for learning. But we need to act on what we know. What prevents this happening?

The systems we are trying to work within are often traumatised too, because of the extraordinary stress around in schools at this time. Competencies are being questioned. Resources are being cut. Different education agendas are being delivered at a fast pace. Troubled pupils are present in all our classes. Staff to pupil ratios are decreasing. Staff care is being overlooked. All of these complexities compromise our own reflective capacity and ability to use ourselves as a strategic tool (Harris, 2008, 2010). We need to find ways of honouring and protecting this capacity as a valuable resource.

Quality relationships provide the necessary vehicles for adaption and recovery. As I've described elsewhere (Bombèr 2007), every relationship has the power to confirm or challenge everything that's gone on before. We now know that good relationships influence the positive development of both the structure and function of areas of the brain associated with social-emotional learning. This development entails increasingly coherent organisation and integration, which are key factors in mental health. A good relationship will provide the continuous, safe base that our pupils so desperately need for such healthy development: someone the pupil can turn to at times of need. A good relationship will also provide the safe haven to which the pupil can return from time to time, in order to then be able to go off, replenished, and fully engage in their different learning contexts. The pupil will be safe and ready to learn and explore his world when he knows that there is someone close by who is holding him in their mind and heart.

Opening up to another person

For pupils with disrupted attachment histories, the provision of an attachment figure in school, *in addition to* the primary attachment figure at home, can make all the difference. These pupils need countless, repetitive, positive and healthy relational experiences in order to literally 're-wire' those parts of the brain that have organised themselves to survive the overwhelming traumatic stress the child experienced in their early lives. What was once an adaptive response to a traumatising environment (that is, the response that ensured survival) now needs challenging in the safe context of the classroom. This is necessary for the pupil to function fully in school, to make the most of all the educative opportunities on offer to him, rather than for him to remain undiscovered behind his habitual defences.

These relationships take time to build and for trust to develop: the pupils themselves know this, as evidenced in interviews with children and young people in care by the charity *Young Minds* in their publication, *Improving the mental health of Looked After Young People: An exploration of mental health stigma* (2012):

> *"There needs to be time to make a good relationship ... before you open up to them."*

"I want one person to support me with everything, not loads doing the same thing"

"Too many people and types of support - I only need one person"

"Needs to be someone I can trust, someone who understands"

(pp.10-13)

These young people also say that the adults best able to engage in this important role with them are those already involved in their lives - their carers, and school staff. These pupils shared how they were more likely to open up to carers and teachers than workers within CAMHS (Children & Adolescent Mental Health Services) (p.3). So we need to be more geared up in our schools to take on these essential roles with the pupils we are supporting to settle to learn. Let's not forget how we are the best placed for these significant relationships to be forged. We are sometimes too quick to refer our pupils on to outside agencies when we (the teachers, the teaching assistants, the mentors, the caretakers, the admin staff, the catering team, the cleaners …) can make such a difference in their lives.

Regulation and developing a sense of self

The regulation of affect/emotion, in other words, the management of our feelings, is one of the primary keys to many kinds of success, and so *affect regulation* must be the primary target of all our interventions. (D. Howe, *comment to* Child Abuse & Neglect Conference East Anglia University, 21/1/2011). Affect/emotion regulation skills normally develop in the context of a good enough attachment relationship with the parent or carer of the child, during their early years.

Affect regulation is the capacity: a) for affects (states) and emotions to be actively and appropriately available - in other words, to know what you're feeling: b) for a person to feel safe and grounded whilst feeling an emotion: c) for the emotion to be experienced at a level that is appropriate to the circumstances: and d) for the emotion to be under the control of cognitive evaluation of the situation, through reflection. But more than that, our capacity for affect regulation provides a basis for developing a secure self structure (Walker, N, *writing for* TAG trauma and abuse group: www.tag-uknet/ra-article10.html).

What normally happens in schools is that pupils with a fragile sense of self and poorly developed self-regulation are expected to engage with and use the external control normally found in schools - just like all the other pupils. External control include the usage of rewards and sanctions. So for example, we expect Simon, a Year 4 pupil, to sit still and to focus on his work and that if he does so he will get ten minutes Golden time on Friday. And we expect Janey, a Year 8 pupil to settle herself, to not become over-excited by the peers around her and to complete her Design Technology project over the next month. If she does she will receive some house points for her tutor group.

But we need to ask ourselves a very pertinent question. How can a pupil who has a background of relational trauma and loss engage with *external* control if he hasn't yet developed a robust sense of self or sufficient *internal* control?

It is clear to us that most of what this pupil needs to learn cannot be learned alone or at a distance. Close proximity and sensitive attuned care are necessary, within a genuine relationship, in order to build up both his sense of self *and* sufficient internal control.

Internal controls imply the capacity to self-regulate. Regulation is learned primarily through the messages we internalise from the significant other people we relate to in our lives, especially in our early years. We discover who we are - what makes me 'me' - my states, sensations and feelings, through the eyes and mind of another person. This is called reflective functioning (*see* p.54). It is this process that gives us everything we need in order to regulate ourselves physiologically, emotionally and cognitively. It is also through reflective functioning that we discover who the other person is - what is in his mind and heart.

We believe that no-one in the educational context should assume that pupils who have experienced relational trauma and loss will have had sufficient, consistent, sensitive care in their home contexts for these internal controls to have come online to the same degree as those of their peers who did grow up surrounded by sensitive, attuned relationships. When the pupil has not been supported to develop such internal controls at home, we need to provide a school environment that recognises this lack, and facilitates their development at school. *Only then will these pupils be in a position to be able to both understand and utilise the external control used in the school setting.*

So why do we merely focus on curriculum, when surely we need to firstly pay attention to regulation? Of course these pupils will not be in a position to 'learn' if they are not first regulated. Optimal learning is only possible when a pupil is relaxed and settled - and this state requires regulation.

We are not saying that our pupils will never be able to use the external control we provide. But we will need to facilitate stepping stones in order to get there, just as we would within any curricular area of focus. These pupils are just not yet ready to make use of our external controls, unlike most of the pupils in our care, those who have experienced a relatively secure upbringing, who are ready. Pupils who have experienced relational trauma and loss are in fact 'working towards' developing a robust sense of self and internal controls. This takes time. And it will take a relationship with a caring adult if it is to be successful.

Dan writes: Our focus on relationships is supported by Paul Tough in his book, *How Children Succeed: Grit, Curiosity, and the Hidden Power of Character* (2012). The author summarises a great number of studies that demonstrate that 'non-cognitive' factors offer at least as much, if not more, to long-term success in life than does IQ or achievement on tests. These factors, which develop within the important relationships in a pupil's life, involve curiosity, self-control, persistence, resilience and general features known as 'character'.

Empathy

Louise writes: Research shows that pupils who have experienced maltreatment such as we described earlier can have significant difficulties with both social understanding and empathy. Some studies also reveal further complex findings; that despite an overall difficulty in emotion recognition, some maltreated pupils are actually *better* than their peers at recognising anger and fear (*see the meta-analysis and systematic review of the literature by* Luke & Banerjee, 2013). These findings make perfect sense when you consider that troubled pupils needed to adapt to toxic home contexts where they experienced extraordinary stress. These pupils would have needed to be skilled in recognising these two specific emotions in order to survive. The other emotions may not have been as important to them at the time but clearly this 'not knowing' will interfere with the many social aspects of life in school.

Because what served them well as adaptive responses in unhealthy, insecure contexts present as maladaptive responses within healthy secure contexts. Professor Judy Dunn has done some excellent work about how social understanding develops in a 'self interested way' (*for example, see* Dunn 1988). But what was protective can become a prison, as we mentioned earlier.

Dr. Nikki Luke who works at the Rees Centre for Research in Fostering and Education has conducted a cross sectional study of 20 maltreated children in local authority foster care and 120 of their classmates within the upper primary phase in eight urban primary schools. Luke & Banerjee (2012) cite the key messages from Luke's work which are that, on average:

- Maltreated children had both more negative and less positive peer-rated behavioural reputations than their classmates (for example, they were viewed by classmates as more disruptive and causing more fights than average, but were also seen as being less likely to co-operate with other children).
- They also had poorer 'social understanding' (the ability to understand feelings, beliefs and desires and their role in social behaviour), even on skills which have typically developed by the age of five.
- In the middle childhood group, there were no difficulties with recognising emotions - but their empathy was poorer in terms of the motivation to act on this recognition and help others.
- Children's difficulties with social understanding and empathy related to their problematic peer reputations as well as more negative behavioural self perceptions (that is, they were more inclined to feel like they were badly behaved).
- The systematic review (Luke & Banerjee 2013) also shows that some maltreated children can misinterpret social situations to assume a hostile intent in people's actions. This is also understood as a matter of adaption to the world they were living in.

All these findings remind us again of why these pupils are so at risk of being misinterpreted, misunderstood and excluded in the education system. With so much stacked against them there are countless opportunities for clashes in meaning. This is why the way we relate to our pupils is going to be so significant in their being able to move towards learning secure ways of being and doing. It is clear to see that we can either hinder or help the adaption process by how we are and how we behave in our relationships with them.

Resistance

When faced with resistance from pupils, some staff, feeling threatened, undermined or even scared, may have behaved defensively, becoming enforcers of power and control. Alternately, we may have opted to back off and to follow the lead of the pupil, either by becoming rescuers or by being overtly compliant (Taransaud 2011). Sometimes we will experience such powerful feelings of disempowerment that we will react with words and behaviours that seem to collude with and reinforce the already isolated world of the pupil. These words can strengthen the internal, negative beliefs of the pupil, meaning that they dig their heels in even further to protect their position. The pupil has formed the view that adults cannot be trusted. The pupil then clothes himself with what Taransaud has termed the 'omnipotent self' (p.11) (that is, a false sense of self or a contradictory presentation of oneself which may come across as hard, cold, powerful, and wanting distance). What gets hidden away is a fragile vulnerability buried deep inside, a vulnerability that needs to be defended at whatever cost.

Sometimes when we experience resistance we pull back, trusting that if we follow the pupil's lead then all will be well and the equilibrium will naturally find its place. But somehow these pupils seem to remain stuck. Rescuing, or being compliant with the pupil promotes a strong message of the pupil's needs being too overwhelming to handle. Such a message frightens the pupil, further causing him to remain stuck within his now maladaptive way of viewing the world (part of what has been termed, the 'internal working model', Bowlby, 1980).

We all need to understand that what is behind this resistance is both real and powerful. We also need to understand how not to become defensive ourselves in response to this resistance. Hard as it can sometimes be, we musn't allow ourselves to be side-tracked from our unique role of facilitating both adaption and recovery. It is only when we realise what's really going on behind the defence systems of pupils that we can optimise the power of our relationships. It is with this in mind that Dan and I have written this book.

If we are able to remain open and engaged with such pupils, rather than becoming defensive ourselves, the child's defensive stance is likely to reduce. Our pupils will then have the opportunity to consistently move onwards towards reaching their potential in school and further afield. At the moment, they are holding onto their defence mechanisms, because it was these mechanisms which may have literally kept them alive. They have buried their vulnerable selves deep down beneath the layers. Our role is to consistently provide a context that is safe, secure and stable, and interventions which communicate our genuine empathy, nurture and gentle challenge, so that this vulnerable self will be enabled to surface. Until it does, the pupil will be restricted in his or her spontaneity, creativity, exploration and learning.

Of course these pupils will resist our attempts to lead them into unfamiliar territory. Why would they quickly remove masks that served such a vital role? Whilst we obviously do need to be very mindful of varying our emotional and physical proximity so that our pupils don't become overwhelmed, we also need to actively engage with their 'window of tolerance'. We need to be slowly, slowly, gently challenging this window of tolerance to extend in size. Some wiggle space is necessary in order for these pupils to grow!

We all know what's good for us: but what we also know is healthy and appropriate is not necessarily comfortable. Let's be honest with ourselves and the pupils in our care about this reality. Focusing on gently challenging that window of tolerance will enable these pupils to take more risks and make more progress than probably they or we ever first imagined.

Dan writes: It is so tempting to think that when a pupil rejects having a relationship with us, it is because he is choosing to do so out of a mature understanding about what he thinks is in his best interests. We tend to say, we did our best, but we can't force it! It's harder to think that our pupil wants desperately to have a relationship with one good adult - just one - to reduce his fears, loneliness, and shame, and to begin to develop a positive sense of himself along with sufficient confidence that he can attain and does deserve having a good life. His resistance to having a meaningful relationship with a teacher, a mentor, or a teaching assistant and so on, is grounded upon his solid belief that he does not deserve one, that he is not capable of one: while at the same time, being terrified of trying to form one and only failing again.

What really matters?

Louise writes: Do these pupils really need more access to study opportunities, better teaching, different reading schemes, more computers, more effective discipline ... ? What if they just needed more access to you and to me? A genuine relationship. Is this a possibility? What if it really wasn't more complicated than that? What if the tool that we had overlooked - ourselves - was the bridge into a world of possibilities, that a genuine relationship with us, perhaps acting as a buffer, could switch on the pupil's 'thinking brain' and integrate it with his 'emotional brain'?

> Relational buffering is needed for those who have experienced relational poverty.
>
> (Dr. Bruce Perry, Conference,
> Centre for Child Mental Health, London, June 2013)

Dan and I would like to invite you into a world of relationship in school, that, in our experience, can open up far more possibilities than we ever first realised. If relationship really is the key, as we believe it to be, then perhaps the money invested into education could be more effectively used for those who have experienced significant relational traumas and losses who fail to respond as we want them to within the school context. We don't need to remain disempowered, going around and around in vicious cycles, continuing to 'do school' the way we always have done in the past.

In some instances, there are even moves to resurrect traditional approaches to a more focused curriculum, and the kind of tighter discipline from the Victorian age that didn't work for this group of pupils the first time around! Maybe we are panicking and proposing tighter controls as a knee jerk reaction to the crisis in our schools at this time? Maybe we don't feel safe in contact with pupils who repeatedly challenge and resist our interventions? When neither adult nor pupil feel safe, both are likely to rely on power in an effort to establish control and a semblance of safety, as we mentioned above. However, the tighter we attempt to control these pupils, the more resistant they will become. Watch and see. What happened to these pupils back in Victorian times? They were excluded. What we are currently doing has clearly not been working: if it were working, would our prisons be so full of those from the care system? A more punitive system is not what is needed.

If we continue as we are, the cycle will merely repeat itself. In light of everything we have learnt from neuroscience, how can we possibly consider it ethical to do so? Our school systems must adapt in line with research, or we will be left behind. Not only will we be left behind, but the pupils who deserve the best will suffer and be impacted for life because of *our* reluctance to do things differently.

Dan writes: To add one neuropsychological finding: both adults and pupils, when they are not feeling safe, tend to see all events as either right or wrong, good or bad. The focus is only on a behaviour and a response - either positive or negative.

When adults and pupils are feeling safe, both tend to be much more likely to search for the reasons for the events, and to be more comfortable exploring what is unique about this event, in order to form a unique response that fits the event. Yes, we are back to safety for all.

Relationships matter

Louise writes: Let's not overlook something that we have known about for a long while. Relationships matter and can make a difference. We are not promising it will always be easy, as it most likely won't be. Genuine relationships aren't easy all the time. They take hard work. But throughout this book, we will explore what it means to be involved with these pupils to a much closer degree than we have had permission for before.

Dan writes: While we certainly will be discussing this in greater detail later, we might also mention here that when we ask educational staff to work hard to develop relationships with pupils who resist them in every way possible, we need to also commit to our staff that we will not abandon them. Rather we will work hard to provide them with the support that they need in order to be successful. If the pupil will be able to change through a relationship with one teacher, for example, then that teacher - to be successful in reaching that pupil - will need a number of other adults to support him or her in a variety of ways.

The way ahead

Louise writes: So together in this book, Dan and I will be exploring the fundamental characteristics of what the relationship between ourselves as adults and a troubled child or adolescent might look like, a relationship that will help that pupil settle, and thus settle to learn. We will consider how we can *stay close* to these pupils

- both physically and emotionally. We will describe what *calm* is and how to facilitate calm both in ourselves and in those we want to calm. The significance of *expression* will be explored, in order to support pupils to truly understand our intentions and motives so that they have more opportunity to connect with others in a meaningful and genuine way.

The different aspects of Dan's model of PACE (playfulness, acceptance, curiosity and empathy) will be woven in, providing us with easy-to-use yet powerful dimensions that will strengthen our relationship and move these pupils on towards adaption and recovery - learned security. We will highlight the significance of *playfulness* and having fun, something that is often overlooked nowadays in our fast paced, serious and demanding schools. We will think through how *acceptance* can be communicated even when the going gets tough. We will be sharing tools that can facilitate *curiosity* on behalf of the pupil so that eventually they can be curious about why they do what they do, becoming increasingly self-aware. Self-awareness is the key stepping stone towards self-control. And we'll consider *empathy* at many different levels, how we can enable those who have previously been misunderstood and excluded to experience being known and understood, often for the first time.

Next we'll reflect on the importance of our *timings*: a sensitively attuned word, touch or look can make such a positive difference. A badly timed intervention can move a pupil into feeling overwhelmed, a state in which he seems to unravel and be unable to 'hear' us. Though nurture is necessary for pupils who have had difficult starts we must not lose sight of the need for *gentle challenge*. Gentle challenge and nurture are needed together and we've made sure to carefully entwine them throughout our book.

Together we will wonder how *creativity* can be used in all of our communications with these pupils. We will think about the importance of introducing the pupil to the concept of turn taking, *following and leading* - a necessary skill not just in school but in life! Because many of these pupils have no idea how to 'put things right' despite our assumptions, we will explore *reparative opportunities* especially in the context of relationships. Together we can provide the stepping stones these pupils need. So many of these pupils have a fragmented sense of themselves and of others, so we will look at how to support them to move towards having *an integrated view* of themselves and others.

These pupils have already revealed resilient features by surviving extraordinary stresses back at home, so now we need to strengthen this by providing further opportunities to extend this *resilience* into other contexts such as school and the wider community. As we are discussing school, we couldn't leave out the task of holding boundaries - *discipline*! We as responsible adults need to help pupils learn to socialise. We need to support them to join in and play their part within existing and new communities and systems, as this will prepare them for living their lives well into the future. But in light of what we know now, Dan and I believe that we must seriously re-think how we practise discipline with our troubled pupils within the context of our relationships.

Finally, we will conclude by considering all we can do to enable us to *persevere* - to remain, and to remain open and engaged and committed, although there will be times of great challenge and uncertainty. Our pupils need us to believe in them, not just for a term or a year, but for their entire time at school and beyond. We can share with them the gift of permanency if we learn how to persevere together with them, despite the odds.

This is the map Dan and I are proposing. We do hope you will join us on the journey! These key characteristics create the kind of relationship that will help our troubled pupils settle to learn.

These characteristics provide us with the keys we need in order to 'unlock' pupils who have lived lives of overwhelming stress. However, they also provide us with keys that are actually good practice for all the pupils in our care. We encourage you to trial them and see what happens. This book will open up many possibilities that you may not have considered before, practices that might have previously been protected for the therapy room only. We have discovered otherwise. In Dan's work amongst families and my work in schools we have found that there is so much we can do to make a powerful difference that can be integrated into normal, everyday life without incurring huge financial costs. We are looking forward to sharing this journey with you, knowing that increasing numbers of pupils will then be enabled to reach their potential, rather than remaining stuck. There is so much more we can do.

If we can understand how our troubled, vulnerable pupils might be interpreting themselves, others and their situation, we will have the keys we need in order to relate most effectively. Yes, we will need to relate, translate, find support, relate and translate again - but watch these pupils thrive. This is our aim.

Relationships matter in school, for all of us. Don't forget your keys!

Chapter I

Stay close

Key Adults act as a 'surrogate secure base' which can contain the inevitable anxiety engendered by the challenges of learning.   (Geddes 2006, p.141)

Louise writes: In our schools, we need to encourage education staff to be physically and psychologically close to pupils who have experienced significant relational trauma and loss. Being close implies physical proximity and remaining open and engaged. Being close communicates acceptance, containment, safety, attunement, attentiveness, responsiveness, structure and supervision. Being close assumes that we are actively present. Being close is how we start to make a relationship with the pupil who has been assigned to us.

However, generally speaking in school we are more familiar with encouraging distance, and even withholding relationships at crisis times within our schools: we all need to start challenging this practice. So in this chapter, Dan and I will be outlining how to be actively present, how to support your pupils to practise *relative dependency*, and how to support the formation of selective attachments. We'll look at resistance - your own, your pupils' and your colleagues' - and we'll explore the challenges that get thrown up if we continue to practise *relational withdrawal* in our work in schools. And we'll look at the kinds of fears some people have about the possibility of over-dependency, enmeshment and child abuse allegations.

Being actively present

Let's explore what it means to be actively present. Being allocated to a pupil but just remaining in the background is not going to be sufficient. We need to be both physically present and emotionally present. How can education staff get alongside a vulnerable pupil? Let's give staff direction to get involved *with the specific intent* of building genuine relationships. This means that you can't just remain a name hidden away in a computer or on the pupil's file! Sometimes schools only engage with the pupils who are known to be vulnerable *at times of crisis*. We'd like to invite you to challenge this practice. We believe we need our pupils to know who we are from the start. And not just known by name, but known as a real life person engaging with the reality of school life for and alongside him or her. Virtual reality won't replace the power of a genuine relationship with you in terms of genuine adaption, resilience, and recovery for that pupil.

Once we're with our pupil, we need to focus hard on activating our attentiveness, so that we notice everything that's going on for him or her in the 'here and now', blocking out distractions or intrusive thoughts. This will mean noticing different cues or lack of cues such as:

- Eye contact
- Facial expression
- Sparkle
- Tone of voice
- Pace of voice
- Shortness of breath
- Body movement
- Gestures

Activity and energy levels

To be able to do this well, we need to support ourselves to remain fully present in each moment we're together with our pupil. It's all too easy to become distracted by other matters or other demands - perceived or real. To help yourself stay focused, keep an eye on your breathing and on keeping your body grounded, so that you can be open and alert. Practicing mindfulness can go a long way in terms of helping you develop your capacity for attentiveness (*see* p.307).

When we are physically and emotionally present with our pupil, we're communicating some very important messages:

Other staff nearby need to be very careful not to inadvertently interfere with the kind of interaction I'm describing. When we take up this role, we need to ask other staff to trust us as we begin to make our relationship with our pupil, and we need in turn to allow other staff to do similar work. Even a ruffle of the hair or a casual comment from a passing member of staff who isn't part of the pupil's close team can unwittingly create distraction. Let's make sure the pupil and their Key Adult have some protected, quality space to be 'together'. Let's honour their relationship.

The beginning of the day is especially important for this but it's easy to get caught up in our preparation. How the pupil begins their day can provide you with vital clues as to the likely quality of the day ahead. Let's not waste this significant opportunity to be 'present'.

In the past, we were warned off becoming too familiar with the pupils in our care. Fears around over-dependency, enmeshment and child abuse allegations were rife (*and see* p.38-42). Now, knowing what we know, we need to be moving into a more balanced view and encourage education staff to stay close. What's the best way forward?

I'll map out the importance of supporting our troubled and vulnerable pupils to practise what I've described elsewhere as 'relative dependency' (Bombèr 2007) in the safe context of school. Clearly, wisdom is needed, and no care work should be entered into without wisdom, especially when getting alongside some of the most vulnerable members of our communities. By wisdom I mean that we need to use our intelligence, insight, reason and judgment in order to reflect upon the most appropriate responses for these pupils. We can't afford to be reactionary or too hasty in our choice of words or actions.

Practising relative dependency

In order to negotiate healthy interdependence, dependency needs to be practised first. Many of the pupils that we are concerned about in this book have not had sufficient experiences of adults -

anticipating their needs

or

responding to their expressed needs

or

meeting their needs

So as children, our pupils learnt quite early on to operate out of a pseudo-independent way of being. They learned to be self-sufficient, to fend for themselves - not to need anyone - to survive. Sometimes we look on and assume this way of relating is merely the pupil maturing fast; but things aren't always the way they seem. In fact, when these pupils are in primary, they can kind of get by. But as soon as the stressors increase, for example when pupils need to followe a greater number of adults in secondary, we can see how things unravel. We would be doing a disservice to these pupils if we were just to leave them in this pseudo-independent state. Is it possible for anyone to relate well, either in school or the working world, if they don't know how to move between dependency and independence at appropriate times, in appropriate contexts?

> *After lunch and now in fourth period, Janine, aged 15, is 'full up' with her teachers telling her what to do, telling her to do this and that. She has had enough of all this power, authority and control. She, Janine, needs to be in control all the time to stay feeling even a bit safe. She can't afford to follow the lead of the adults or to allow her vulnerability of 'not knowing' to surface, because who knows what will happen next? The pressure gets too much. Janine loses it by swearing and exiting the room, slamming the door violently.*

Sometimes we need to follow instructions. Sometimes we need to give instructions. Sometimes we need others to lead us or to provide for us. Sometimes we need to lead or provide for others.

Unfortunately there are no fast tracks for this kind of learning. It comes through experience. The only way is to engage in the experience of relating, and this takes time. Practising relative dependency is one of the biggest 'asks' for these pupils in our schools. They need to learn through experience that relying on a trusted other person can be rewarding, satisfying and productive. When they start to realise this, they can then move into a healthier place of *interdependence*, using both dependence and independence appropriately.

At the same time, we need to be mindful that some other vulnerable pupils will be indiscriminate in their attachments, connecting closely with whoever is passing by. This needs to be attended to as well, as what we need to be encouraging in school is *selective attachments*.

Dan writes: It seems that the function of these indiscriminate attachments is to induce relative strangers to 'like' the pupil, so that he or she will be safe, or at least feel safe. These children feel they are constantly responsible for their own safety and their overly familiar behaviour will achieve it, to a degree. They don't trust that a Key Adult (KA), a particular attachment person, will anticipate, respond to, and ultimately meet their needs. This tendency is common with children who spent their early years in an orphanage. It is also present with children who have experienced significant neglect in their lives.

Encouraging selective attachment

Louise writes: Many pupils will need us to direct them back to one or two staff - their Key Adult (KA) or back-up adult, or to their small team - form tutor, school counsellor, Key Adult and INCO (inclusion co-ordinator). Such direction isn't done with anger, nor as a sign that the pupil is or has done something 'wrong'. Rather the message - that the Key Adult or team will be of greater help and support for the pupil - needs to be communicated with positivity and confidence. Of course, routine requests and immediate situations might best be managed by the closest educator, but the child needs to be turning to their Key Adults for important learning experiences, and for comfort and support. We advocate that this way is best, even if it means a slight delay, so that the Key Adult or pupil's team have opportunity to respond as best they see fit, to work in an integrated way. This is because someone else getting involved runs the risk that the team's good work could be unwittingly undone by other people who are not 'in the know'.

For our support work to be effective we need the whole school community to be aware of the value and benefit of selective attachments. The whole school community needs to be aware that encouraging indiscriminate attachment can actually put vulnerable pupils more at risk.

So boundaries will be crucial *(discussed later on in this chapter and in Chap.16)*. Some staff will find the boundaries hard: they can feel as if they are rejecting the pupil in some way by sending them off to someone else. Other staff may have their own unmet childhood needs around needing to be wanted, and so may struggle in this area too. This is why it's so important that, as education staff, we attend to our own personal histories as we go along. You'll notice that Dan and I will be stressing this throughout this book: none of us can afford to let our own relational traumas and losses become enmeshed or acted out in the school context with our vulnerable and troubled pupils. As education support staff, we all need to stay aware of our own 'drivers' and 'triggers', so that we can be sensitive to the need to adapt our responses where appropriate - even if this means going against our natural more familiar responses, on occasion. Let's make sure *we* get the support *we* need, so that we can stay regulated and focused on our pupils.

With all the best will in the world, there will be pupils who will find these support interventions really hard. As we've explained, and we'll keep pointing out, this is one of the biggest 'asks' for a troubled pupil - to trust the grown-ups. Though we can explain we're working with their best interests at heart, there will undoubtedly be resistance.

Resistance

Liam, aged nine, has been sat at his desk for a while staring at his blank paper. He is clearly unsure as to how to get started. Pat, his KA, approaches him at a gentle pace, coming to sit alongside him. Turning his back to her, Liam mutters, "I don't need any help. I'm fine. Leave me alone".

Getting and staying close to your pupil is not likely to be an easy process; your support focus on staying close will most probably be resisted. Why wouldn't it be? Distrust and suspicion are 'evidence-based' from the child's real life experiences, and hard-wired into his or her responses. All of us do what we do because of what we have lived. However, with sensitive care and gentle challenge, pupils can be introduced to relative dependency over time, so that they can start to develop in this area and not remain stuck as a result of their past experiences with adults.

From time to time you may feel like giving up. The pupil's resistance can be really difficult to work with, especially when you may not be receiving the kind of appreciative responses you're familiar with in similar interactions with most of your other pupils. Being met with a cold stare or rejecting behaviours can leave you with powerful negative feelings; these can have a profound impact on your sense of well-being, and even confidence. We need to be mindful of this process; it's likely to happen to even the most skilful support person with even her most compliant pupil, at some point. Let's not underestimate that impact. Whether you are a Key Adult, a teacher or a Headteacher, such rejection can affect you. All of us want to be effective, and so regardless of how professional or experienced we are, we may feel it on a very deep level. Be aware that you may start to doubt your worth and value, and question whether there is any point in what you're doing at all. You may even begin to dislike the pupil. It's natural. We're human.

Perseverance is necessary *(and we'll come back to this at the end of the book in Chap.17)*. So find some support. Use your networks to re-build your confidence. Once you've made it through the 'first line of defence' you'll find, as the vast majority of us do, that the work really does become easier. When you're prepared for resistance, you'll know that you don't need to take this defence so personally. Then you won't allow it to impact your relationship with the pupil.

Dan writes: Yes, Louise, we are human. We need to have empathy for ourselves when we find ourselves pulling back from a pupil who is constantly challenging and rejecting our efforts to be engaged with him. It might help to know that this experience of discouragement, and a tendency to 'give up' when our pupils don't respond to our invitations for closeness, can also be explained by our emerging neuropsychological understanding about the workings of our brains.

Attachment behaviours (of the child) and caregiving behaviours (of the adult) emerge from the identical regions of the child and adult brains. Both attachment and caregiving behaviours are supported in the brain through a positive response by the adult (to attachment behaviours) and the child (to caregiving behaviours). This is obvious when we note how a child no longer seeks to form attachments with particular adults following a history of abuse and/or neglect. However, it's equally real that an educator's caregiving behaviours are placed at risk if your pupil doesn't respond in a reciprocal manner to your intention to provide for his care. The regions of your brain that are responsible for providing care are supported and enhanced when they experience a favourable response from the pupil you're caring for. To support these regions of our brains when the pupil is *not* responding, it's essential that we receive care from other members of the educational staff (*see* Chap.17, pp.343-4).

Louise writes: Some pupils' window of tolerance (Siegel, 1999), their capacity for having you close by, will be extremely limited. So you'll need to think about giving your pupil breaks from the intensity of intimacy with you from time to time. If you don't, your pupil may well tip into becoming overwhelmed, and then this could compromise his or her growing feelings of safety around you. So let's all be mindful of what Dan and I think of as the *dance of attachment* - a dance which, as for ourselves with our partners and friends, involves both togetherness and separateness.

We need to pay extremely careful attention to the pupil's body cues. Try not to be so involved with tasks that you fail to notice what the pupil might be trying to communicate to you. In most cases, body cues such as the way your pupil does the things listed below will give you a lot of information, letting you know what might be going on emotionally for him. The way he -

- looks away
- starts to slouch in his chair
- starts to yawn
- rocks back and forth on his chair
- starts to speak more quietly or even becomes hard to hear
- raises his eyebrows
- bites his lip
- … (something else you've come to know he starts doing when something's going on)

At the same time as noticing these things, we also need to be aware of our own body cues. Our posture, gestures, voice tone, rhythm, and intensity, and our movements toward or away from the child, may be communicating an attitude that is open and welcoming, or closed and defensive.

As you learn more and more about the pupil's history, and how this history has shaped them, the more available you can become to engage in what can often be a very painful process for both your pupil and you. Some of the Key Adults Dan and I have worked with have named this process the 'defrosting' stage! In order to defrost something, warmth needs to be applied. The duration of application of warmth is significant. If it comes and goes, the ice remains as it would if an object were frozen from the inside out. If, however, warmth is applied consistently over a period of time then the defrosting is sustained. So to keep your own flow of warmth steady, hold onto the fact that there is a vulnerable, frightened pupil locked inside the iceberg!

Many Key Adults have had the rewarding experience of being part of this process. Words are often insufficient to communicate the sense of awe and wonder they experience as they watch a pupil 'come to life'. To see these pupils really start to thrive.

Dan writes: I agree completely, Louise. When we experience this process with one of our very troubled pupils, we realise completely the meaning of our professional lives. It is so much more than a job. We will have been part of the recovery process of a really troubled child or young person. This realisation is so rewarding.

Louise writes: Slowly, slowly, step by step, we start to earn the trust of the pupils in our care so that they can begin to allow themselves to be dependent, and for us to lead. Many have grown old before their time, and have not had this experience of allowing another human being in.

Relational withdrawal

There are times when the pupils in our care may move into feeling overwhelmed through experiencing an overload of stress, shame, fear or panic, or a combination of all four. This is how he or she may be feeling: but what we may see is quite extreme behaviour, such as:

SITTING AT THE TOP OF A TREE OR ON A ROOF   *SCREAMING*   HIDING ALL OVER THE SCHOOL

swearing   **damaging stuff**

RUNNING OFF   *biting*

spitting   **painting themselves all over**

masturbating   KICKING

GROWLING   LOCKING HIMSELF IN THE TOILET

SELF-HARM, FOR EXAMPLE HEAD BANGING

This is not the time to pull back or withdraw from the relationship with your pupil. Contrary to the common belief out in schools, this is the time when our pupils need us most. What they don't need is for us to leave them when things get tough. We have used *relational withdrawal* as a sanction for too long in our schools, through the use of 'ignoring' and 'time out' types of response to difficult behaviour. This has got to be challenged within our school systems. Not only does it compromise what we are trying to teach troubled pupils in terms of dependency but it also compromises their behaviour further, and means they are left without the necessary tools and strategies to bring about reparation. Your pupil needs you to provide a human bridge back into safety, security and stability. Let's not leave them at the very time they need us most. Please read what we're saying about reparation (Chap.13, p.257) for more information on this much needed support work, which will also move our troubled pupils on in their emotional and social development.

Our pupils' behaviour is compromised when relationships are withdrawn from them; in other words, when the pupil is ignored, put outside the room, moved to another class or excluded. Even if the intention was to enable the pupil to calm down, you may well have noticed how things can often get much worse.

Sîan starts screaming, then she starts darting about the classroom when the teacher states that the class are to turn away from her, and everyone is given instruction to ignore her.

Ben kicks his foot through the nearest pane of glass when he is told that he is going to be secluded in the isolation unit because of his misbehaviour.

Everything we've learnt about developmental trauma and loss suggests that relational withdrawal can actually re-traumatise our pupil, triggering off very powerful feelings linked to abandonment, isolation and neglect. This is why we then see even more disturbed behaviours.

Dan writes: Some professionals worry that if we remain close to our pupils when they 'misbehave' we are reinforcing the problematic behaviour, and that it will only occur more frequently. Our experience, as well as those of many others in the fields of psychology, child development and education, have not found support for this worry. When children are routinely provided with attention in their daily lives, they don't misbehave in order to get attention. When we stay close to children who are frightened or sad, we don't reinforce their fearful or sad behaviours. Why then do we think that it will happen when we stay close when children are angry?

'Time in'

Louise writes: Troubled and vulnerable pupils also have great difficulty managing their emotional states, often lacking the ability to achieve such 'regulation' alone (*for discussion of regulation and co-regulation, please see* Chap.2). They need an adult nearby, who is emotionally regulated themselves (in other words in a calm, alert, stable state) in order for the adult to co-regulate the child's emotions. So in fact we will need to facilitate *'time in'*, especially at times of difficulty. 'Time in' will involve a member of education support staff being alongside the pupil - not withdrawing from them. The pupil will need time to either relax, process information or to 'regulate' their states, sensations and feelings: in other words, time to get themselves together. It's as if they need someone to *gather them in* out of the panic or alarm. For this purpose, it's best that you remain close by. Move into another space so that you can engage in 'time in' together. A safe space: a multi-sensory area is best placed for this.

So the only 'time out' Dan and I encourage is for the adults, when they need time to restore their own reflective capacity (*see* Chap.2 p.63 *for information on 'swap-ins'*).

Inherent fears that need to be challenged

I   OVER-DEPENDENCY AND ENMESHMENT

If dependency is being encouraged, there is a risk that the pupil may become overly-dependent or enmeshed with the member of education staff. However, usually the pupil is *so* pseudo-independent that this risk is greatly reduced. Your role is to support them to move more into an equilibrium, rather than take away their independence.

If you're using appropriate and healthy boundaries within your support work, the possibility of over-dependency is also greatly reduced. Clearly state your role and responsibility, motives and intentions on a regular basis, to ensure there is no room for misinterpretation.

PUPIL   *I want you to take me home and be my new mummy.*

KEY ADULT   *You are letting me know that you would like me to take you home and be your new mummy but I can't take you home or be your new mummy. I am your Key Adult in school. I just work with you in school. My job is to help you to settle to learn. But I am honoured that you consider me to be a person who you would want to be your mummy. Thank you!*

PUPIL   *Why don't you come with me after school to the skateboard park and I can show you my tricks?*

KEY ADULT   *You are letting me know that you would like me to come to the skateboard park with you after school as you want to show me your tricks, but I can't come with you after school to see your tricks, as I'm your Key Adult and I work here in school with you. My job is to support you to settle to learn, but I expect that your tricks are incredible.*

Be prepared to pull in further boundaries as time goes by, in relation to the kind of responses you get from your pupil. In this type of relational support work, not all interactions can be prepared for. Your interactions with one another are unique. We believe it is important to receive supervision to do this work, especially when you're working with a pupil with severe relational damage. This supervision is best provided by a professional with therapeutic experience and expertise. Ideally, such a supervisor needs to be someone from outside the school staff, for example a school therapist, clinical psychologist, educational psychologist with therapy training, or a CAMHS therapist.

II   CHILD ABUSE ALLEGATIONS

It should go without saying that we need to be highly ethically responsible in all our education practice, so all tools and strategies should be clearly documented and reviewed. All support work should be managed and supervised so that there is clear accountability. Everyone needs to be clear as to why support is being used. This demands good communications in school, good staff care and sufficient training.

There are a couple of specific areas that need attention here: the use of touch and the use of boundaries.

a)   Touch

For too long now we have shied away from using healthy and appropriate touch in schools, in the name of protecting ourselves from allegations. Fear has led the way, rather than common sense. But by engaging in this stand-off approach we are, in effect, contributing to the discomfort and stuckness of those of our pupils who have experienced significant relational traumas and losses.

If we facilitate healthy, safe touch, then our pupils will experience being grounded, feeling soothed and comforted, experiencing our acceptance, and being in a better position to be able to contain their own strong emotions. Healthy, safe touch also facilitates the child's ability to more accurately perceive an adult's intentions/ motives in the interaction.

So let's include touch within our written individual development plans, being transparent about what we will do and when, together with the benefits. Let's also be transparent with our pupil as to our intentions for touching him, as well as making it clear that he will not be touched if he chooses not to be. Your written plans will include an awareness of the need for safety for both the educator and the pupil. When you do this properly, you won't be leaving yourself open to misinterpretation. Let's create consent forms for those with parental responsibility to sign. This is important and necessary work.

Dan writes: I agree completely that we need to revisit the need for appropriate touch in our interactions with our pupils, and its role. There will always be the need for clarity, so that our pupils, our educational team, and our pupil's parents and carers understand the nature, intentions, and boundaries for any interventions that involve touch. Finally, there are good reasons to believe that when we are able to develop a meaningful, supportive, relationship with our pupils, the likelihood that they will make a false allegation about our interactions with them is likely to greatly decrease.

b)   The use of boundaries

Louise writes: As mentioned earlier in this chapter, boundaries are very important in this work amongst troubled pupils. Good line management and supervision in school can really support education support staff in providing the necessary frameworks for ensuring healthy and appropriate interactions as the pupil's developmental needs change over time. We are concerned that some staff would rather shy away from quality, close relationships than deal with the more challenging work of engaging with and managing boundaries. We would actually go as far as to say that we need to move away from focusing on 'managing behaviour' to managing 'our boundaries', as this would have a much more effective relational benefit for these pupils. For example, let's look at what might happen with Sîan and Ben from p.37.

Mr. Perrins organises Sîan's team to re-group, together with Sîan. They go through all the support structures in place for Sîan so that she is really clear as to the tools and strategies she can use when she feels overwhelmed. They ensure she is clear about where she can go, who she can be with to support her and what she can do herself. Mr. Perrins suggests they also try out a few new activities in Sîan's Calm Box over the next few weeks.

Ms. Todd organises Ben's team to re-group, together with Ben. She asks each member of the team what they are expecting from Ben in order to keep him safe. Using different words, they all repeat the fact that Ben needs to stay in his Ben zone at school during playtimes and lunch together with Ms. Todd, and that Ms. Todd will include his friends in that zone over time.

(*see* Bombèr 2007).

Boundaries are necessary for life both inside and outside school. Boundaries support our pupils into healthy and appropriate ways of relating, which in turn leads them to be able to make healthy and appropriate contributions towards our shared society, whatever their skills, abilities and work interests.

These pupils don't need our sympathy. It is not helpful to rescue them. They need our support to gently challenge them into the world of secure attachment where roles, responsibilities, motives and intentions need to be examined and understood in order for the creation of new neural pathways to become a reality. Our pupils need the tools necessary to stand up and be all that they were intended to be.

Dan and I are interested in genuine and lasting change, not superficiality. How we relate to these pupils in school matters. Really matters.

Chapter 2

Stay calm and bring calm

Those who have been overpowered, humiliated and abused experience a catastrophic loss of power. They will seek redress, sometimes by rendering others similarly powerless. (Batmanghelidjh, 2006, pp.53-4)

Dan writes: 'Stay calm and bring calm'. Easier said than done? Yes, we know! Yet we need to say it. Our emotional states are so contagious! When we're tense, others around us tend to become tense. When we are happy, we tend to make others a bit happier. If we as educators are feeling angry, our pupils will tends toward anger, or at least toward a tense, defensive state, raised to protect themselves from our anger. Such states reduce our vulnerable pupils' readiness to learn and our ability to influence them, without resorting to power and control.

So, we talk about calmness, though we acknowledge that it can be hard to initiate and maintain at times when other people are in a different emotional state, particularly the kind of state which actives our anger or tension. By calmness, we're not suggesting a need for a quiet and slow state. We are referring to an open and engaged state of mind that is welcoming and receptive to those around us, even when *they* are angry and tense. We're referring to maintaining this state and inviting the other person or people to join us, rather than our joining them in their state of distress. Such calmness may be animated, playful, and lively. Or it may be soft and gentle and quiet. What we are saying in this chapter is that if we are able to stay in this state most of the time, we will be able to bring the same state to our pupils and colleagues.

In this chapter, we will be discussing the importance of our emotional and physical presence in our pupils' lives if they are to be able to settle to learn in our schools. If we - the educators - are tense, agitated, irritable, and angry (regardless of the source of these emotional states) our pupils will not be able to remain engaged, relaxed, co-operative, and focused on learning. We might be tempted to say that our pupil's behaviours 'made' us agitated and angry. And then our pupil might say that because we were angry, don't like him or were unfair to him, he became angry and acted poorly. It is embarrassing to think that we are now engaged in the argument of *"He started it!"*

Regardless of our pupils' behaviours, when we are able to maintain our own emotional stability we will be in a much better position to assist our pupils to demonstrate an appropriate emotional state themselves. Starting with our own calm and confident presence, we will be more likely to initiate, build, repair, and maintain our relationships with our most troubled pupils, than if our emotions are often being triggered by their behaviours.

We use the terms *'regulation'*, *'dysregulation'*, and *'co-regulation'* in this chapter and elsewhere in this book. These words often refer to our emotions, but may also relate to our thoughts and behaviours. When we are *'regulated'*, we are in a position of mental and physical integration where our thoughts and emotions are influencing each other to remain focused, moderate, and stable. We are able to be aware of the demands of the present moment, consider the options, and respond in a sensitive and complete manner. In contrast, when we are *'dysregulated'* we are reacting impulsively to a situation, without considering the relevant factors that are important in making the right decision as to how best to respond. When dysregulated, our emotions and behaviours tend to 'get away' from our mindful awareness and control. When regulated, it is as if we have a thermostat that keeps us grounded and focused on maintaining a moderate range of emotion where we function at our best. When dysregulated, our thermostat is broken and we are subject to intense emotional expressions, distracted thinking, and impulsive actions.

'*Co-regulation*' refers to ability of one person to influence the regulatory state of the other. If our pupil is dysregulated and we are able to remain regulated, our mental and emotional state is likely to influence his to become regulated again. We are not likely to be able to effectively assist our pupils in maintaining a consistently stable level of functioning, if we find ourselves frequently becoming dysregulated.

Louise writes: School life has the potential for a lot of angst. Working within such a large, busy community there will inevitably be times when our patience is tested. Most of us try our best to stay calm in tricky situations. During teacher training, we were taught to expect calm from pupils, but few of us were given the tools to teach us how to calm ourselves or how to teach pupils how to regulate or calm themselves. We know that there are many troubled pupils in our care who seem very dysregulated. At the same time, many of us recognise that a situation can equally be made much worse in schools by dysregulated adults. Many of we education staff are desperate to know how to be and what to do to improve this situation.

As well as the ordinary stresses and strains involved in school life there are extraordinary difficulties as well. There are pupils included in the school community who haven't had sufficient, sensitively attuned care in their early years which would have enabled them to learn to self-regulate - self soothe and self calm. In fact, many children and adolescents have had overwhelming experiences to try to cope with, which have usually involved some kind of disempowerment. So it's not surprising that these pupils are going to get into power struggles with us, especially when they experience stress. Some of these power struggles can easily knock us off balance if we're not mindful of this dynamic. We could find ourselves reacting very differently to the way we normally do, and being anything but calm!

It's important for us to consider that pupils with backgrounds in relational trauma and loss experience feelings very deeply: they've often been wounded to the core. Their anger can quickly move into rage, sadness into despair, fear into terror. Guilt into toxic shame. If we meet these pupils in a reactionary way and attempt to fight fire with further fire, we have a disaster waiting to happen! And yet, rather than staff being reprimanded for their reactive behaviour, and then helped to address what triggered them into dysregulation and supported to do things differently, our pupil might get permanently excluded for how *he* behaved, even though this may have been because he was triggered into panic reactions by the staff member's response to him. This is neither right or ethical.

I'm sure we can all think of examples from school practice when we have experienced the consequence of being around dysregulated education staff: it's not a pleasant sight! The observer usually has a strong sense of something being very wrong. None of us like to admit we've behaved in a less than 'good enough' way - but we've all done it, at some point or another. If I (LB) look back at some of my own early teaching, I can see there were times when I communicated my impatience with some of the pupils in my care. I was shocked by some of their behaviours. I was frustrated that after all my hours of preparation over the weekend that some of my lessons seemed to get sabotaged. Sometimes I was far from calm: irritated and annoyed, I would snap. Through good staff mentoring, support and further training I learned better ways of relating to these pupils. I feel grateful that I've now had the opportunity to pass on what I learned back then, and what I'm learning as I continue. There's always so much to learn about how to relate most effectively!

However, regrettably, some staff still seem oblivious to the impact that they have on the vulnerable pupils in their care. Sometimes staff reflect on how disastrous outcomes could have been avoided, and we notice that particular pupils seem to behave worse when around particular staff. Have you ever wondered why?

Of course it could be that there is something about this member of staff that is a 'trigger' for the pupil's distress, no matter how able or calm the teacher is. For example, the teacher's voice, her hair colour, something about how she moves may remind the pupil of the person who abused him. But, alternatively, perhaps the pupil doesn't do well with this teacher because it's the staff member herself who is feeling overwhelmed? Maybe this member of staff hasn't developed the capacity yet to manage stress well, or is so stressed herself that she has lost her capacity to be resilient? Maybe she has never had the opportunity to resolve her own personal unprocessed traumas and losses?

Unconsciously, we assume that as education staff, we all have a coherent sense of ourselves, have 'resolved' our own personal histories, and have a relatively secure attachment style of relating. But not all staff have had the training, support, opportunity for insight or wherewithal to get to this point, and all of us are still learning and growing. If we have unresolved trauma and loss in our own early backgrounds, we need to be seriously aware that pupils who have experienced significant relational traumas and losses will awaken buried traumas and losses in us. In our training, we were never told that our own histories, our own capacity for self-regulation could have such a profound impact on a troubled pupil who is themselves dysregulated. Phillip Riley based at Monash University has written widely on this theme (2010): he concludes that teachers' own attachment styles affect the formation and maintenance of classroom and staffroom relationships, that the attachment processes going on impact teachers' and pupils' emotional responses to educational tasks and that these two factors then influence classroom behaviour, particularly the management of pupil behaviour. These matters are well worth considering.

Dan writes: I am so grateful for the chance to have 'do overs' in my personal and professional life. They are crucial in building and repairing my relationships with particular pupils or clients or friends and they are crucial if I am to improve in my career and my relationships in general. I am thinking of a teenager who yelled at me that I didn't have a clue about what was best for him, and I reacted with sarcasm that he didn't have a clue either. I am thinking of a 12 year old who said that he did not want to see me for therapy, and I replied defensively, as I stood up, that he should give me a call if he changed his mind. It's tempting to think that I was young and inexperienced then and would never react in those ways now. Experience may make those reactions less frequent, but doesn't stop them completely. Experience could also make them more frequent, if we experience an increased sense of discouragement over our failures in making a difference or lead to our becoming less idealistic or motivated to do our best. We're human. We can only try to do our best most of the time and to do as little harm as possible during the hard days that challenge us from time to time.

Now, to turn back to what we might strive to attain during our good days, when we want to make a difference and when we feel proud of our roles in the lives of young people. As we're stressing throughout this book, we become much more effective as educators when we have a meaningful relationship with our pupil, and such a relationship will be facilitated when we approach each pupil in every situation in an open and engaged manner. This manner is interfered with when we approach the pupil in anger or defensiveness. Either stance will create defensiveness in the pupil and undermine any efforts to initiate and maintain a reciprocal discussion.

Louise writes: Dan, I know that some education staff are concerned that if they stay too calm then the pupils in their care won't learn from their experiences. I've met some who believe that expressing their rage and disgust in short bursts may actually shock these pupils into behaving! What do you think of this?

Dan writes: Louise, I do believe that there is a limited role for anger in influencing a pupil in an immediate situation where the pupil's behaviour is harming another person. If one pupil has another child or young person on the floor and is about to kick him, the educator seeing this is wise to immediately respond with a loud voice that conveys anger at what the pupil is doing. Remaining calm then would be likely to minimise the seriousness of the situation and the pupil's aggressive behaviour. However, this anger must not be rage or disgust shown towards the pupil himself, or the pupil is likely to escalate and/or enter shame and be at greater risk in the future of engaging in similar behaviours. The pupil might be just more careful not to be seen when he's doing it!

The important thing in any situation is that the educator *needs to be in control of his anger,* so that he knows what he is saying and he can stop it when its role in managing the situation is over. Then, if the educator focuses on the behaviour (*"Kicking is not allowed in our school!"*: in other words, not *"You coward!"*) followed quickly with an alternative behaviour that the pupil should do (*"Tell me if you have a problem with him"*) then the intervention may be successful.

The most important part comes next. The educator needs to repair the relationship with the pupil that he just became angry with. The anger is likely to have activated shame and rage in the pupil. If the educator is able to engage in relationship repair, the pupil will be more likely to recognise that the educator's anger has to do with his (the pupil's) behaviour, not his person, and that the relationship between them is still strong. The educator might say something like this:

> *"I just expressed anger at you for what you were doing to Mark. I know that my anger is hard for you. And I also know that your anger at Mark was very big and you might have hurt him badly. I care about Mark and I care about you. I'm going to help you to manage your anger better and when*

you do, that's going to help you in many ways. You'll learn and I'll help. We'll get through this together".

Co-regulation

Calmness is an underlying feature of the open, engaged stance that we recommend. However, when we recommend calmness, we're not suggesting a detached manner, with a monotone voice and ambiguous facial expression. This would reduce the pupil's sense of being connected with us and will most likely increase his anxiety. Rather, we are speaking of calmness as having more variable, expressive features. To us, the core feature of calmness is the open and engaged state that we have been describing.

Louise writes: Yes, these pupils need us most at times of difficulty, so it's not helpful to withdraw relationally, as we said in the last chapter. We do tend to speak a lot about 'staying calm' in school, but I know that it'll be unfamiliar to consider 'calm' as being animated or expressive, especially to those working in the secondary context. Vulnerable pupils need our connection with them; an active relational presence will support them.

Dan writes: When the pupil is agitated, our calmness is expressed by being animated, but regulated. That is, there is a degree of energy in our communication that is similar to his, but this energy is grounded, integrated, open and engaged, not frantic nor with sharp edges. When the pupil is angry, our calmness is expressed when we speak with greater intensity and more quickly, while still being regulated, but not angry or defensive ourselves. If the pupil is frightened, our calm, regulated state is best expressed with a quiet, confident and expressive attitude. When the pupil is sad, our calmness is best shown in a gentle, delicate manner, of coming close to the pupil and softly making him aware of our presence and support.

The central feature in all of these descriptions of calmness is that we are regulated emotionally and available to assist the pupil in whatever (often dysregulating) emotion that the pupil is experiencing and expressing. Our state of regulation will facilitate his regulation. This is known as *co-regulation*, and is what parents do with their babies. Babies have such difficult times with their big emotions. They wail and scream and fuss! The world just seems too hard for them. When his parent is present, cuddles, and rocks, often in the same rhythm as the baby's movements and wails, while remaining calm and focused on supporting him in his distress, the infant often moves into the same rhythm as the parent, now calmer and with less stress. The parent's movements and voice show the infant that the world is not so bad and that they will manage any stress together.

The same holds true in close relationships between two adults. When one says, *"I just want you to listen!"* often she means that her emotions are strong and unsettling and she wants to experience someone with her, showing a calm confidence that whatever stress she is experiencing will be handled together. No advice or verbal reassurance is called for, just a good friend's safe presence, co-regulating any emerging emotions.

Our brains are designed for such co-regulation. The central regions of the brain that deal with significant emotional relationships with others - the pre-frontal cortex, anterior cingulate cortex, and insula - are very sensitive to the emotional expression of others and respond to those expressions with the same rhythmic movements of our face, voice, and gestures. These regions are central to our ability to experience empathy for others and to have an intuitive sense of the other person's inner life of thoughts, emotions, and wishes. These features, in turn, generate trust and the sense of companionship that lie at the heart of our important relationships.

Louise writes: Being able to calm ourselves requires that we have a sense of what's going on in our own bodies, hearts and minds. This requires a certain level of self-awareness. We also need to know what works for us in order to bring calm when we become dysregulated; ordinary life is stressful, never mind working in a school environment with many hurting pupils, so we need to know what to do to stay in or swiftly return to a stable state.

Something that has really benefited many support staff is coming up with a small 'fan' of reminders of what they can do when they feel stressed. A 'fan is a loosely-bound set of small cards that describe your possible options for staying calm. For example: breathe deeply, step outside for some air, press the pause button, have a cup of tea, swap in with someone else (*see* p.63), use your stress ball, go for a walk around the block, put on some hand cream, splash your face with water … regardless of status, role, responsibility or experience we all need a stress plan!

It is important to start with this knowledge, as self-awareness will give you what you need in order to get alongside some very troubled pupils. Also, if you're aware of the following two possibilities, then you can prepare yourself and won't be fazed.

Our capacity to remain calm is adversely affected when we are taken by surprise. What we often find in working with pupils with relational trauma and loss is some kind of shock, and some kind of rejection. So be aware of the *'shock factor'* and the *'rejection factor'*, and brace yourself!

THE SHOCK FACTOR

In support work we're going to be shocked - by swearing, spitting, shouting, rage, screaming, freezing, mocking, hysteria, masturbating, sarcasm, dissociative episodes, cruel words, self-harm, cruel acts, lack of remorse, unusual activities, coldness, indifference, hopelessness, helplessness - the list is likely to be long. So let's get prepared. If we act out our shock, it could well make things worse. When you're shocked, what will you do? How will you hold on?

THE REJECTION FACTOR

From time to time we may experience the pupil attempting to push us away. Often the pupil won't even be aware of what he is doing. It's often an unconscious response or a defence mechanism that comes into play as a default response, which is usually left unchallenged. Bring it out into the open: *"It's as if you are trying to push me away at the moment"*. Be clear about what you sense going on: *"I wonder whether you might be trying to get me to experience what it feels like to be you"*. Bringing it out into the open in this way can often disempower the emotional intensity around whatever is happening. Ensure you let the pupil know how you will respond to this.

> *"I'm not going anywhere. You matter to me. However much you try and push me away I don't give up that easily. I'm sticking around because I care."*

Why do pupils behave in these ways? Why shouldn't they? If we'd been hurt to the degree that they have it would be crazy to allow someone to mean something, to get close: it would be far too scary. There is a great deal of courage required in this kind of recovery. This is no walk in the park!

I believe that good staff care is fundamental in allowing education staff the space to firstly become regulated, and secondly to remain so, despite even the most difficult of circumstances. Staff care involves both a personal and corporate responsibility (Bombèr 2011, Chap.15). Once we've reflected on our own ways of remaining calm by managing our own stress levels, we can then look to the vulnerable pupils whom we want to support.

> *"Roy, I can see that things are getting a bit tricky right now. I can see that you are getting agitated as you seem quite preoccupied and your fidgeting has increased. Come on, let's take a break. Let's get some air and do some physical exercise first to get ourselves settled ready to get on with the learning".*

Dan writes: Our state of regulated calmness is characterised by our reflective functioning in which our mind is focused on the child. Reflective functioning refers to our ability to turn our mind to the inner life of our pupil. Over time, we develop an intuitive sense of his thoughts, emotions, motives, and wishes, based on the subtleties of his non-verbal expressions, his words, and our history with him. We then use this sense to decide how to interact with him in a manner that might prove to be in his best interest. We are noticing the child's non-verbal expressions - the intensity and rhythm of his voice, his facial expressions and the look in his eyes, his movements, gestures, and posture. We are thinking of the immediate situation, the other pupils, the expectations on the child, recent events that he experienced, our history with him: and we are openly exploring in our mind what he needs from us. Focusing on him and trying to sort out what is in his best interests - if we are to do it well - requires that we remain in an integrated, regulated state with a confident presence and clear intention to be of help, not to create defensiveness. That's all!!

Yet, calmness also requires that we be aware of our own experience (turning our reflective functioning toward our own inner life), as Louise mentioned above. Starting with our body: we can ask ourselves if we are anxious, angry, feeling inadequate, struggling to control a tendency to verbally attack, or to create and win a power struggle? We can notice our own gestures, voice intensity, and movements, and try to imagine how they are being experienced by the pupil. If we truly are committed to maintaining an open and engaged dialogue within a safe relationship with the pupil, we will work to maintain a broad view of the child or adolescent, our relationship with him, and the immediate situation, rather than a narrow view that is only intent on stopping a behaviour.

At the same time, sometimes the first priority - for the sake of safety for all concerned - may well be to stop the behaviour. But such acute safety needs are more the exception rather than the rule in situations that require your involvement. Often you'll be able to use the stressful situation as an opportunity to strengthen your relationship by successfully loaning your own emotional regulation and reflective skills to the pupil when he truly needs your help. Such crises need not weaken or cause a break in your relationship with the pupil. They may deepen the relationship instead, by showing that you are available during his hard times. You won't attack him, nor walk away, and you won't leave him alone to despair. His relationship with you is bigger than any conflict and one of the key features of your relationship is to assist him, to stand by him, when he is struggling.

Seven year old Robert got into a fight with another boy, Hank, before school started. Robert did not respond to Ms. Stanton's firm words for him to stop and she had to take him by the arm and escort him away. In his anger, Robert hit Ms. Stanton's arm and swore at her. She brought him to the corner of the room and he turned his back on her and stared out the window. In an agitated voice and with tears he yelled that the other boy, Ms. Stanton, and the school were all stupid and he hated being there. Ms. Stanton responded with animation that things were very hard for him right then and it was a difficult way to have to begin the day. As he calmed down she quietly wondered if how she might be of help and she mentioned a special project that she had planned for the first period. After he took a deep breath she gently placed her hand on his shoulder and wondered if he would help her to get the materials ready for the project. He turned, now focused on the project, and walked with her to her desk. While taking things from the drawer, he reached out and gave her a quick hug. He was not only a great help in the success of the activity, he went out of his way to show Hank how to assemble the parts of the project. His relationship with Ms. Stanton helped him a great deal in regulating his emotion and becoming successfully re-engaged with his class, and even with Hank.

This process holds true in all aspects of our lives. When we have a conflict with a good friend there is more danger to the relationship if we pretend nothing happened and continue relating with each other than if we address it. This takes courage - bringing up a conflict that was painful for one or both, facing shame or fear of loss of the relationship. But when we choose to face the conflict, after the anger or tears and sense of vulnerability, the relationship is likely to be stronger. There is safety in knowing that you are both committed to doing what is difficult in order to preserve the relationship. The same is true in our relationships with our pupils. When we are willing to face ridicule or rejection in order to assist our pupils in resolving a conflict with us or with their peers, our pupils are likely to trust that we are truly committed to our relationship with them and to their educational success.

Louise writes: I think we're sometimes too quick in schools to *manage* behaviour rather than seeing it as presenting vital educative opportunities around regulation, around enabling our pupils to settle to learn. I feel very strongly that we should be focusing on assessing our pupils' capacity for regulation in our schools, rather than on managing behaviour. Once we have assessed this capacity we then need to create a plan to either raise their awareness of dysregulation and the tools they can use to become regulated again, or we need to give them some alternative tools that they can use, practising them together on a regular basis, before expecting them to go off alone and self-regulate.

Everything that Dan and I are saying here implies slowing ourselves down. There is often considerable pressure on us both internally and externally to sort something quickly. But the reality is that we don't always have to. In fact, the more we slow things down, the more reflective we can become, and the more reflective our pupils can become. It's reflective work that seems to precipitate change. My experience has been that reacting to situations seems to just bring either further disturbance, or compliance, rather than real change.

I think it's important to highlight that although many of us don't like conflict of any kind, that it is through conflict that often some deep work goes on in the development of our relationship with our pupil. What is key is not the absence of conflict, but the way in which it is navigated and what is learned en route. In the next section, we'll look at some of the practical things we can do to facilitate calm in our dealings with our pupils .

Facilitating calmness

Emotional regulation is important as it allows learning to occur and enables greater variety of thinking strategies to be available. Without developing emotional regulation and mentalisation skills, pro-social behaviour cannot develop.   (Schofield et al 2012, p.4)

I   CREATE PAUSES

Schools are often very fast cultures. Efficiency leads the way at the cost of very many vulnerable pupils. Often the stress caused by this fast pace causes pupils to melt down, and the recovery time from these meltdowns can be long. Let's build in pauses from the start through to the end of the school day.

If these pupils haven't received sufficient experience yet in order to build up their own reserves of regulatory tools, we are going to have to step in. The *relationship* between a member of the education support staff and the pupil will provide the vehicle through which to experience and learn regulation. Our pupils are in our schools for many hours, weeks and years. According to Dr. Tina Rae, a renowned UK educational psychologist, author and educational consultant, learning how to manage stress shouldn't just appear on the curriculum before GCSEs, but from an early age, and Dan and I agree.

Learning how to recognise and cope with negative automatic thoughts, to re-frame negative thinking, to undertake behavioural experiments, to utilise relaxation techniques and mindfulness approaches, and to make stepped approaches to recognising and managing the anxiety and stress associated with the learning process, are essential life skills. The earlier these are taught and practised, the better for every child and young person, in terms of preventing more significant problems in the future and in maintaining (their) overall well-being on an ongoing basis.

(Rae 2013, personal communication)

But 'stress management' isn't just a cognitive exercise. We wish it were, as then it might be learned more quickly! We can't learn about self-soothing by reading a text book and completing some exercises. We learn through experience. We learn by first having had the experience of someone soothing us through their empathic response to what we are experiencing (*the importance of empathy will be explored in* Chap.8).

II SETTLING TO LEARN

Before engaging in any kind of interaction, especially learning, we need to ensure that the pupil is regulated or calm. It's clear that if the pupil is dysregulated, we're not going to get very far. We need to 'learn the child', be aware of what calms them and what is too much for them. We need to take on the role of sensory detective. Sensitive care involves assessing the sensory context of the pupil, assessing what causes further dysregulation and what brings calm. It may be that too much intimacy causes disregulation and therefore we will need to ensure that the pupil has some 'breathers' away from his KA from time to time to enable his tolerance of closeness to grow. This will help him become used to the dance of intimacy, to the coming together and the moving apart. We all need a rhythm between time together and time apart.

III WATCHING OUT FOR SENSORY OVERLOAD

A pupil can easily move into sensory overload for a number of different reasons: because of over-excitement, over-stimulation, too many transitions, being triggered by a sensory reminder from another time and place, to name but a few.

So let's remember that even positive sensory experiences can be sometimes too much; these pupils can easily move into a feeling of being overwhelmed with transitions and too much to process. Remember these pupils need a lot of time to process all the different cues that they are taking in. For example, Max who goes berserk on the Natural History Museum trip or Maddie who goes and hides under all the coats in the cloakroom when she is given a certificate and a clap from everyone in assembly for completing her work well. Our task is to learn the pupil, and to ensure that they receive a 'balanced diet' of sensory stimulation. We need to also be wary of any indicators that might show us that the child is being triggered into a sensory memory, also known as flashbacks. We *don't* want to re-traumatise them, as this won't be helpful. Learn the pupil in your care to identify possible trauma triggers.

Our whole school environments and classrooms are often very sensory places. Our lessons are often full of multi-sensory tools and strategies. We need to be aware that whilst these pupils do respond best to multi-sensory learning (as they often tune out of auditory learning, especially the human voice in times of stress) they will also become agitated from time to time when it all gets too much. Let's build in some pauses and some downtime.

IV   SENSORY BREAKS

These pupils need regular sensory breaks integrated into the everyday life of school in order for them to make the most of everything on offer to them. Often the clues for what they need will be in what they show us through their behaviour. Much of the time, the pupil himself is likely to be seeking some kind of comfort because he's feeling un-comfortable, for some reason. This has to be our starting point.

Let's integrate sensory breaks into the usual school day. These can either be high- or low-energy based, depending on the pupil. You can use sensory materials or exercises known to shift the existing state or sensation that a pupil is currently experiencing. For example, Linda is seeming very anxious and shut down in her literacy lesson. To help her get energised and to start becoming more vocal, her KA gets her bouncing on a space hopper in the infant playground. Linda starts laughing. And Sanjeep's KA Mike has noticed that Sanjeep is becoming really hyper-active in Maths, so in order to get him grounded, Mike goes with Sanjeep to the climbing wall for 15 minutes and gets him to hold his whole body weight using the hand grips. *These activities are called sensory breaks. They can either be subtle or explicit in nature, like the examples given.*

You may be surprised to discover that this is the first time that anyone will have come alongside a pupil like this to give them any feedback or to show them ways to help themselves get back to a state of calm and comfort. For many of our pupils, it'll be the first time that they start to realise that they can control and change their states, sensations and feelings. Once a pupil becomes aware of how these can be changed and the effects of these changes, then he is in a position to start controlling himself.

Often in schools we expect our vulnerable pupils to control themselves before they have anyone working with them on self-awareness. These pupils need our help: for new and healthier neural pathways to get established in their brains, they need us close beside them, as Dan was describing above in the process of co-regulation. It literally can't be learned alone. So it's really not enough to direct a pupil to go and calm down. So much more is required of us than that.

What our pupils need is someone to get alongside them, to co-regulate and to give them some kind of an exit strategy. An exit strategy could be a tool, a resource or an activity. When vulnerable pupils don't have an exit strategy, they tend to move into familiar fight/flight/freeze responses - their only known line of defence against uncomfortable feelings. There are many simple ideas you can pass on to them. For example, breathing techniques and tapping games, for example The Butterfly (in which you cross your arms over your chest and alternate tapping your chest as if moving his wings): access to a safe space, to a Calm Box or through high energy activities *(see Bombèr, 2007 and 2011)*.

Do check out *The Scared Gang* (Bhreathnach, Alder Tree Press, 2011), a great series of small story books giving ideas of how to regulate through a variety of characters such as *Frozen Frank, Run Away Ronnie, Fired up Freda* and *Busy Beatrice*! Jenny Mosely (Positive Press, 2008) has also developed fantastic resource books such as *The Big Book of Calmers* and *The Big Book of Energisers* too, so there is lots out there to inspire you and get you started.

Here are some more simple examples: using a straw to drink water to calm down, chewing a sweet when angry, engaging in some movement such as crawling or hanging upside down to calm, slowly washing hands and applying deep pressure on drying our hands to alleviate stress. I'm sure you could add to this list! These pupils seem to learn self-regulation in the most effective way when they experience co-regulation with a primary or additional attachment figure (that is, the individual who provides a consistent, empathic and attuned relationship over time) - rather than with a variety of different adults: so this has implications again for assigning Key Adults to these pupils, as we've described above.

Check how the pupil is after any sensory intervention, as they should be calmer and more relaxed, or, if they were withdrawn or de-energised beforehand, more focused and alert.

V   WHEN IS ENOUGH?

Attempt to monitor both your and the pupil's stress levels. Don't keep going regardless. Decide what breaks are necessary. Back-up adults can be very helpful in extremely demanding cases, whereby lessons or parts of the day are covered by another person, freeing the Key Adult to have other, less challenging times in the day, to prepare support work, to meet with outside agencies and to attend support groups/ consultations and trainings.

VI SWAP-INS

Be very mindful of the pupil's *window of tolerance* (*see* Introduction, p.17), and his feelings about proximity. There may well be times when we need to reduce the intensity of what's happening for our pupil - and that might include being in relationship with us! Set up a plan whereby if you were to say 'swap in', another member of staff would know what this means. Hearing those words, your colleague would literally take over and you would swap into their role or task for a while. This works best when the swap-in is with someone from next door. We model taking time out for five to ten minutes. This time out for staff can be invaluable in both diffusing intensity, pre-empting any heightened stress response and in allowing each other to become grounded and come back to clear thinking again. At times of high stress, our capacity for clear thinking goes.

As you can see from this chapter, we need to shift our focus to remaining calm, as this will determine the pace of the pupil's developmental growth and could be pivotal in terms of how they manage school and the countless opportunities available to them. Co-regulation will naturally lead to self-regulation through a lot of repetition. Let's give it a go!

Dan writes: Finally, by way of looking at an example in-depth, let's think of a difficult situation and consider two ways of responding to it. The first represents reacting from a defensive stance, where the educator is close to dysregulation himself when he approaches a dysregulated pupil. The second represents an educator who was able to successfully maintain a more open and engaged, calm and regulated state while approaching the same dysregulated pupil.

14 year old Paul was having a hard day, beginning when he observed his parents' silent treatment of each other, his argument with his mother about when he needed to come home after school, and continuing at school when a friend laughed at him as his teacher confronted him about a missed assignment. He barely focused on the lesson in Mr. Slade's class and when his teacher asked him to focus on the lesson and quit distracting the others, he exploded that he'd do what he wanted. Just then the class ended and Mr. Slade asked him to stay for a few minutes. As Paul sat angrily in his seat, Mr. Slade handled a few small obligations with other students and then approached Paul.

MR. SLADE   *You will not act like that in my class! You will not talk like that to me again or you will regret it! Who do you think that you are? Some big shot who can do whatever he wants?*

PAUL   (yelled back) *I don't have to do what you tell me. I said that I'll do what I want and you'll just have to deal with it.*

MR. SLADE   *That attitude will get you nowhere!*

PAUL   *And you're a fat ass!*

MR. SLADE   *You just got yourself a trip to the Headteacher's office and a few days suspension. How do you think that will feel, Mr. Big Shot?*

PAUL   *If I get a break from seeing your ugly face, that will feel just fine!*

This led to a temporary suspension from school and a strained relationship with Mr. Slade that continued throughout the year.

In no way would Mr. Slade be considered to have *caused* Paul's challenging behaviours. However, Mr. Slade's impulsive reaction may well have *contributed to the escalation* of his pupil's behaviours.

How might he have responded differently? As the other pupils were leaving the room and he was handling small details, Mr. Slade might have quickly:

i)   assessed his own emotional regulation. If he was irritated, he would need to calm, possibly focusing on his breathing, establishing a sense of being open and engaged.

ii)   reflected on Paul's immediate behaviours as well as his past history with Paul and his knowledge about Paul's life (apart from his relationship with Mr. Slade himself).

iii) thought for a moment about approaching Paul in a way that would reduce Paul's defensive posture and possibly lead to some successful communication between the two of them.

Mr. Slade was mindful of the need not to escalate the conflict and he realised that he had to begin with his own emotional and mental state.

MR. SLADE   *You seem to be having a tough day.*

PAUL   *So!*

MR. SLADE   *I'd like to know what's going on.*

PAUL   *None of your business!*

MR. SLADE   *Were you annoyed at something I said or were you annoyed about other things?"*

PAUL   *Everything about school sucks! There's nothing about you or anyone else here that I feel good about.*

MR. SLADE   *I'm sorry, then, Paul. Coming to school must be really a drag for you.*

PAUL   *Why would you be sorry?*

MR. SLADE   *Because you're not happy with what's going on in your life now. And you seem to be all alone with it.*

PAUL   *That's just how it is. So I deal with it.*

MR. SLADE   *Would you be willing to work with me to at least make my class a place where you can relax and feel good about things?*

PAUL   *Why should I trust you?*

MR. SLADE   *Maybe because I don't want to fight with you. I just want to get to know you.*

PAUL   *We'll see.*

MR. SLADE   *Great. We'll see together.*

Conversations like that are not unrealistic, when the adult is able to remain open and engaged, calm and regulated, in spite of the anger and defensiveness shown by the pupil.

Even troubled pupils have brains that strive to connect with others, if only they have a reason to feel safe and trust their teacher. With the neurological realities of co-regulation on the side of the calm and engaged teacher, pupils often find themselves moving toward a co-operative dialogue that has little room for anger and defensiveness.

Chapter 3

Be expressive

Louise writes: In this chapter we'll be looking at how important it is that we are expressive on every level in working to build relationship with troubled pupils. We'll reflect on the challenges *neutrality* present for these pupils. This will lead us into exploring the significance of the way we use our faces, voices and bodies. We'll not only think about the significance in terms of the meaning communicated, but also unpack how we can affect regulation through modulating the sounds we make and by matching our pupils' expressions. The careful and sensitive use of 'ourselves' can make such an incredible difference to how a troubled pupil experiences school and whether he or she is in a position to 'settle to learn'.

What we communicate through our body language, especially our eyes and face, is so, so important. Yes, I know: at university teacher training, many of us were directed *not to smile* during the first term - to remain slightly distant and neutral in our stance in order to maintain control. When I hear newly qualified teachers saying they are still hearing this advice, I'm horrified. *Neutrality is not at all helpful for the pupils we are talking about in this book.* Whilst at the time I thought it was very good advice as it would probably communicate that I was 'the boss', despite feeling a little unsure as I started out in my teaching career (unsurprisingly), I now realise that this *"Don't smile"* was very bad advice and really didn't help me when I stood in front of my year six class in East London, where there were many troubled pupils. Neutral faces are anxiety-provoking for many children and adolescents who have experienced significant relational traumas and losses. Many of these pupils will interpret neutrality as anger. When anger is suspected, many of these pupils can tip into fear, panic and even terror at times. We are then more likely to see unwanted, challenging behaviours. This really isn't our aim!

Dan writes: I recall a study in which abused children were shown a variety of faces that show various emotions - sad, happy, excitement, anger, worry, and so on - along with many ambiguous faces, that, when shown to a control group of children, were described as showing a wide variety of emotions, or simply *"I don't know"*. When the children with a history of abuse saw the ambiguous faces, they were very likely to describe them as being angry (Pollak & Tolley-Schell 2003). So yes, our troubled pupils will see us as angry when we have a neutral stance! When pupils have been physically abused by their parents, they became hypervigilant to any signs of anger in the facial expressions of *all* adults. In fact, even when an adult isn't feeling much of anything (in other words, being neutral), our abused pupil is likely to notice the smallest sign of any possible emotion and interpret it as anger. Such hypervigilance is an important survival skill for children who were at risk of physical abuse if they failed to notice an early warning sign of aggression in their parents' faces.

Also, there is also an extensive line of research known as the Still-Face Experiments that demonstrate how intensely infants seek and respond to the facial expressions of their parents (Tronick 2007). As the parent and infant begin to communicate non-verbally with each other through their facial expressions, they quickly match each other's expressions, developing a synchronised dance where each is 'attuned with' the expressions of the other. When the parent - following the instructions of the experimenter - becomes 'still' and inhibits all facial expressions, the infant finds this to be very stressful, often becoming frantic in his efforts to elicit a response. He may begin to drool, move his arms and legs rapidly, appear frightened and in distress. After a minute or two many infants become listless, disengaged, and seemingly dissociated from their immediate stressful experience. The infant appeared to be experiencing abandonment by his parent. Being unable to elicit a contingent response to his expressions by an interested parent, he often became disorganised emotionally, cognitively, and behaviourally - to use the language from the previous chapter, extremely dysregulated (*dramatic examples of Tronick's Still Face research may be found on* YouTube http://www.youtube.com/watch?v=apzXGEbZht0).

These experiments are now monitored closely so as not to create 'too much' anxiety in the infant. They demonstrate clearly how not only infants, but also the vast majority of us, feel safer and more engaged with any person we're with when that person is not ambiguous or neutral in his expressiveness, but rather quite clear and demonstrative about how he is emotionally engaged with us.

Louise writes: This proves why it is so important that we get this message out to our schools, since so, so many people still use still faces and neutrality as a technique for 'good' classroom management. It works with those pupils who have experienced good enough care. But for the vulnerable pupils we are focusing on in this book, this strategy can have disastrous effects, as Dan so eloquently describes.

When I (LB) am out and about in secondary schools where one pupil has access to many teachers, each having a different teaching style, I'm often told that there are a few lessons in which a particular pupil is not settling to learn. I'm told that the pupil must be just 'playing a game', as they do seem to be able to hold it together in some classes. I tend to ask the same important question. How does this particular member of staff address the class? Time and time again I've noted how often the pupil cannot settle in the classes where the teacher takes a neutral stance.

In these classes, the pupil I'm observing 'acts up'.

What are our pupils communicating when this happens? I believe they are communicating that they are unsettled and in some cases perturbed by what they are sensing in the other person - the teacher. For a pupil already operating from a survival mode, the neutral face, anger or rage can trigger off a panic button in their internal alarm system. Once panic or alarm is experienced, the pupil activates their learned survival strategies or tightens up their defences. Ideally we don't want to be triggering all this in our classrooms! Ideally we want to be doing everything possible in order to keep their anxiety levels low, so that their exploratory system - the brain and hormonal circuitry geared towards learning - is freed up to come online. We've been taught neutrality and objectivity. We've been advised to not get too involved. Let's challenge these approaches, and ourselves, for the sake of our troubled pupils.

Dan writes: Yes, being expressive when we speak with, and interact with, our pupils helps them to feel safe with us, because we are not being ambiguous. They know how we are responding to them. They know how we are experiencing them at this very moment. Hopefully, we're experiencing them in a positive manner. Of course being clear that we dislike a child will not help that child to feel safe with us! We need to be clear that we dislike a child's behaviour, not who he is. If, however, you realise that you truly do dislike this particular child, you might reflect as to the reasons for this and then on ways to begin to like him. Maybe you might need to work a bit harder to discover something about him that you can like. Or you might realise that he reminds you of someone else who you have had difficulty relating with elsewhere in your life. Just becoming aware of any such negative associations to someone else may help you to begin to see him differently, and to be open to liking him. Still struggling? It might help you to seek support from a colleague or supervisor to safely explore possible reasons for your dislike for the pupil, and ways to change this emotional response to a more favourable one.

Being clear that you like a pupil, while you may dislike his behaviour, will help make him feel safe. You can remain interested in him, curious about the reasons for his behaviour, intent on helping him to manage the situation better the next time. When you give expression to this interest and your desire to be of help in your non-verbal expressions, he is more likely to be able to accept your limits, and even annoyance, around his behaviour.

And yes, too, when you are aware of liking a pupil, there is no value in concealing it! Vulnerable pupils need to experience themselves as being 'likeable' to good people. Giving non-verbal expression to your delight in your pupils, your fascination with their ideas and interests, and your compassion over their struggles and challenges, goes a long way in building trust within them toward your motives and desire to be of help to them.

Finally, I'd like to add that as we are expressive, we are presenting who we are, what is unique about us. It is through expressing our uniqueness by which our pupils know that we are communicating and sharing qualities of ourselves as adults who take an interest in them, that they truly come to believe that our engagement with them is more than a job.

Louise writes: This is crucial. It's so sad when pupils say that the staff are only alongside them because they are getting paid to be there. Engaging in relational support work in schools is so much more than a job. It has to be. Only those wanting to build genuine relationship need apply! These pupils will see through any half-hearted attempts to join with them. They deserve our efforts and ourselves. They deserve a taste of humanity this time round. A taste of humanity costs more than mere hours being allocated.

We can learn from other cultures in this respect. In the West we do tend to focus on efficiency over relationship. When I lived out in Bolivia, as part of an international, voluntary group working with street children, I was blown away by the focus on relationship over efficiency. For example, the bank closed on the day of our departure so that the staff could engage in a considered goodbye with the group from the UK. I guessed we meant more to the staff there than just our accounts. We can express our relationship with others in so many ways. A very significant way is through our faces.

So let's show what we mean with our faces. When we are around babies and toddlers, many of us naturally become more expressive but we often lose this capacity when faced with pupils who are older chronologically, though emotionally and socially immature. We need to remember this capacity and allow it to surface again, this time with these pupils - whatever their age. Let's raise our eyebrows, over-exaggerate our smiles, modulate our tone and pace of voice, and sparkle! Think toddler! Let's be captivating in our communications!

So for example, we might use a wide-eyed look, a cheeky grin and sparkly eyes when gently challenging a 15 year old about whether he will be able to cope on the residential or not when he is anxious, and you know he will be able to cope because he's so much stronger emotionally and socially these days!

Dan writes: I sometimes think that educators - and therapists - should have periodic training days in which they take lessons from story-tellers. We could all learn more from how they convey the meaning of a story, and how to hold the child's rapt interest in the story through voice prosody, facial expressions, movements, and gestures.

Louise writes: Perhaps as educators we forget that we're involved in communicating all kinds of stories. The story of life. The story of science. The story of history. The story of literature. We could go on! We're all engaged in our own stories and the stories of others. And, it is important to add, the story of our time together with our pupil.

We need to be explicit in our motives and intentions, not assuming that our pupils will understand what we mean. We know that many troubled pupils will find it difficult to pick up on ordinary social cues. They tend to miss many of them because of being preoccupied with matters to do with assuming danger and the need for survival. With this in mind, we are going to have to exaggerate much of what we would usually do more subtly, in order to help them to notice!

> *For example: "Stacy you have managed to complete that work that you were struggling with. That must be such a relief!" with a big smile, open face and raised eyebrows, communicating excitement, pleasure and interest followed by exhaling slowly and loudly and a big stretch - as if releasing tension!*

So, as you can see, every detail counts, from the way we articulate our words through to how we modulate our voices. Everything matters to your pupil, so ensure they are 'hearing' something important and that you are communicating what you actually mean.

Matching expression

In schools we're probably most familiar with 'rescuing' vulnerable pupils away from their uncomfortable feelings. This seems to be the accepted practice. We've been told to calm these pupils down, basically by directing them to *"Calm down!"* But despite our best intentions to reduce the stress of the situation this way, many pupils have escalated their behaviours. The likelihood is they are doing this because they haven't felt heard.

> *Craig (aged five) is desperate to play on his bike at first break but you have just been told that no children must go out as it is wet play. Now Craig is whimpering in the corner. You tell him to stop being silly, to calm down and go and play with the jigsaws. You state how the other children aren't causing a scene. The next moment Craig throws the Lego box across the floor and retreats quickly under the table with his hands over his head, sobbing uncontrollably.*

What is it that our pupils actually desire most of all? To be heard. Just like the rest of us. To be understood. By at least one person. Rather than deflecting their difficult feelings away, we need to engage with them. We need to 'match their affect', to use Dan's phrase. We can do this by not only *reflecting back the feeling* of what the pupil is communicating but by *matching the bodily expression* (the affect) of the pupil's feeling in our own non-verbal communications too. When we are able to match the intensity and rhythm of our pupil's voice when he is angry (without being angry ourselves), the pupil is likely to feel that we 'get it'. In this way, we can let the pupil know that we understand what he is sharing with us through his behaviour.

Dan writes: Yes, when we tell pupils to *"Calm down!"* when they are upset, it's likely they won't calm down and won't feel understood: they may even express their distress even more forcefully.

Imagine you're at home with your partner and you are experiencing anger, sadness, or fear, and your partner repeatedly tells you to calm down, or says *"It's*

OK!" or *"It's not so bad"*. Most likely you will not feel heard. You probably wouldn't feel understood or supported by your partner. It will seem that your partner is simply focused on telling you what to do rather than being with you so that you don't feel alone in dealing with your distress. You're likely to want your partner's engaged presence and empathy much more than his advice and intent to 'fix it' - or to 'fix' you! When your partner *matches your affect* - but not your emotion of fear, anger, or sadness - himself, you are likely to feel both understood and supported.

So when your pupil is in distress and you see your role as helping him to experience your support by being emotionally regulated, available, and responsive to him, you will be able to provide him with your emotional strength so that his emotional dysregulation becomes regulated too (matching your regulated emotion). If two individuals are interacting and one is emotionally dysregulated and the other is emotionally regulated, either both will become regulated or both will become dysregulated, often within minutes (as I have described above). That's how our brains work - they seek synchrony with the other person's brain. It is our responsibility as educators - and our gift to our pupils - to remain regulated emotionally when our pupils are not, so that they can lean on us and become regulated.

It is very different, and much less helpful, when we teachers react to our pupils with our own anger, fear, or withdrawal when they are in distress. This is likely to cause a reaction in turn that becomes more escalated than it was originally. The pupil's emotional state would have caused a similar emotion in us, which caused an even stronger emotional reaction in him, which caused an even stronger emotional reaction in us ... and so on until our pupil is excluded, and we consider other careers. Let's use our capacity to co-regulate constructively, be expressive in our communication, and take a different journey together.

Not that this is easy! It forces us to utilise our own emotional strengths and regulation skills. Strengths that we may routinely use at home or with friends but forget to use at school because of our focus on calming and fixing our pupils, rather than being with them in their distress while remaining emotionally available and strong ourselves. To do this means that we need to be safe with our colleagues and managers. And that we understand how to expressively match the child's affect without reacting to his emotion.

Louise writes: By suggesting this matching of feelings, we're not encouraging you to lose control, or to let yourself get overtaken by your feelings; but rather to communicate on every level that you have 'got it'. You are showing that you have really understood what the pupil is trying to communicate, and how important it is to him, at a deep level. Letting the pupil know this includes using our posture, our tone of voice, our pace of voice …

- *"Wow, you are letting me know you are so, so very angry right now,"*
  … said in a loud, strong, firm voice - fast in pace, lowering intonation with your words 'very angry'. Standing in an interested, open and engaged manner.

- *"You are letting me know you are so, so sad at the moment,"*
  … said in a quiet, gentle voice - slow in pace, exaggerating the word sad to draw attention to this specific expression. Sitting at the same level, matching the posture of the pupil in a less intense way, slouching, hands clenched …

When we have used this very basic principle amongst some very troubled pupils out in schools the positive impact has been considerable. Try it out and see for yourself! It can make all the difference. And have a look at our Empathy chapter.

Dan writes: As Louise and I write elsewhere in this book, matching affect is often very effective in helping our pupils know that we truly understand their experience. We're not angry when we match the affective expression of anger in our pupils, but our voice and face demonstrates the same intensity, rhythms, and general expressiveness of their anger. When we match the affective expression of anger, without being angry ourselves, the child experiences empathy for his anger and this will often help him to regulate and reduce it. This takes some practice, though we do it without thinking when we're with babies. When they become upset or fussy, we naturally become more animated and our voice becomes more intense. And we also behave this way when we're with little children and they are excited about something.

Louise writes: Yes, up to now some very basic principles that can actually make the world of difference in the life of a vulnerable pupil have been overlooked in our schools. *Whatever it takes* must be our motto! We need to allow our vulnerable pupils the opportunity to truly understand what we're doing and why. Otherwise, in the midst of so much possibility for misinterpretation and misunderstanding, we are simply setting them up to fail.

Chapter 4

Be open and engaged with PACE

Dan writes: There is a great deal of interesting research emerging from neuroscientists who study the brain and the rest of the nervous system, which both Louise and I feel is relevant for educators. One particularly fascinating area involves the polyvagal theory of Stephen Porges, a neuropsychologist located in Chicago. Understanding something of this theory can provide us with an awareness of how the functioning of our minds, as educators, may enable our pupils to use their minds in ways that enable them to better relate with us and learn about themselves and their world. We hope that understanding the 'brain science' will enable you to recognise the importance of maintaining your own 'open and engaged state'; and to see how central it is to your pupils' capacity to settle to learn.

For two centuries, according to Dr. Porges and others (Porges et al, 2011), the autonomic nervous system has been considered as consisting of two parts: the sympathetic branch, which involves activation, *increasing* arousal and mobilisation, and the parasympathetic branch, which involves *reducing* arousal and creating immobilisation. The sympathetic branch has been studied in great detail because of its importance in understanding aspects of heightened arousal, such as fighting or running away.

Porges has proposed a new model for the autonomic system that involves three hierarchical levels. Firstly, when the organism (or person) is under the greatest stress, it becomes extremely immobile and has a high pain threshold, as might be helpful under great threat and in preparation for death. Many animals, for example, feign death when captured by a predator. Secondly, under less stress, the sympathetic or mobilisation system is activated for fight or flight - active efforts to create safety and reduce harm. When this system is active, the organism is in a defensive mode, focusing on self-protection. However, when the organism is already safe - and this is true for mammals - the individual utilises the *social engagement system* in the brain, which is activated by the ventral vagal nervous circuit (as opposed to the dorsal vagal nervous circuit which is responsible for immobilisation). So at this third level, when we're feeling safe, the ventral vagal circuit is activated, leading to an 'open and engaged' state (Porges, 2011). This state invites communication, understanding, and joint interest in the immediate situation. It's the state that our pupils need to be in in order to best learn what we are teaching them. And most importantly, it's also the state *we* need to be in ourselves, as educators, if we are to provide the best help for our troubled pupils.

Louise writes: This has significance and potentially enormous benefit for all of us working out in schools. We're on the frontline in our classrooms, as we stand up front, leading and teaching 30 plus pupils, who will have experienced many different types of care before coming to us. So we should be informed, so that we can integrate the latest findings into our practice. But those of us involved in education seem to have been left behind in terms of the latest research: we don't really know why. Many of us were aware that pupils respond in very different ways, but we haven't had a clear framework to understand what we were observing in our classrooms. Without this kind of understanding, we might view stressed responses as very unnecessary, and may even label the pupils as misbehaved, believing we need to engage in behaviourist systems in order to get them back on track.

So I believe that Porges' work has significant implications for both how we run our school systems and how we relate to the pupils in our care, especially those who are already in a stressed state before they even come to us, because of what is happening or has happened at home. The presence of, and, more importantly, the *experience* of safety, seems to have a profound effect on pupils. We not only need to consider the pupil's own internal stress system and their current stress levels, but we also need to consider how we as educators and how our school systems might aggravate or calm stress. I am curious about the stressors out there in the school system, and I'm curious about what brings calm and the kind of 'open and engaged' state Dan describes.

Dan writes: Yes, if we are to be able to have a meaningful influence on the pupil with whom we are engaged, it's crucial that we're able to remain in this open and engaged state, rather than a defensive state. If we instantly regard our pupils' defensiveness and challenges as threats to us as educators, the open and engaged state from which we can positively influence our pupils will be undermined.

What we must also remember is that our safety as educators may be threatened by our relationships with other adults and educational practices. When we experience continuous criticisms, evaluations, and high performance expectations without sufficient support and training, as well as an educational atmosphere that focuses on weakness and errors rather than strengths and successes, we are not likely to feel safe and not likely to be able to remain open and engaged during the course of our educational day. Relationships matter, and they matter a lot - at all levels. This applies to Headteacher and teacher, teachers among themselves, educators and parents, adults and pupils, and pupils among themselves. Interpersonal safety in all these varied relationships must be a given if we are to be able to maintain the open and engaged manner of relating and learning that is at the heart of all successful education.

The open and engaged state that is associated with the ventral vagal circuit gives priority to human interactions over other sensory input coming from the environment. Why? Because other people are most often associated with threats to our safety. Once we ensure that we are safe with the other person, then we become open and engaged with him or her. Once this happens, we also become interested in and want to explore and learn more about other features of our environment, including the academic content presented by our teachers. The polyvagal theory of Stephen Porges is congruent with the full range of attachment theory, beginning where the young child turns to the parent for safety and ending where the young child is now safe to explore the world. Without safety, the pupil can't be truly interested in learning about the world. With safety, the child uses the same mental activity (being open and engaged) that helped him to experience safety, to now learn about the world.

Louise writes: I understand that this will mean that the pupil is then in a position to utilise his exploratory system, to go off and be curious: to learn. This is our priority in schools. *To settle pupils to learn.* To make the most of all the educative opportunities they have. Yet so many can't settle to learn. They seem preoccupied.

Dan writes: Well yes, when we're in a defensive state, we notice other people only in so far as we are alert to someone else as a threat to our sense of safety. When a pupil feels defensive, his readiness to learn about anything apart from threats to safety is greatly restricted. When a pupil is receiving an angry scolding from a teacher, his mind is focused on how to become safe in the present (that is, how to stop the scolding) much more than how to prevent it from happening in the future (in other words, how to manage the incident differently the next time). So human interactions in the context of safety create the best environment for learning.

Louise writes: I have really noticed this as I've carried out observations in school. I've noted time and again how troubled pupils seem to become further dysregulated and agitated when the teacher is impatient, irritated, angry or even raging in relation to a pupil or their class. How the pupils don't seem to be focused at all on what the teacher is attempting to communicate. Both the pupil and teacher seem to end up in a vicious cycle that often seems to spiral out of control.

Dan writes: When the pupil is defensive we will only be successful in having him focus on the one incident for the purpose of staying out of trouble in the future. His mind will be narrowly focused on remembering and verbalising the 'coping skill' that he is being told. He won't be able to learn from this experience because he will be defensively focused on safety with his teacher, rather than making sense of what he did, what he might do differently, and why.

However, when he feels safe, we will be far more able to help him to reflect and talk about the incident in an open manner in order to more deeply understand what happened with regard to its meaning in the context of his life. This activity of making sense of an incident is much more effective than memorising some kind of behavioural script for dealing with a similar incident in the future.

Mr. Drake saw Stan copying the work of another student so that he could present it as his own.

MR. DRAKE	*What are you doing!* (in anger) *That's not your work and you're trying to present it as if it is! You're cheating! Don't you know that you're being dishonest!*
STAN	*Yes, sir.*
MR. DRAKE	*Then why are you doing it?!*

STAN   *Forgot to do it last night.*

MR. DRAKE   *Why didn't you just tell me? You're in a lot more trouble now for stealing his work than if you had just said that you hadn't done the assignment.*

STAN   *Yes, sir.*

MR. DRAKE   *Simply tell me the next time, instead of trying to use someone else's work!*

STAN   *Yes, sir.*

In this example, Mr. Drake's quick anger and judgment immediately caused Stan to react defensively. Stan's primary focus during the above interaction most likely was to end the scolding from Mr. Drake and leave the room. If there was a chance that he could lie successfully about what he had done, most likely he would do so. If he could not lie, he probably would acknowledge his mistake, apologise, and agree not to do it again. By saying those things, Stan would end Mr. Drake's lecture sooner but most likely his motivation to do what he said would be weak. His primary motivation would have been to end the scolding.

If, however, Mr. Drake was focusing on helping Stan remain safe and not become defensive, he most likely would have approached him much differently than the above dialogue.

MR. DRAKE   *Stan, what are you doing there?* (said with a conversational tone, not conveying anger or shock)

STAN   (tries to cover the other student's paper but is not successful. He looks down but does not respond.)

MR. DRAKE   *You seem upset now and I think that I know why.* (After another ten seconds of silence he continues) *I think that*

you did not get to your assignment and are now copying
someone else's work in order to hand that in. Do I have it
right?

STAN (Nods his head to indicate that Mr. Drake is right.)

MR. DRAKE *And now that I know, you seem to feel really bad about what*
you did.

STAN *I'm sorry, Mr. Drake, I really am. I just had so many things*
to do at home last night that I didn't have time to do it.

MR. DRAKE *Yeah, I know the feeling. Sometimes everything just seems*
to be waiting to get done and I can't get to it all.

STAN *So, will you overlook this one time?*

MR. DRAKE *No, Stan, I don't think that I can do that. But I'm willing*
to help you to work out how to be sure it does not happen
again.

STAN *Just do it.*

MR. DRAKE *Yeah, that's an option, though it might not always work.*
Another is to let me know about your not getting the work
done and see if we can work something out.

STAN *That's harder than it sounds.*

MR. DRAKE *Because?*

STAN *You'll think that I'm just making up excuses.*

MR. DRAKE *Maybe, if it happened every week. But even then I'd*
probably see if we could figure out how to handle it. You
seem to be worried that I'd think that you're lazy and not a
very good student.

STAN *Yeah.*

MR. DRAKE *I know you better than that, Stan. So often I know that*

you're doing your best. Sometimes not. Like all of us.
Right now I'm disappointed in what you did to try to hide
your mistake, but I'm not disappointed in you, Stan. I
respect the person you are. Now I'll be giving you some
things to do because of what you've just done - not doing
your assignment and copying someone else's work - but
we'll get through this, and I'll still value the person you are,
Stan. I'll still be proud being your teacher.

In this dialogue, Mr. Drake was likely to have assisted Stan in becoming safe after his initial fear and shame over being found out. This would help Stan to be open and engaged in the dialogue, address what he had done with a true desire to address the problem, and then re-establish his relationship with Mr. Drake. Most likely this dialogue would reduce the likelihood that he would try to use someone else's work in the future, while the first dialogue would only be likely to make him become more secretive about what he did that was wrong, while also reducing the importance and benefit of his relationship with his teacher.

Louise writes: Everything Dan is describing here rings so true in school! How many pupils have just said back in parrot-like fashion what we have wanted them to say? And yet we have this sense that the true message is not really being digested. So often it's clear that the reflective part is missing. We see the evidence of this when the same situation happens time and time again. Where's the real learning? And what also worries me is that I've come across school staff who might try this approach ten or 15 times before even considering that maybe another approach might be required - as if no-one has ever supported them to know there is an alternative. At the end of which, all too predictably, they're disillusioned, exhausted and too stressed to engage their own reflective capacity - never mind the pupil's! It seems that an overhaul in terms of how we 'do school' is long overdue, for all our sakes.

Dan writes: We know that if the educator approaches a child in an angry (sympathetic system activated) state the child is likely to immediately not feel safe; he will unconsciously and automatically activate his defensive state, and not be receptive to exploring and learning about the incident being discussed. If the child approaches the educator in an angry state, the educator is also at risk of reacting in a defensive state, again causing open, reciprocal dialogue to be very difficult. In this instance, it is crucial for the educator to inhibit the tendency to become defensive, to remain open and engaged; while, at the same time, being focused on assisting the pupil to become open and engaged as well, prior to focusing on his anger, what happened to trigger his response, or possible alternatives to how the incident could have been handled. *It is the educator's ability to inhibit both her angry or defensive tendency to relate with the pupil that will enable her to facilitate a reciprocal, open and engaged state in the pupil. This, in turn, will make it possible for her to have a positive influence on the pupil.*

Louise writes: I've always been interested in the different responses that pupils present depending on how the teachers relates to them. I know there has been some discussion about this within schools. But I think up to now we have restricted this thinking to maybe quite a simplistic interpretation, maybe seeing simply a positive correlation between being calm and organised and the pupil responding better. Pupils do seem to do best around teachers that exhibit these characteristics. However, Dan has described something a lot more complex than merely just being calm and organised, and this really does need our attention. From what Dan is saying it seems that we need to be encouraging one another to inhibit what might feel familiar to us to do 'in the moment'. To remain grounded and together, regardless of what comes our way. And to be able to match the pupil's affect as we talked about in the last chapter, which won't always look like 'calm and organised'. That's a tough order, isn't it?

Dan writes: Yes, it is a tough order, and requires that educators are given the care that they need in order to provide such a degree of care for their pupils. An educator needs to feel safe with senior leadership, including the Headteacher, and her colleagues if she is to enhance the safety of her students. She needs relationships with colleagues where she is accepted and valued and is able to scream and cry and express despair without judgment. In that setting she will be able to acknowledge her mistakes and her struggles to accept her pupils and so find the inner strength to become again the educator that her pupils need her to be.

Also, according to Porges, telling a child to *"Listen to me!"*, *"Look at me!"*, *"Sit still!"*, or *"Calm down"* is telling a child to do something that is often not under his conscious control. Rather, these activities are bodily, visceral, states, made much more possible when the pupil is safe and his neurological social engagement system is activated.

Louise writes: I know that many teachers will be especially interested in this, as it's all too easy to think that these pupils are engaging in behaviours that are conscious and controlled, especially when we're feeling stressed ourselves. Because of this, many troubled pupils get punished.

Dan writes: Yes, and punished unfairly I strongly believe. Pupils most often don't have the neurological maturation to be able to *consistently* inhibit their dysregulated, impulsive, behaviours, though they are able to do so periodically. The ability to consistently inhibit strong competing action tendencies requires the maturation of areas of the dorso-lateral pre-frontal cortex, and this region of the brain doesn't fully mature until the individual is in his early to mid-20s. These inhibitory behaviours are likely to be more responsive when the child is feeling safe than when he has become defensive. They will be less responsive with troubled pupils. Asking or telling a troubled pupil who is not safe in the present to be calm is likely to be a very unrealistic expectation.

This degree of interpersonal safety is likely to be present when the child feels that he is being accepted by the adult, not being evaluated or judged. Yet, of course, the educator does need to evaluate the child's behaviour! When a pupil's behaviour - lying, stealing, ridiculing or hitting another pupil - does not reflect the values of the community, the teacher needs to comment on it, and make clear expectations for appropriate behaviour. However, to be effective in having an influence in the future expression or inhibition of this behaviour, it is crucial that the child has a relationship with the educator in which he experiences acceptance of his self - his person - even when his behaviour is being evaluated. Our relationship - when it communicates that we unconditionally accept the child - will enable the child to remain safe and socially engaged when we need to evaluate and comment on his behaviour. Acceptance is so essential that we will speak about it a great deal more in Chapter 6.

Louise writes: What Dan has just said has implications for how involved we become with the pupils in our care. Our schools have become so overstretched with stressed systems and curricular demands that we often don't have the time necessary, or make the time, in order to engage in the kind of quality relationships you're suggesting. However, it sounds as if we have to get to a place within our school systems whereby we can start to honour relationships more than we have been. For a pupil to experience acceptance for his personhood is going to mean that we become involved. Porges' work seems to be giving us permission to get close to the pupils in our care, underlining what we were saying in Chapter 2: the opposite of teacher training guidance!

Dan writes: I believe that Porges' work not only gives us permission to be close to our pupils but also gives us the reasons as to why it is so important to do so. Such closeness - as is also true with secure attachment - facilitates healthy relative dependence, independence, and interdependence (*see* pp.28-30, p.239).

Along with the importance of acceptance in the relationship, Porges' research goes further in helping us to understand how to influence the behaviour about which we have concern.   The social engagement system remains active when the adult speaks to the child with a relaxed, modulated, rhythmic voice, rather than the monotone voice that is characteristic of a lecture.   As we described in the last chapter, the modulated voice is one that may be described as a 'story-telling' voice that is simply describing an event, understanding it, but not evaluating nor judging the child.

Louise writes: This is interesting too!   During observations I have noticed that the troubled pupils do seem to do better around teachers who are animated - serious implications for teacher training again.

Dan writes: Yes, we definitely need to be more expressive, but not in an artificial way.   Rather when we clearly express our interest and intentions in a way that fits our personality and culture, our pupil is likely to experience our genuine interest in him and our awareness of qualities about him that we are responding to that make him unique.   When we are neutral in our stance, our pupil is more like to experience us as simply 'doing our job' and to not believe that he is having a positive effect on us, that we could genuinely enjoy being with him and watching him grow.

This new neuropsychological knowledge both describes the necessity of remaining in our 'open and engaged' neuro-circuits when interacting with our pupil in order to have an influence on him and his behaviour, while also suggesting possible characteristics of such interactions. We believe that these characteristics have four central components: playfulness, acceptance, curiosity, and empathy (PACE - *see* Hughes, 2009, Golding & Hughes, 2012). While playfulness may not always be present, depending on the immediate emotional state of the pupil, when it is present, it facilitates a light, rhythmic, engaged interaction that poses little, if any, threat to the child. Acceptance provides the foundation of the child's experience of safety and his willingness to enter into relationship with the adult. Curiosity - when the child is open and engaged - enables him to make sense of the meaning of his behaviour without shame and fear. The educator's empathy enables the child to experience his stressful emotions without dysregulation or denial. These characteristics will be discussed in greater detail in the next four chapters.

I routinely bring parents into my therapy room and demonstrate for them how they can be open and engaged with their children, during both the relaxed times but also times characterised by conflict and discipline. Troubled children respond so well when their parents, foster carers, or adoptive parents relate with them in a manner that takes their 'troubles' into account, rather than reacting to them. Louise and I have both experienced that pupils respond equally well when their educators do the same.

Chapter 5

Be playful and have fun!

Prone to action, and deficient in words, these 'pupils' can often express their internal states more articulately in physical movements or in pictures than in words.   (Van Der Kolk 1996, p.195)

Louise writes: Words often seem to be the primary means of communication in school nowadays, especially in secondary: and yet there are many other ways of communicating, of relating, and we need to re-visit some of them. Vulnerable pupils need a wide range of alternatives if they are going to be able to engage with us.

A Key Adult and pupil (aged eight) use Theraplay together in their 1:1 withdrawal session in order to build relationship. The KA collects two cushions and a feather and the two of them proceed to blow the feather backwards and forwards on their cushions. From time to time, the feather floats to the floor and neither of them are swift enough to catch it. They both laugh and have another go!

A Key Adult and pupil (13) play football together each day. They don't say much, but there is a lot of eye contact, physical interaction and laughter.

Laughter releases the all-important hormone oxytocin which is well documented as countering the negative impact of the stress hormone that is in plentiful supply in those who have experienced significant relational traumas and losses - cortisol. High levels of cortisol can be toxic, not only killing off brain cells and compromising the pupil's immune system but interfering with the connections between the left and right hemisphere of the brain. These connectors are necessary in making the most of school and all the opportunities available there. So we need to consider how we can facilitate the production of oxytocin as a vital component of any pupil's stress management plan!

Dan writes: Allan Schore said that the region of the brain that is active when we laugh is never active when we are feeling shame (1994). Since most troubled pupils, if not all, experience a pervasive sense of shame, and since shame greatly impedes their ability to learn from their mistakes, becoming engaged with these pupils in reciprocal laughter might be seen as an important educational activity. Also, Mary Dozier, a psychologist at the University of Delaware, and her colleagues, have developed an important intervention programme which assists high-risk mothers to develop a relationship with their young children in a way that promotes attachment security in the child (Bernard, et al 2012). The programme coaches facilitate the mothers' ability to experience *delight* with their young children. Dozier has found that reciprocal delight enables the relationship to develop in very important ways.

Louise writes: In this chapter, we will explore the numerous benefits of integrating playfulness into both the primary and secondary phases of education. We'll look at the current fears around this and reflect on the different interventions that will help settle vulnerable pupils to learn, based on the work of Dr. Bruce Perry.

Playful interactions dampen down the impact of stress and enable the higher level parts of the brain to come online. This means that the pupil can then be open and engaged - in a position to think, to reflect, to learn …

We need to give each other permission in schools to smile, to laugh and to have some fun together: to play. We all need to play. Many of our schools have become far too serious, probably as a consequence of the fast pace and ever-increasing curricular demands imposed by education legislators who are far-removed from the classroom. Belinda Harris from Nottingham University claims that many school systems are traumatised (2010): if that's the case, then no wonder we have all got so serious! The sparkle needs to be restored! And it can be, even in secondary provision, when expectations and demands increase massively.

One 15 year old adopted pupil summed it up well when she said:

"Why do teachers just moan at us? Why can't they make our learning fun? I'm anxious enough as it is. I do not need any more anxiety. I then can't hear anything. Crack a joke every now and then. Smile. Let us know it's going to be OK. It makes all the difference. I feel my anxiety melting away. It means I can then relax and hear you."

Dan writes: Many troubled pupils have difficulty with signs of compassion and care, but they're able to remain engaged and increase their trust with adults with whom they have experiences of joint smiling and laughter. Eye contact in the context of laughter tends to increase pupil's connection with us, more so than does a supportive discussion.

Troubled pupils have difficulty regulating all of their emotions, both positive (joy, excitement, affection) and negative (anger, fear, sadness). If we're able to help them to regulate positive emotions through playfulness, this is likely to increase their ability to regulate negative emotions as well.

Finally, Louise, I think that when we are playful with our pupil we are strengthening our relationship so that he may well continue to trust us when we set a limit or ask him to focus on a task. Playfulness shows that we truly like him, even if at times we need to have expectations that might lead to conflicts. Playfulness shows hope and confidence that no matter what, we will get through this and still like each other.

Louise writes: There seems to be a paradox here, as the exploratory system in each and every pupil is much more likely to come online to its full potential once a pupil is relaxed; and yet this can sometimes seem contrary to what we're attempting to do in schools. Somewhere along the line we learned that pupils need to be anxious in order to give their best. We don't want them to feel *too* relaxed. What might happen? There is a cultural expectation that stern discipline is all that is needed in order to get results.

We have moved so far from the actual truth, so let's challenge what's happening. What if we were to allow or even encourage playfulness? What if we protected quality time for playfulness? What if we started measuring our schools' success by smiles and laughter? Would we see an improvement in learning? My guess is that we would.

Dan writes: Yes, mild anxiety tends to increase a pupil's performance more so than does no anxiety or high levels of anxiety. If a pupil is quite relaxed and we introduce mild anxiety, his performance is likely to improve. What we need to remember is that our vulnerable students tend to maintain a core state of a high level of anxiety already, which is itself already interfering with performance. For these pupils, inducing mild anxiety might well move their already too-high level into extreme anxiety that could well be dysregulating, and cause increasing behavioural disturbances. For these children, we need to work to *decrease* their habitual level of anxiety so that it becomes mild in order to improve their performance.

The limitations of everyday language ...

Louise writes: There is a lot of emphasis put on the use of words in both spoken and written form in schools, and yet words do have their limitations. There are some feelings and experiences that are best communicated through other media such as music, dance, art, playfulness ... Even writing can be tackled more playfully and creatively than perhaps we do currently.

Dan writes: Remember too that the work of Stephen Porges (*see* Chap.4) indicates that the spoken word, when it's expressed in a manner that contains a lot of modulation and rhythm - much like story telling - can easily have a playful quality to it. This quality can facilitate the open and engaged state of mind so crucial for learning. Words don't have to be spoken within the stern monotone of a lecture. How we talk is so important.

Louise writes: Some pupils who have experienced relational trauma and loss don't want to use words or don't have the necessary words to communicate what they need to express. We probably all know pupils who actually engage in incessant chatter fuelled by anxiety, not really communicating much at all - yet increasing anxiety! So let's ensure that we give our pupils a balanced and varied diet of many different forms of expression. Let's be mindful of incorporating playfulness and fun into our interactions.

Neither does our support need to be serious all the time! In fact, the more playful we can be within our interactions together, the better. Basic, childlike humour is a bonus whatever the age of the pupil, as humour can diffuse anxiety. However, we need to be wary of sarcasm or irony: many troubled pupils won't understand these kinds of humour - both need higher level functioning in order to be understood and enjoyed. Some of these pupils are not developmentally ready for this yet. They may experience sarcasm as us laughing at them; it's often this kind of wit, however mild or kindly meant, that gets met with a defensive response. Many of our vulnerable pupils take language literally.

Below is a list of six important characteristics, all beginning (usefully) with 'R', - which Dr. Bruce Perry believes need to colour our interventions amongst troubled pupils (Conference, June 2013, Centre for Child Mental Health, London): Dan and I find these helpful. The six R's encourage us to let our interventions be:

- *Relational*
- *Repetitive*
- *Rhythmic*
- *Rewarding* - fun
- *Relevant* - developmentally (emotionally and socially)
- *Respectful* - of the pupil, family and culture

Remember too that our pupils may not have had much experience of being in the presence of grown-ups who, to use some jargon, 'manifest positive affect': in other words, people who are calm, open, friendly and approachable, who actively show that they are interested in the pupil, enjoy them, want to help them learn and are willing to have fun with them. In fact many of these pupils will have been overlooked, scorned or dismissed in their early experiences. Imagine how strange it would be then to come into this other, warmer, playful world - none of us would be able to trust or to adapt to that overnight.

Let's open up new possibilities for our pupils. New experiences pave the way for new neural pathways. Within these interactions let's also be mindful of the power of rhythm, which may be an 'R' in Perry's list unfamiliar to some readers. Rhythmic interactions include such things as:

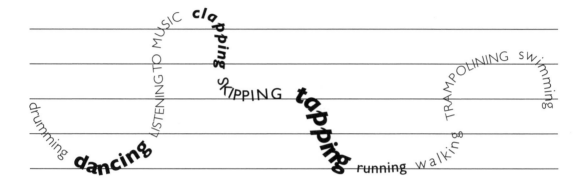

These interactions are known to have positive effects on pupil's states of readiness for learning. Such activities don't have much status in schools and are even being taken off the curriculum in some cases, in order to make more space for what is considered 'core curriculum', such as literacy, numeracy and science. Surely the core curriculum also needs to include a focus that deepens positive ways in which our pupil views himself, others and the world?

If the pupil isn't settled within himself at his core, how can he realistically settle to learn? Another paradox: *if we neglect rhythmic interventions* in the more academic subjects, we are, in effect, restricting the capacity of the pre-frontal cortex to work to its full potential, as it needs to. A good balance is needed for health. Perry goes further (*ibid*), recommending that we should think about facilitating rhythmic sensory breaks throughout the school day for short bursts in order to optimise learning. He suggests that sensory breaks quieten down the lower parts of the brain to enable other parts to be fully activated.

Rhythmic interventions such as those listed overleaf seem to reach parts of the brain deep down within in the cortex, which positively affects the 'higher', more sophisticated parts of the pre-frontal cortex. So the deeper down we go, the more on-line we become further up! So let's not stay in the shallows, but let's go deeper, so that the thinking and reflective parts of the brain can be impacted!

> *When I go into schools to take classes nowadays I take a Djembe drum with me. I start rhythms off and the pupils follow me by matching my rhythm whilst clapping. Individual pupils start rhythms off and the rest of us follow. It's fun. I use the drum in between my talking and their engaging with words. We engage in conversations together through the drum. We often smile! This playfulness stills the class, enabling them to take in key messages about inclusion, as that's often why I'm there. The drum also stills even those who are fidgety, inattentive and usually disruptive. I wish every class had a Djembe drum. Oh the music we could create, and the learning that could come!*

If we want the pre-frontal cortex to come online to its full capacity then we must pay attention to the roots!

Learning from Winston

> *At the time of writing I have just acquired a three month old kitten called Winston, who is quite a handful but also very entertaining. I've not only had to learn the dance of attachment with him to tune into his needs throughout the day, but I've also had to set up a play routine at regular intervals. I've found that the more play I can facilitate and join in with,*

the less likely he is to engage in aggressive play - scratching and biting. Not only this but the more able he seems to stick within the limits that I set him. This has been a steep learning curve for me! But you know what? Both Winston and I have benefited from this process. I can't just sit at my computer screen for hours. I have to take a break! These bursts of playfulness have stimulated my mind to write.

Dan writes: Louise, the well-known and respected neurologist, Jaak Panksepp, has found that play in young animals, like puppies, kittens, and rat pups, facilitates their development in many ways (2012). If play was suppressed when they were young, their overall learning, social, and sensory-motor skills were deficient in adulthood. Panksepp strongly believes that the rough-and-tumble play of childhood is crucial for the overall development of children and that too often, educators try to suppress such play, because it makes the school environment more difficult to manage. We need to learn how to 'manage' the increased energy that results from a play-friendly school. Maybe our needs for control and order could become a bit less rigid: and maybe we educators need to be more comfortable with incorporating a more spontaneous and flexible structure into our school programmes.

Louise writes: So let's give ourselves permission in school to play, not just setting up activities but joining in as well. Play is so therapeutic in the widest possible sense, and yet it has slowly taken more and more of a back seat as the national curriculum has taken up our full focus. We need to challenge this.

The meaning and value of play need to be resurrected. Playfully.

Chapter 6

Communicate acceptance

Louise writes: Gott (2009) contrasts two views of challenging behaviour. Here's the first (I've changed 'child' to 'pupil'):

> The behaviour must change. The pupil must change his unacceptable behaviour. The pupil must learn that she has to fit in/adapt. The pupil is old enough to realise that we don't behave like that. That's how the world works. We are preparing pupils for the real world.   (p.58)

We could add to this stance. We could add: *"There are no excuses. Pupils will soon start to realise the consequences of their actions and start taking more responsibility for their choices if we get more determined in our use of rewards and sanctions, authority and control, and continue to adhere to our whole school behaviour policy. We just need to toughen up."*

Now let's look at the contrasting view that Gott presents. Yes, the behaviour must indeed change. But our troubled pupils are not able to fit into the main school behaviour policy - yet - because they have a fragile sense of self and they do not have sufficient internal controls developed - yet. Adverse circumstances and extraordinary stress have compromised their development. There are even physical differences in the brain as a result of this, meaning there are a number of significant vulnerabilities present. It is possible for pupils to move forwards developmentally and to learn healthy and appropriate attachment behaviours. The pupil will need a number of relational capacities if they are to 'cope in the real world', as Gott puts it. And as she concludes, 'attitudes may need to change in order that the pupil can change. School approaches may need to change ...' (p.58).

When I'm out and about in schools, some senior managers tell me that certain behaviours are totally unacceptable. These behaviours include screaming, punching, lying, spitting, swearing, kicking, damaging property and the like. However, some senior managers have a very different take on what's going on - seeming to link these behaviours to so much more than merely unacceptable ways of relating. Interestingly, the level of tolerance and the understanding of what lies behind such behaviour varies enormously from school to school. In a Guardian article (16/2/13), the Children's Commissioner for England Maggie Atkinson was quoted as saying

> ... there is a gap in the knowledge of the children's workforce in what ordinary child development should look like and what child development looks like if there is a delay or physical condition.

I would add that there is a gap in knowledge around the impact of relational developmental trauma and loss too. Atkinson goes on to state that in their initial training and once in their posts, teachers should ensure that they understand what brain development looks like, what social development look like and what emotional difficulties looks like.

In some schools, I am firmly told that *"Something needs to be done"*, that 'something' being to communicate explicitly, not only to the pupil in question, but also to their peers, that these behaviours are unacceptable. Many times, the communication of this explicit message has seemed to aggravate the behaviours further; but, despite this, senior managers clearly feel they have no choice but to continue to make the same interventions to deal with the issue.

Sometimes this results in exclusion. The levels of exclusion in the UK are very high at this time. These exclusion figures not only include legal exclusions but illegal ones too. New research published by Contact A Family (The Guardian 19/2/13) found that out of 400 families of children with disability or additional needs, 22% of the children are illegally excluded once a week and 15% every day (for part of the day). The Chief Executive of this charity describes how a lack of understanding in schools can actually facilitate escalation to such a point that the school then feels that they have no other option than to exclude.

When I ask them about why they continue with what doesn't seem to be working, senior managers repeat that these pupils need to know that what they are doing is unacceptable. The managers' intention is to reduce the level of inappropriate behaviours *by helping these pupils to connect cause and effect*. This might seem a reasonable aim. However, regrettably, what the new learning from neuroscience has shown is that pupils who have experienced significant relational traumas and losses *will not be able to make this connection through this approach*. We now know that the pre-frontal cortex concerned with making connections, especially regarding cause and effect, is severely compromised for these vulnerable pupils. In fact this 'explicit communication' seems to further entrench the very behaviours it was intended to reduce.

Many staff make assumptions about the level of social understanding, empathy and reflective capacity of the pupils in their care. They assume they are self-aware enough in order to make healthy and appropriate choices. Right choices. They assume that these pupils are able to utilise cause and effect, making connections so that they can adapt their behaviours.

This is so far from the truth. So many of our troubled pupils are under-developed in these significant areas. Many do not have the necessary *internal* controls - yet - in order to make the most of the *external* controls being imposed on them within a school context. With the lack of understanding around these pupils, it's easy to see how staff can become angry with what seems more like defiance than developmental vulnerability.

I'm curious about how we can work together to improve this situation. Interventions used to reduce unacceptable behaviour vary significantly from school to school as well, especially at the level of acceptance and the kind of approaches used. Sometimes this even differs within classes in the same school. I'm curious about these differences too. I'm especially interested in how these differences impact on a pupil's well-being, their behaviour and their development.

As I've queried elsewhere, why is it that a particular pupil is open and engaged in one class with one teacher, but seems to fall apart in another? Why is it that in one school a pupil is excluded, and another pupil remains for exactly the same misdemeanour? Why is it that in some schools, an initial behaviour escalates and yet in other schools, the same initial behaviours can be stilled?

A lot seems to depend on the interpretation of this word - acceptance. What is acceptance? And what affects our acceptance? More importantly, what impact does acceptance have, if any? In this chapter, we'll be navigating our way through these questions. We will also explore how we can increase our communication of acceptance by thinking together through the challenges that we will face. By the end of the chapter, you may conclude with us that we all have to adapt the way we 'do school': our updated thinking must affect practice. Let's start by accepting where we are currently, within our own understanding.

What is acceptance?

In schools we seem quite wary about the word 'acceptance'. We assume acceptance means that we must overlook behaviours that are shocking, disturbed, dangerous or inappropriate. This is not what Dan and I are advocating.

We believe that though we may not agree with or condone certain types of behaviours, that there is a pupil hidden beneath the behaviours who needs to be acknowledged, seen and heard. The pupil becomes our central focus - *not* the behaviour. We're curious about why a pupil might do what they do; evaluation is always secondary. The pupil comes first. His personhood is always first in our thinking. We need to clarify that this doesn't mean that we merely excuse behaviour either. We use our reflective capacity to enable us to create a framework in which to *interpret* behaviour. Once we have our framework of understanding in place, we're then better placed to be able to facilitate interventions that will actually make a difference, rather than assuming that one size fits all. Fortunately or unfortunately, each pupil is unique. Time and effort will be needed to understand this particular pupil.

According to my Concordance, acceptance has a number of different meanings. For the purposes of this book I've chosen four which I believe best match what is needed within support provision in the school context. You'll notice that they seem to connect to *personhood* rather than *behaviour*.

- AFFIRMATION

    affirming the pupil's sense of self, the intrinsic value of their life
    and their capacity to make a positive contribution to their world.

- WELCOME

    welcoming the pupil in, regardless of difference, of 'presentation
    of affect' (expression of feeling). Letting the pupil know explicitly
    that they belong, no matter what.

- BELIEF

  believing that whatever the pupil communicates in the 'here
  and now' is valid and worth taking notice of and reflecting
  on. Believing that there is some kind of meaning in the pupil's
  behaviour that needs to be understood.

- ACKNOWLEDGEMENT

  acknowledging a pupil's situation - both past and present. Being
  aware of the impact of relational trauma and loss upon this pupil.
  Being aware of behaviour as communication.

Dan writes: Louise, I believe that the core of our acceptance of the pupil is
this strong and unconditional focus on what you are calling his personhood, not on
what he does or doesn't do. We communicate acceptance when we do not judge,
evaluate, or criticise our pupil's inner life. What he thinks, feels, wishes, intends,
perceives, values, remembers, and is interested in, is accepted as being part of who
he is now. We don't place '*should*' on any aspect of his inner life. If he feels fear,
sadness, anger, or shame, we don't argue with him about his emotions. Rather,
we accept whatever it is, have empathy if it's hard, and then work to understand it
and any implications of the feeling. If he says that he hates another teacher, our
response might be something like:

> *"My, that must make it hard being with Mr. Jenkins - if you hate him. My
> guess is you don't feel close to him, would be reluctant to talk with him,
> and might even not feel safe with him. Is that so? What do you think that's
> about - your hating him? Have you felt that way long? Are there times
> when you don't feel that way?"*

We're not suggesting that we make all of those comments, just that we stand near the child and his inner life, and help him to reflect on it, making sense of it, and seeing it again. Now, with our experience of his hatred, that feeling he has is likely to begin to shift and soften, and he is likely to begin to wonder about Mr. Jenkins in a more open manner.

What affects our levels of acceptance?

Louise writes: As I've worked alongside staff across the phases over the years, I've become aware of a number of features that can compromise our capacity to communicate acceptance.

How we have been disciplined ourselves, our own training and how we are managed, all seem to really affect our value systems around what is acceptable and what isn't. Also of course we tend to interpret what we see through the lens of our own previous experience of relationships - our own attachment lens. For example if we didn't experience warmth or care in our early years, we will tend to use an *insecure attachment lens* in which to interpret ourselves, others and our situation. Those who had good enough care are likely to use a *secure attachment lens* in order to interpret themselves, others and their contexts (*discussed in detail in* Bombèr, 2007).

Unless someone encourages us to think outside our own narrative and understanding of the world we tend to be shocked by behaviours that we and our peers wouldn't have ever engaged in: we naturally tend to judge others according to our own experiences. We tend to put in disciplinary measures according to our own interpretations, not always taking account the interpretations of those whose experience has been very different to ours. For example a pupil who comes from a shaming, abusive background 'wearing' an insecure attachment lens in school is more likely to be treated with scorn and disbelief as he over reacts to slight stressors - swearing and behaving aggressively to a member of staff for example, who may themselves be 'wearing' a secure attachment lens, and not understand why he is upset.

In addition, troubled pupils can unconsciously awaken past or present traumas that lie unresolved or suppressed deep within us. When we are reminded of another person, another time and another place, some very uncomfortable and sometimes painful feelings can surface. When working with these pupils we can easily feel deskilled, disempowered, even out of control. These are uncomfortable feelings to manage. Sometimes the intensity of these feelings move staff into feeling overwhelmed. Sometimes staff dispel their discomfort by restricting their 'window of tolerance' when relating to troubled pupils, often increasing their level of power and authority over them (*and see later on in this chapter for how we can take responsibilities for our own histories*).

Our school systems are stressful for even the most secure people amongst us, as they are extremely demanding places to work emotionally, mentally and physically. If, for example there's also a residential trip away to manage, and it's nearing the end of the term, stress and fatigue are going to reach toxic levels. This combination can affect the reflective and care-giving capacity of educational staff supporting troubled pupils, meaning that acceptance is going to be low on our agenda. Survival is going to be the priority for everyone within an already stressed system.

What impact can acceptance have?

From experience, it's clear that the troubled pupils who remain in school making progress developmentally and academically are the ones who have been saturated with acceptance with a capital A! They are the ones who sense deep down that staff really care, really value them and affirm them for 'who' they are. They sense that there are staff rooting for them on every level, sharing their emotional experience of the highs and lows together. They sense that the staff have curiosity about them, a willingness to learn together, to attempt to understand why they (the pupils) do what they do. They sense that despite feeling a deep sense of pain, loneliness and their own sense of being overwhelmed, there is something about these members of staff which contains them. They sense hope. It's as if has someone has deeply understood what they so desperately needed without them ever having put their request into words.

We might keep this in mind each time a pupil's behaviour becomes increasingly challenging. Acceptance - when it is unconditional, continuous, and clear - creates safety for our pupil and is fundamental in maintaining the strength, value, and meaning of our relationship with him. Acceptance conveys confidences that our relationship is *'for better or worse'*. We might have a bad day, he might have a bad day, we both might have a bad day, but we'll get through it together. Acceptance conveys a commitment to our pupil and the relationship, *regardless of his behaviour.*

Acceptance enables: evaluation disables

In schools we sometimes believe that we have a free licence to evaluate everything about a pupil, but we don't. We must communicate our acceptance to our pupils as a matter of priority, far above all other agendas.

I wonder what would happen in our schools if we really learned how to fully communicate acceptance to all pupils, regardless of their starting point, regardless of their actions? Accepting a pupil as a human being doesn't necessarily mean that we agree with his values, beliefs or actions. Accepting a pupil means that we affirm him, we welcome him, we believe him and we acknowledge him. That is a huge difference, but this difference isn't usually communicated in an explicit way in our schools, so staff and pupils alike can become confused and agitated by the apparently conflicting intentions and motives of others.

Dan writes: That accepting our pupil's inner life doesn't mean we are necessarily agreeing with it, is a key point. We are simply understanding it and helping our pupil to understand it more fully and deeply himself. Through our acceptance, he is more likely to continue to share his experience with us, giving us a greater opportunity to have an influence on his experience. But this influence will not be through evaluating it to be wrong. Influence will come from the acceptance that provides our pupil with the safety needed to explore his inner life with us in an open, rather than defensive manner. It will then be for him to decide if he will join some of our thoughts, perceptions, values with his and in doing so, allow us to influence the development of his inner life.

Louise writes: For anyone working in any care-taking role, acceptance is an essential quality. For a pupil to know that someone will remain alongside them despite their attempts to do everything to push the other person away, both consciously and unconsciously, is powerful. If a pupil experiences acceptance, he is more likely to stay open and engaged. If he is open and engaged, he is more likely to engage his reflective capacity and to hear what you have to say. If he can hear what you have to say, there is potential for change.

The opposite is true for a pupil who does *not* experience acceptance. Evaluating personhood disables a pupil in terms of his reflective capacity and his ability to make new meanings or to adapt. Evaluating personhood activates defensive strategies which in turn means that the pupil remains stuck. How can our pupils possibly have the opportunity to move on in their thinking, and thus their behaviour, when merely engaging the primal part of their brain linked to survival? When personal judgments and personal evaluation are involved, the kind of thing I described above that the senior managers were attempting to do to link cause and effect will always be severely compromised.

Struggles communicating acceptance

Dan writes: How many times have we said:

"I'm not angry with you, I'm angry with what you are doing! You need to try harder!"

And then our pupil yells back at us defensively, or walks away, sulks, and avoids us for the rest of the day. So much for the value of communicating acceptance. What went wrong?

First, we may have drifted into the habit of being annoyed every time our pupil misbehaves. When our anger is that consistent, he will most likely experience us as not accepting who he is, imperfections and all. He may believe that we will accept him only if he is perfect. He may well believe that we accept him when he is being 'good' but not when he is being 'bad'. For acceptance to be experienced as acceptance, it needs to be unconditional. When your anger is reserved for more serious misbehaviours, such as hurting another child, but not for routine behaviours, such as not completing a task, then your pupil will sense that your anger is specific to his behaviour and not to his personhood whenever he misbehaves.

Second, our anger may not have remained focused on his behaviour - whatever he did - but rather moved into a deeper aspect of his sense of himself - his effort. We said that he did not try hard enough. How do we know that? Maybe he tried very hard but wasn't successful. Maybe he is not trying the right way of doing something. Maybe he was overwhelmed by a major stress, loss, conflict, or trauma that we know nothing about. Much better to take a 'not-knowing' stance as to the reason for the behaviour that you are evaluating.

Third, we may well have still been angry, as evidenced by our voice, face, gestures, and posture. As he experienced our anger in the here-and-now, he is not likely to be able to differentiate his self from his behaviour. Communicating your acceptance is best done when the anger is gone.

Let's think a bit about how we might communicate acceptance more clearly when relating with a pupil in the situations described above. We'll start with the less serious behaviour - being late for class. Suppose we begin with: *"Harry, I notice that you have been late for class a few times this week. What's that about?"* Our voice is relaxed and conversational. Our face is warm and inviting. We are open and engaged with him, showing that we're interested and want to have a conversation with him about being late. Our question is also open-ended and non-judgmental. It's not the stern, intense, *"What's that about?"* that conveys that we have already judged that there could be no valid reason for not being on time for class. Rather, it is 'not-knowing'. We truly don't know why he was late, and we want to understand that before we make any judgment or give any recommendation or consequence for the behaviour.

If we approach Harry in this way, more than likely he will try to tell us why he was late. If he says that he simply did not notice the time, we might continue wondering why he thinks that he forgot. This might be a good line of questioning whether he is seldom late or if he is late often. Again, there is no judgment about him being late, simply a desire to understand and be of assistance if this is a challenge for Harry. If we choose to address the behaviour with a recommendation or a 'consequence' that follows from the reason, he is going to be much more likely to accept our guidance or directive if our voice remains relaxed and modulated, rather than moving into a stern monotone.

In our exploration of Harry's being late for class, our overall manner suggests that we were accepting him and we were engaging him within the overall nature of our relationship, rather than seeing him as a problem or seeing the problem as more important than him and a threat to our relationship.

Let's now explore communicating acceptance when we are addressing a more serious behaviour with Harry - hurting another child. Here the appropriate first response might well be anger, which stresses the seriousness of the behaviour. A more relaxed first response could erroneously suggest that we are not that concerned about the behaviour, and that its impact on the other child is not that important. However, the anger, when expressed effectively, will focus on the behaviour, the reason, and an alternative behaviour:

> *"I am angry that you hit Jake! He needs safety like everyone here does, including you! If you have a problem with him, you tell me about it, you don't hit him!"*

The behaviour is now stopped, your response to its seriousness is clear, and here comes the tricky part. If we truly want Harry to know that we are angry with the behaviour *while accepting him*, we now need to repair the relationship. We accept him, and our relationship with him is still extremely important to us; it's strong, and it has not been broken, in spite of his behaviour. Our voice becomes relaxed, modulated, open, and engaged. We convey empathy for any stress caused by our anger and let Harry know that we will work with him on managing his anger better.

> *"I realise it's difficult for you when I get angry with you. You might even wonder if I don't like you now. I still care a lot for you, Harry, and we'll get through this. I'm going to work out ways with you to handle things better without hitting other kids. We'll get it done."*

We've been told by others that such an approach might 'reinforce' the pupil's aggressive behaviour. That hasn't been our experience. Such 'reinforcement' might be the case if we have a poor relationship with the pupil, and the only time he gets our attention is when he misbehaves. But if our relationship is strong and ongoing, he will not be aggressive to get from us what he can get for free. Instead, though our pupil's behaviour may elicit our anger, the strong continuity of our relationship may be the central factor in him being motivated to reduce his aggression toward his peers.

How can we increase our levels of acceptance?

Louise writes: If acceptance does have such a profound impact on our pupils' well-being, then we're really going to have to find ways to increase our own capacity to provide it. Here are some thoughts about what will help:

I   TAKING RESPONSIBILITY FOR OUR OWN HISTORIES

It may be that we need to gain further understanding about why we do what we do. The more self-aware we are, the more likely we will be able to make sense of why certain dynamics might unsettle us or stress us out. We can do this by journalling, talking with close, trusted family and friends, or by seeing a counsellor/psychotherapist. Once we're clearer about our own histories and how they have impacted us, then the more available we will be to communicate full acceptance to those pupils in our care. Having someone alongside us, empathising with our own journey through life, will increase our capacity to empathise. We all need to know we can find full acceptance somewhere in our lives.

II   ACCOUNTABILITY

When we're involved in support work of vulnerable pupils it's wise to have someone or some others to check in with from time to time. It's good to be around other people who can listen and can also gently challenge our practices, encouraging us to be reflective and to consider our actions in the school context.

III   DEVELOPING OUR UNDERSTANDING

a)   The pupil's story

It is time for us to reflect on our pupil's story, to attempt to understand why he does what he does, remembering as ever that behaviour is communication. Let's develop our curiosity. Let's encourage our pupils to start to develop their own curiosity.

b)   Things are not always the way they seem

Let's remember that it's not always helpful to interpret what we see through our own attachment lens as we might misunderstand completely what is going on; our response may then make things worse, without that being our intention.

c)   No to judgment

We need to be so mindful in schools of our over-dependence on judgment as a means of supporting pupils to know the difference between right and wrong, to make connections between cause and effect. Many of the pupils we are concerned with in this book are not able to manage this - yet. Pupil A may 'unravel' in front of us after a minor criticism or what appears to be a judgment of him as a person. However, Pupil B might just 'get over it' quite quickly and adapt his behaviour in the way we're hoping. So it's quite clear that something else is going on for Pupil A that needs to be explored, reflected on and considered. This implies that we might have to adapt our usual educational practices along the lines we've been suggesting.

Once pupils have developed a more robust sense of self and some internal control, they will probably be able to accept some judgment/evaluation, but many will still need a very different approach to begin with, especially those who have internal toxic shame (*see* Chap.13, p.250).

IV   SLOWING THINGS DOWN

In our schools we are often quick to react. These pupils need us to slow ourselves down. Before engaging in *action* we need to communicate *acceptance* loud and clear - as a preventative, on-going way of being and relating. Let's encourage each other to stay with uncomfortable feelings for longer than we do. We are stronger than we often realise. Remaining alongside someone, rather than evaluating and judging, is a skill, but one well worth practising. Let's find ways to settle ourselves into tolerating and managing the uncomfortable feelings that will inevitably arise.

V   USING SPECIFIC SCRIPTS

The scripts opposite have proved helpful within support work in schools to communicate acceptance.

Acceptance enables: evaluation disables

Dan writes: I believe that this is so important, Louise, that I'd like to say it again. By accepting our pupil's inner life, we are not necessarily agreeing with it. We are simply understanding it and helping him to understand it more fully and deeply himself. Through our acceptance of his inner life, our pupil is more likely to continue to share his experience with us, giving us a greater opportunity to have an influence on it.

Louise writes: As you can see, Dan and I view full acceptance as key to developing authentic relationships with our pupils, and the most fruitful and rewarding way forward for all.

SCRIPTS FOR COMMUNICATING ACCEPTANCE

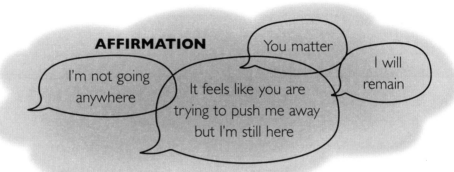

AFFIRMATION

You matter

I'm not going anywhere

It feels like you are trying to push me away but I'm still here

I will remain

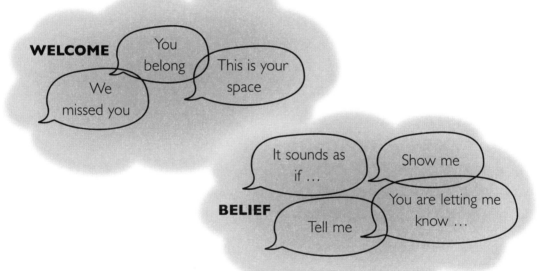

WELCOME

You belong

This is your space

We missed you

It sounds as if …

Show me

BELIEF

You are letting me know …

Tell me

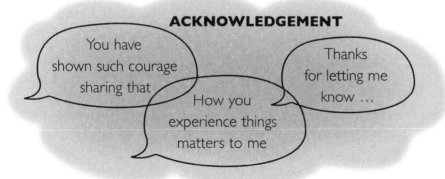

ACKNOWLEDGEMENT

You have shown such courage sharing that

Thanks for letting me know …

How you experience things matters to me

Chapter 7

Be curious, without judgment

Dan writes: As we noted in Chapter 4, the state of mind that the neuropsychologist, Stephen Porges (2011) described as being 'open and engaged' is central in maintaining an attitude toward our pupils that facilities both safety and the readiness to explore and learn about their world, including the world presented to them in the classroom. Focusing on being open and engaged in a bit more detail, we will be presenting how curiosity is central to this attitude toward our pupils. Being open and engaged with our pupils places us in a stance where we have no presumptions about their motives, interests, thoughts, or feelings that are influencing their attention and behaviour. We are in a 'not-knowing' stance toward our pupils, in which we approach them in a state of curiosity, wanting to get to know them, including the organisational details of their minds and hearts. Curiosity is helped greatly by empathy when we focus on our pupils. We'll be looking at the neurological systems that facilitate empathy - and thereby enable our curiosity to be more successful - in Chapter 8 (p.141).

How we use our minds as educators will have a great influence on how our pupils use their minds. So to encourage our pupils to be curious toward themselves, and their learning tasks, we'll need to start by being curious ourselves about our pupils and our relationships with them. This may well be challenging in light of the many, many expectations that are placed on educators throughout the course of any given day. We have so much to accomplish that we may be tempted to take shortcuts in our interactions with our pupils, and assume that we know the reasons for their behaviours when we really don't understand the history and context for them. So we are asking for something more. To slow down, observe our pupils and get to know them. How we value that experience when other adults take the time to get to know us! Just having others try to understand our hopes and dreams, challenges and satisfactions, as educators, can make all the difference when we approach each day, term, and year.

Louise writes: One of the greatest gifts we could ever give someone is that of our empathic curiosity. For us to take the time out to truly understand another person is invaluable. Often our schools are such fast, busy places that we don't take the time necessary to think about who someone is, what makes them who they are and what motivates them to do what they do. Sometimes we're prone to react rather than respond, simply because we haven't allowed ourselves or our staff to have the breathing spaces necessary to reflect within a school day. We all need to be able to engage our reflective functioning so that our school communities can function well. Let's honour and protect the time it takes. Let's allow and create pauses, and facilitate supervision space as well. Curiosity won't thrive without time, space and energy.

Dan writes: Yes, if we were to pause, maybe we could then be interested in the objects and events and people we encounter in an open and engaged manner, being receptive to the meaning that they have for the pupil in our care, and being willing to allow that pupil to have a possible influence on us. Imagine that while we focus on directing or limiting a behaviour that we are concerned about with one hand, we use our other hand to wonder and be curious about the meaning of the behaviour in the context of the immediate situation and the pupil's history.

Curiosity at its richest involves a deeply integrative act of our minds and hearts to fully experience another person, an object, or an event. We approach the other with a deep interest in knowing what it would be like to walk in his shoes. We are fascinated with the pupil's hopes and dreams, fears and passions, trying to understand them as fully as we are able. We are searching for what is unique about him so that we can know him differently than we know anyone else. Who truly is Susan or Taylor, Camille, or Derek? Curiosity involves acts of discovery, searching for the underlying strengths and vulnerabilities of this particular child. We'll learn how he sees himself, others and his world through the lens of his earlier insecure attachments. At the same time we'll discover what makes up the source of his persistence, stengths, and resilience.

Louise writes: The significance of someone other than you having a go at 'walking a mile in your shoes' speaks volumes about care, value, worth, appreciation, acceptance and dignity. If a pupil experiences these amazing qualities from us, then the opportunity to move on in their development will be incredible. The very experience of someone getting alongside these pupils in this way will not only fill them up with the essential 'nutrients' that they need in order to grow optimally but will also give them the capacity to know who they are for themselves.

Dan writes: We believe that while our curiosity stretches from one area of knowledge to the next, it needs to begin and end with our pupils. Our pupils who have experienced family relational trauma, shame, and loss are likely to have little curiosity for who they are, what they think, feel, or want, why they do things, or why they succeed or fail. Their lack of self-reflection and self-curiosity is likely to relate to two central factors.

First, their home environment was not likely to have facilitated such reflective functioning. Their parents were not likely to have conveyed interest in what they thought, felt, or dreamed about.   There were likely to have been way too few conversations about what family members believed, wished for, or wondered about. Their parents were likely to have been preoccupied by many things that didn't involve their child, and they were not likely to have been interested in what their child was interested in. Most likely these pupils don't or didn't have confidence that they resided in the minds of their own parents, that their parents actively remembered and thought about them. They may have doubted that they were important to their parents and questioned whether they were of value at all, to anyone.

I (DH) am now thinking of one of the abused children that I became engaged with in psychotherapy. Tom entered foster care when he was four after having been exposed to considerable physical and emotional abuse by his parents throughout most, if not all, of his early years. Now, aged six, he had lived for two years with foster carers who were very patient with him when he responded with rage and defiance whenever they set reasonable limits and expectations on his behaviour. After his daily aggressive outbursts, he would quickly say that he was sorry and then refuse to discuss it further. Efforts to do so were only met with more anger and minimising what he had done. I was not much more successful with Tom in treatment, though Sherri, his foster carer, was present to support him.

During one session, I expressed sadness that Tom had such a hard time earlier in the day when he hit Sherrie after she would not let him play with something of hers which was easily broken. Within the flow of the dialogue I wondered why Sherrie would not let him play with it. He replied quickly that she didn't like him. I wondered - if that was correct that she did not like him - why. He replied that he was bad. I expressed empathy over his belief that he was bad and wondered what made him think that. Tom replied that he knew that he was bad because he often hit Sherrie. I then wondered if he first thought that he was bad when his father used to hit him. He began to cry and allowed Sherrie to put her arm around him and comfort him.

Afterwards Tom sat quietly for a while, and then asked me why his father used to hit him. I acknowledged how confused that must have made Tom, and that it made sense that he would think that he was hit because he was bad. I suggested that rather than that, it most likely was because his father did not know how to be a father and he would not let others show him how to care for his son better. Tom continued to sit with Sherrie's arm around him as he seemed to reflect on the meaning of his father's anger and his own subsequent anger toward Sherrie. His emerging curiosity about both enabled him to begin to create new meanings for them. He could then accept Sherrie's limits more easily while also accepting her comfort.

Second, our pupils were likely to have made sense of these realities by assuming that they possessed little inherent worth themselves. They developed the assumption that their parents were right - that they (the pupils) were bad, boring, stupid, or unlovable. Given this harsh self-concept, they were not likely to want to experience the shame of these realisations. They didn't think about their inner lives because they already knew the answer - the answer given to them by their parents' words and actions, namely that they were bad, boring, stupid, or unlovable.

Our pupils will not begin the journey of challenging the beliefs about themselves they developed so early on in life, on their own. Why would they? Their parents' experience of them was seen as being objective reality. Their parents could not be wrong. The shame that they developed in response to their parents' poor care of them prevented any wondering about their inner lives. Our pupils' sense of shame is generally so strong and rigid that it does not leave room for the possibility that their inner worth could be different.

Telling them something different - that they are pupils who are clever, liked, and cared for by their teacher - is likely to be met with disbelief and may well lead to swearing and hurling a nearby computer. They are likely to assume that everyone in the educational staff has to say that - it is their job. Or they have tricked the teacher into thinking that. Which deception certainly won't last. Or that the educators are trying to trick them, so that they will be 'good' and make the educators' lives easier. Why would they trust us? They trusted their parents and where did that lead? Suspicion is very evident when getting alongside troubled pupils.

If our pupils are to develop, deepen, broaden their sense of self, it will be through our curiosity - a curiosity that does not judge, but rather wants to discover who this child is. This curiosity is not a cognitive belief or argument that we can prove through gathering facts. Rather it needs to be based on our experiencing the child's unique strengths and vulnerabilities and communicating these experiences to the child in an expressive manner where our words and non-verbal expressions are clear and congruent.

Louise writes: We build up a picture of who we are through the eyes and mind of another person, usually the first people who cared for us. If a pupil has experienced this other person as frightening, abusive and neglectful, then he will have been left with a very distorted image of who he really is. If, subsequently, he meets another person who is caring and responsible, someone who actively wants to make a relationship with him and get to know him as Dan has been describing, then he will have the possibility of acquiring a more accurate sense of who he is. This is what is necessary for adaption and recovery. Our 'internal working models' of ourselves and the world are not fixed states but are malleable, continuing to be shaped throughout our lives through our experiences with others. The process is complex when the person is viewing life through an insecure attachment lens (Bretherton & Munholland 1999), because his resistance to change will be powerful. However, as Taylor says, 'humans are evidence-seeking creatures', (Taylor 2013, p.41). So let's make the most of this plasticity, and provide our pupil with lots of evidence of who he really is - a worthwhile, lovable individual.

Strengths and vulnerabilities

Dan writes: If our pupil is to develop within our relationship with him, what strengths and vulnerabilities might we discover as we get to know him? They are likely to involve many of the following:

STRENGTHS

☆ Courage to face difficult challenges

☆ An openness to finding the strength to acknowledge a weakness

☆ A desire to have a better life

☆ An integrity to try to 'be true to oneself' even if he does not
   know yet who he is

☆ A willingness to keep trying and not give up

☆ A compassion for someone else, whether it be a child, adult, or animal,
   whether someone in his life or someone in a movie or book

☆ A sense of humour and playfulness

☆ An ability to elicit a sense of delight, interest, and care from a good person

☆ A desire to understand and make sense of his behaviour and his life

☆ His unique gifts, whether they be interests, knowledge,
   or an openness to learn

VULNERABILITIES

- A hesitation to trust others and a tendency to see negative motives for others' actions
- Difficulty regulating and integrating strong emotions
- Difficulty making sense of the hard times of the past and reducing their impact on the present and future
- A sense of shame that makes it difficult to learn from mistakes and to develop hope for the future

Our pupil will not discover these qualities in himself - he will not even focus his mind on their possibility - if his education staff are not curious about him. We need to find his strengths. They are there, though they may be hidden under many problem behaviours and challenges. We will only discover these strengths and vulnerabilities if he is willing to give expression to them, and he will only do that if he feels safe with us. Safe in the knowledge that we are not judging him; we simply want to understand him.

That special someone

Louise writes: Dan, many of us remember that one teacher who got alongside us - I wonder why we remember? Could it be that they not only believed in us but that they took the time to really get to know us, to be curious about us and about all that we could be? What if they awakened the 'life' that was there all the while, just waiting to be found? It makes sense that if someone was wounded within relationship that relationship will be the vehicle towards adaption and recovery. We know now from neuroscience that neurons connect up, coming online, in the presence of quality relationship, so let's take note of this and adapt our practices in schools, by providing the kind of relationships that support this development.

Curiosity in action
Dan writes:

Ms. Grant had been pleased with the steady progress that Jenny had made in her class. A quiet girl who sat passively and did not make much effort at the beginning of the year, Jenny had responded well to her encouragement and assistance and now worked quite well independently, often with considerable success.

Jenny was mostly ignored by her classmates and one day after she did particularly well on an assignment, Ms. Grant announced to the class how well Jenny had done. She said that Jenny would be able to skip the next assignment and spend some extra time on the computer. Jenny sat at the computer but did not play any of the available games. To make matters worse, over the next days Jenny seemed to have returned to her passive and withdrawn manner. Ms. Grant had some free time before classes began the following day and she took Jenny aside. After becoming engaged with her in a light conversation, Ms. Grant began wondering about the change in her behaviour.

MS. GRANT *I noticed that you haven't seemed to be that interested in your classwork the past few days. What do you think that's about?*

JENNY *I don't know.*

MS. GRANT *I don't think that you've done any of your work since I let you work on the computer. I wonder if that had anything to do with it.*

JENNY *I didn't want you to.*

MS. GRANT   *Oh, OK. Though I'm a bit confused since you usually like to use the computer. Why don't you want me to let you use it now?*

JENNY   *I like to use it.*

MS. GRANT   *Help me understand, Jenny. Why didn't you want me to let you use it after you did so well on your work?*

JENNY   *I wanted to.*

MS. GRANT   *Wow, this is confusing to me. Maybe to you too. Did part of you want to use it and part of you not want to?*

JENNY   *Yes.* (with some animation)

MS. GRANT   *Why do you think that you felt both ways about it?*

JENNY   *Because you told the other kids that I did well!* (tears)

MS. GRANT   *And you didn't want me to? I was praising you! I wanted them to know how well you were doing!*

JENNY   *I don't want you to.*

MS. GRANT   *I'm sorry, Jenny. I guess that I should have asked you first if it was OK. Why do you think you didn't want me to tell them when you did well?*

JENNY   *I don't know.*

MS. GRANT   *So we're both not sure ... Do you think ... Do you think that maybe you're not used to the other kids noticing you? Maybe you worried that they wouldn't like you for doing better than they may have done. Or maybe that they'd make fun of you?*

JENNY   *Yeah.*

MS. GRANT   *Thanks for helping me to understand, Jenny. Maybe for now we'll keep it between you and me - how well you're doing. And I won't mention it to the other kids. We can decide sometime in the future if we'll tell them or not. Would that be OK?*

JENNY   *Yeah!* (with clear relief, and a quick return to her successful classwork)

In this example, Ms. Grant asked a series of questions, demonstrating curiosity at each stage as she better came to understand Jenny's behaviour and then how to respond to what it meant. In so doing she enabled Jenny to better understand her own behaviour as well. Such curiosity most likely would improve their relationship and Ms. Grant's ability to better meet Jenny's academic, social, and emotional needs.

Louise writes: Yes, I completely agree Dan. So here I'd like to introduce some further ideas that can be interwoven together with this kind of dialogue, in order to promote further curiosity in our schools.

Additional support interventions that facilitate curiosity

Let's express our curiosity about the pupil out loud, gently encouraging him to be curious about himself. It's important that we keep things in this order: the adult being curious about the pupil in the first instance, before expecting the pupil to be curious about themselves. This is the natural developmental order within a healthy care-giving context.

- modelling thinking
- wondering out loud
- using commentaries
- noticing out loud

- the Hand of Options
- video interactive guidance
- being curious about contradictions
- linking up the missing pieces

I   MODELLING THINKING

Tap your head and say that you are thinking …*"Um … I'm having a think about this …"*. Show curiosity on your face. This type of communication can be very helpful, especially when things get tricky.

II   WONDERING OUT LOUD

Have a go at guessing the possible states, sensations and feelings that the pupil might be experiencing, in the kind of tentative way an attentive parent might do with their baby. It can be helpful to use the phrase, *"I'm wondering if …"*

Be aware that you may well not interpret your pupil accurately, as things are not always the way they seem. For example, fear might be behind an angry face. As you become more familiar with the pupil in your care, you'll find that your guesses may be met with acknowledgement. These tentative wonderings can start to encourage curiosity by building awareness and connection, so that our pupils can start to make some sense for themselves of what might be going on internally.

> *Mona Lisa (ten) is smiling and saying she is fine when you ask how she is. However, you notice her eyes are welling up and she seems really sad. "I'm wondering if you might be feeling really sad, as even though you are smiling, your eyes seem very sad."*

Some pupils might express their fear about you doing this; they may experience your wondering aloud as intrusive - as if you are seeking to not only *read* their minds - but to *take over* their minds. Ensure you let the pupil know that you are not a mind-reader, that you are merely trying to understand how they might be feeling right now. Let them know that you may have got it wrong, that you are just guessing. It is important that our intentions and motives are explicit as some pupils have traumatic experiences of previous adults being very controlling and intrusive in their interactions with them. Even if you're certain that your guess is accurate, if your pupil says that you are wrong, don't argue or express scepticism. Instead, thank your pupil for clarifying that and wonder what he thinks is more accurate.

III   USING COMMENTARIES

Describe what you can see with your eyes in an open, engaged manner. Tilt your head to show your curiosity. Again this is quite typical behaviour of an attentive parent with their baby or toddler. However, this is not so common with an 11 or 15 year old, but there are many out there who still need this type of attention in order to experience the healthy and appropriate curiosity of a grown up. You may well find that commentating like this encourages the pupil to let you in on what they're doing. Your curiosity will be seen as an invitation to openness and vulnerability in the pupil. Pupils who would otherwise have been quite hard to read or get close to have been known to begin developing genuine connection at these times. It makes sense. If the pupil experiences you as being genuinely attentive in your curiosity, the more engaged they become.

> *"Saleem, (nine) you are cold right now. I can tell, because look at your arms! They have goosebumps all over them! And you are shivering. You are standing there without your jumper or a coat. You don't seem to realise that you are cold."*

IV   NOTICING OUT LOUD

Many troubled pupils have a very restricted view of themselves, others and their worlds. Many have had lies said about them concerning their personhood (*"You're an idiot"*, *"You're useless"*, *"You shouldn't have been born"*, *"You're no fun"*, and so on). Many have lived in toxic shaming environments. Many haven't been noticed, cared for or attended to. If this is the case of course they're not going to necessarily be aware of everything that makes them who they are, what makes them tick, what makes them sparkle. Many of these pupils are too aware of their faults at the expense of their strengths. Many of these pupils scan for danger at the expense of not noticing what brings safety. One of our support roles is extending their vision so that they can have the opportunity to start to notice so much more. Asking questions such as: *"Did you see that?", "Did you notice when...?"* or making statements such as: *"I notice that you ... "* will start to enlarge the pupil's radar, opening up further explanations along their journey of discovery. Whilst journeying, they won't be able to help picking up many treasures along the way.

Shona (aged 12) is in her 1:1 weekly session with her KA, Magda, who says: "I have noticed that you are coming to the inclusion department a lot at the moment, much more than you used to. Is something bothering you? You only used to come up here for your sessions but I think I've seen you nearly every day. It might be that you are anxious about something."

V   USING THE HAND OF OPTIONS

Another helpful strategy is what I've called the 'hand of options' (Bombèr 2011, p.186). A way of speculating about and discussing possible alternative explanations for other people's motives and motivation, this tool supports pupils to be curious like us about how they see themselves, others and their world - allowing the capacity for updating! Many of these pupils can seem quite stuck and really benefit from us supporting them in becoming aware that there might be much more in the present that they are missing.

Being curious together with a pupil about what another person's motives or intentions might be opens up a wealth of possibilities. Often these pupils will assume the worst. Let's support them to realise that things are not always the way they seem -

well, not through a lens of distorted perception, anyway! Remember we are working at introducing this pupil to the world of secure attachment where there are so many more interpretations then merely negative ones.

> *"OK, so when Laura says she doesn't want to come to your house tonight, you're thinking this means she can't be your friend. I'm wondering whether there might be any other possible meanings? What if her family have something special planned for her to do tonight? What if she's expecting an important phone call? How about if she has been told by her parents she can only stay out once a week after school? Or if you have also invited someone that Laura doesn't feel comfortable with? Or what if she's too tired and just wants to crash in front of the telly in her pjs? We could go on ... there are so many possibilities. We can't assume the worst as we just don't know. Any of these possibilities could be true. Everyone behaves so, so differently".*

Encourage Key Adults to point to their thumb first to acknowledge the pupil's interpretation and then to point to their other fingers one by one to map out other possibilities. This is a helpful tangible anchor of the idea of alternatives. These pupils need lots of repetition, but once they start getting the hang of this idea for considering what is going on in the 'here and now' it's as if a light bulb is switched on, meaning that interactions no longer need to remain persecutory. This type of curiosity can bring the possibility of hope where there might have previously been despair.

Dan writes: The hand of options is a wonderful concept, Louise. I wonder if it might also be applied to what a pupil thinks about his own motives or intentions. When a pupil teases one of his classmates, you might ask why he thinks that he did that. He might reply with annoyance: *"Because I felt like it!"* or *"Because I'm* *stupid"* or *"What do you think!"* His first responses to your curiosity about his behaviour are often triggered by shame and anger. If you don't react to them and make some guesses on your own about his motives, he is likely to be open to the possibilities that you present. These might open his mind to the complexity of his motives which are not shame-based. For example, you might say:

> *"That's one possibility. I wonder too if you might have teased him because you were a little angry with him yesterday. Or maybe because he's been spending more time with Ronnie lately and you've been feeling left out. Or maybe you've had some hard times yourself recently and you wanted someone else to have to struggle a bit too. I've noticed that you've had some pretty hard times recently."*

The pupil might deny the validity of all your guesses, but he might keep them in his mind and reflect more in the future about his various motives.

VI   VIDEO INTERACTION GUIDANCE (VIG)

Louise writes: A tool that can be very beneficial in schools for this purpose is VIG. VIG is a great tool for supporting social and emotional well-being in pupils. VIG can be used in at least three ways with these troubled pupils. It can support the Key Adults supporting the pupil to be curious about what they are doing, what their pupil is doing during interactions, and for the pupil themselves to reflect upon why they do what they do.

This powerful tool deepens curiosity. Like looking in a mirror, we can become aware of what might have remained unnoticed or had been forgotten. For more information on VIG, please visit www.videointeractionguidance.net

VII   BEING CURIOUS ABOUT CONTRADICTIONS

There will be times when the pupils in our care will state something that is contradictory to what you know of them, or they will actively sabotage success, as in the example of Jenny, above. At these times we need to be curious about why they are doing this, in a gentle, sensitive way. We can extend our curiosity not just by using words but by using visual cues too. If we're curious, curiosity can be caught! Every time we're curious we give the pupil opportunity to modify their beliefs and values about themselves. In order to extend curiosity visually, set up a *book/portfolio of success* or a *jar of strength* for the pupil that you can refer to at these times. I describe below how to create these.

a)   Creating 'My Book of Success'

Encourage Key Adults to create books or portfolios of success in order to capture any moments of health - health in the widest sense. The book could include:

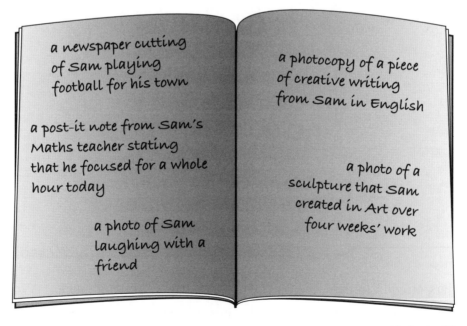

a newspaper cutting of Sam playing football for his town

a post-it note from Sam's Maths teacher stating that he focused for a whole hour today

a photo of Sam laughing with a friend

a photocopy of a piece of creative writing from Sam in English

a photo of a sculpture that Sam created in Art over four weeks' work

My Book of Success

This book needs to be guarded so that your pupil doesn't sabotage everything he has achieved until now by damaging or trashing it. It can be referred to at regular intervals, since troubled pupils often forget the 'good stuff'. This book is used to support connection-making, as previously described above, since these pupils respond best to visual cues as reminders. As humans we seek evidence, and these visual cues provide some.

b)   Creating 'My Jar of Strength'

Encourage Key Adults to set up transparent containers to visually represent everything that is making this particular pupil strong. By strength, we mean their resilience - so everything that they're capable of, everything they can contribute. For example, in one pupil's jar of strength there were post-its naming the following:

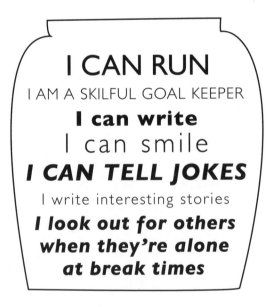

My Jar of Strength

These jars provide further visual evidence of what is growing inside. A lot of our support work seems to be to bring out into the open what's usually left hidden.

VIII   LINKING UP THE MISSING PIECES BY BEING CURIOUS!

We can attempt to make sense of why a pupil might be doing what he's doing by joining up the pieces, creating a narrative. There will always be missing pieces, but take a guess, and start to make links through making connections.

Start to have confidence in what you know about this pupil, encouraging the pupil to join with you in this act of exploration. Remember though that you are their travelling companion through school, not through the pupil's own mind, and so it is OK to be wrong! Our pupils can start to learn that it's actually interesting to understand why they do what they do. They can start having the confidence and dignity needed to dare looking at themselves. This requires great trust, as previously their sense of self may have brought them intense self-loathing and self-disgust.

It is really rewarding when you hear a pupil processing why they do what they do in front of you; some of them will start to do this as you encourage this kind of dialogue together. Look out for comments such as:

"I wonder why I did that?"
"I think I might have thought that because ..."
"Ah, I know why I did that now!"

Tom (aged 15) popped by to see his KA in the inclusion department after English. "Sir, it was really weird in that lesson, I got all wound up and I don't know why. I wasn't hot like I get. I wasn't getting wound up by anyone like I usually am. I don't know but I think I might still be thinking about the autobiography work from last week. Do you think I might be? It could be that, I reckon."

Chapter 8

Be empathic

The hardest

What was the hardest (thing about your life)? ...
The hardest is being
asked that question
and finding the answer
written in a report
but not in anyone's
mind and heart.

Your sweet persistence ...

It was your gentle presence -
your sweet persistence -
in touching me with your smile and voice
and teaching me that these touches were called
comfort, care, compassion, companionship.

(from Hughes, 2012b)

Dan writes: It is hard to overstate the importance of empathy. The importance
of experiencing - both knowing and feeling - that another person, with both mind and
heart, wants to, and is able to, experience - both know and feel - the qualities of your

mind and heart. Our pupils need to experience our empathy if they are to experience value, understanding, safety, and the desire to learn when they are with us.

Most of our pupils respond to our empathy as we might hope, but our troubled students are less likely to do so. It's difficult for them both to experience our empathy for them and to experience empathy for others. Our empathy for them often generates anxiety and confusion. They mistrust our intention - are we expressing empathy in order to make them be good and obey? They expect our empathy will not last when we truly get to know them. Our empathy may make them feel vulnerable, and because they don't want to experience that state, they resist our empathy for them. Having experienced little empathy themselves in their family, they're not likely to be able to experience empathy for others in any deep and consistent manner.

When our pupils don't respond positively to our empathy, we tend to have difficulty continuing to experience and communicate empathy for them. Empathy - along with much of our life that is important to us - tends to continue to function well when it meets with success. When our pupils value it and respond well to it, it is much easier for us to continue to express it. When, however, they reject it - and our genuine caring and interest that underlies it - we are likely to become vulnerable ourselves, and become at risk of shutting down our empathic presence in their lives, and focus instead on 'doing our job'. Yet empathy is central to any relationship that we want to establish with our pupils, and we won't be doing our job well if our capacity for empathy closes down (*see* Chap.17, *including how to help ourselves re-open this capacity*).

Here I would like to note that when our expression of empathy is rejected in any of our relationships - with our partner, child, parent, friend, or colleague, we are at risk of withdrawing our empathic expression, despite our best intentions. If this occurs often enough, our relationship becomes stressed and we may be more distant or we may become more irritable and impatient. When we reach out with empathy to another person, we become vulnerable to the experience of rejection - and without thinking about it - are at risk of beginning to relate with that person in a more defensive manner. This process is likely to occur in our relationships with our pupils as well.

What to do? First, we'll talk about what empathy actually is, along with its roots in the structure and functions of our brain. We will also be considering how troubled pupils do not experience empathy for themselves or for others very well. Second, we'll describe why empathy is so important in being a successful educator for these pupils. Third, we'll explore how we might more effectively enable ourselves to remain empathic with our pupils, and how we might encourage our pupils to utilise our empathy for safety and new learning in the classroom as well as to develop empathy for others.

What is empathy?

Empathy is more than a feeling that we have for someone's distress. It isn't something that we 'give' to another person as we would give them information or a gift: empathy is an experience that we have *of* another person. This experience involves a *reflective* component - a cognitive awareness of what the other person might be thinking or of what is bothering him. It also involves an *affective* component - an emotional experience of the person's emotional state that is associated with what he's thinking about. Empathy requires us to truly experience the unique experience of the other person and then respond fully and clearly to the person who we are experiencing. When we are able to experience both his mind (thoughts) and his emotions (heart) and we communicate this experience to him, he is likely to sense a bond with us that will serve as the foundation of our relationship with him. As he senses that he is understood by us, as he feels 'felt' (as Dan Siegel (2012) so nicely describes how we experience another person's empathy for us), in the school context, our pupil is then likely to be able to begin to settle and attend to the educational activities that we are presenting to him.

Research is clear about the central value of this quality in so many areas (Elliott et al, 2011). For years, we've known that empathy is central to the success of psychotherapy. Patients in our hospitals who have a nurse rated high on empathy report less pain than those with nurses who demonstrate less empathy for their patients. Programmes developed for youth at risk for legal, educational, and mental health problems achieve better results when their staff demonstrate higher levels of empathy. Yet too often we fail to highlight the importance of empathic interventions in our efforts in our schools to reach pupils, especially those who have experienced relational traumas and losses.

Louise writes: I wonder, Dan, whether this is merely an oversight on our parts - not realising or not understanding about the importance of empathy, or whether there is something happening in our schools that actually prevents us from relating in this way? In school, it is so easy for us to simply go through the motions without remaining emotionally connected. We may continue behaving this way for a number of reasons. Maybe other staff would frown upon us for becoming 'too involved'? Maybe we would lose some credibility amongst other colleagues if we didn't take a hard line? Maybe this way of working doesn't fit the school ethos?

I wish I could tell you that the following example doesn't happen much, but unfortunately it does.

I met with the senior manager in a secondary school recently to discuss Albie's challenging behaviour. I attempted to describe why he might be in a real state right now. This is what she said, pretty much verbatim, in response to my carefully crafted, empathic narrative. She presented a deadpan face, showing no warmth, no understanding, no empathy.

"We are a school. We cannot tolerate this kind of behaviour. There is

no excuse. He needs to know that this is unacceptable. He is running rings around us. I am going to exclude him. He needs to learn that he cannot behave like this in a school environment. We are not a therapeutic community".

My heart sank. I knew what this decision would mean to Albie. It would lead him into an escalation of fear and panic. I had been working with Albie's Key Adult for a long time now. He had been doing so well but then something had kicked off with another member of his family which had unsettled and unnerved him. Echoes of the not so distant past had reminded him of why he had needed to be so defended in the first place. Defences he had started to leave behind had been taken up again because he was anticipating the possibility of further vulnerability - of further pain. I couldn't say anything to support this senior manager to see Albie as I saw him. She just wanted him out.

Engaging in one's own emotion isn't a necessary requirement for work in schools at the moment, whereas there are many other expectations that need to be adhered to. We may have been allocated a pupil to work with that we didn't actually opt to work with: we may not have experienced any choice in the matter.

Equally, in a busy system, with a large number of pupils, crowd control can sometimes take priority over an individual's needs. We may be so overwhelmed ourselves that the pressure on us in schools has meant that we have closed down our emotions in order to 'survive'. How many times have I heard staff counting down the days till the holidays, or when asked about their day, force a smile and say *"I survived"*. No wonder it's hard to stay open and emotionally connected. Yet this is what these pupils need from us, for us to be not only physically present but emotionally present too. A stern face, a stern attitude at these times can appear cruel to a pupil like Albie, and we can understand why. Our troubled pupils have already had an overdose of people who have been:

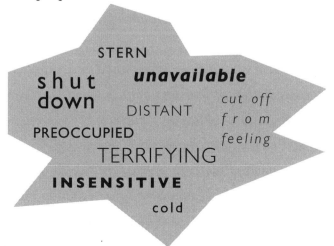

when they were in the hands of parents, step-parents, aunties, uncles and grandparents. We have the opportunity to relate in the opposite spirit:

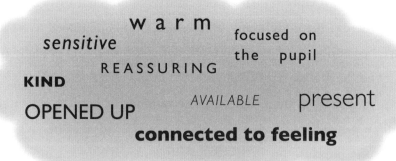

I wonder what a difference there would be in behaviour in school if we related in this way? Why not give it a go and trial this approach in your school, noting any differences as you go along?

By engaging in empathy in the ways we're describing, you are communicating that something meaningful is happening (at an unconscious level) that the pupil can pick up on. You will be building a bridge that will provide the scaffolding necessary for the pupil to take the risks inherent in learning, and in developing further. This makes such sense. Empathy is the foundation of safety. We need to attend to safety in our schools; the consequences of not enough emotional or mental safety for pupils are only too obvious in the current high numbers of exclusions.

The neurological foundations of empathy

Dan writes: For too long philosophers, theologians, and scientists have believed that humans are by nature selfish and competitive. *Survival of the fittest* was a phrase thought to explain the competitiveness evident in many of the ways in which we relate to other people. It led to the long-standing educational philosophy that our animal desires needed to be tamed in order to train us in developing habits of altruism and companionship. This philosophy never quite fit my experience both of my own thoughts, feelings, and interactions with others, nor of my perceptions of the behaviours of my friends and relatives. Yes, under difficult situations, we might act in a self-protective, defensive, manner. Yet, when things seemed safe, I noticed that we were often sensitive, caring, supportive, and spontaneously self-sacrificing for no reason other than the satisfaction that seemed to be inherent in altruism. I often thought that the cruelty and selfishness that I saw was not inherent in human nature but rather reflected the life of a person who had seldom been safe, and rarely, if ever, experienced good care.

Louise writes: Yes, from the moment I began teaching, I started to notice the connection between disturbed behaviours and childhood deprivation that Dan is describing. When I got alongside some of the pupils in my care that I was concerned about, I was taken aback by the things they disclosed which they were living through or they had lived through. Horrors too disturbing to even listen to as an adult, never mind experience as a child. The other pupils in my classes who had experienced 'good enough care' were just so different. They seemed to be constantly wanting to engage with others in a collaborative way. They seemed quite excited by the prospect of having not just one friend, but many. There was something about these lucky ones that embraced life - life in all its fullness. However my troubled pupils engaged in behaviours that kept others at a distance. Some pupils were so frightening that their peers were frightened of them, actually physically withdrawing when they came within a certain distance. These types of behaviours were clearly adaptive for another time, another place, another person … but not here, in school. Here in my classroom they were maladaptive. These pupils seemed to be rejecting life in all its fullness. It was as if they had given up and were living in despair - in all its emptiness.

Dan writes: The exciting knowledge that we have acquired over the past 20 years about the nature of our brain and neurological system has greatly challenged the assumptions that we are fundamentally selfish by nature. We may compete with other species, but we are literally 'designed' through evolution to support the survival of our own social species through communication and co-operation. When we experience conditions of scarcity of our basic needs, we do compete, with other humans, for the limited supplies available. However, when we are safe and our needs are met - something that didn't occur often in previous generations - our brains begin to focus on co-operation. Our survival is enhanced when we develop the systems in our brains that lead to experiencing empathy for others, communicating with others, and co-operating for the common good. Our brains are wired for relationships!

When I first became aware of this I realised that experiencing empathy for others was not a matter of will-power and self-discipline to do what was not natural to do.

Rather it was learning how to re-awaken the areas of my mind *that were present, but which had closed down.* To establish my own sense of safety so that I could attend to the needs of my pupils or clients. Nor was it a cognitive process where I could simply *decide* to act more empathically, and I would easily do so. I came to realise that the safety that I needed to activate my relational brain was itself *only activated through supportive relationships which nourished me.* Within the safety of my relationships with my partner, friends, and trusted colleagues, I could allow my brain to do what it was designed to do - namely, connect with others in deeply emotional and reflective ways.

Yes, we are moral, altruistic, social mammals. Without such an intricate neurological system, which functions to enhance complex relationships, our societies would not have evolved as they have done. We would most likely still be isolated clans, competing for seemingly scarce resources.

Since some of the old assumptions remain strong today in our educational community, let's now take a moment to review the new findings from our increased knowledge of the structure and functioning of the brain.

Our neurological system - our brain and the nerves which extend from our brain to all regions of our body and back again - is designed for empathy. There are thought to be a minimum of eight brain structures that are central in our readiness and ability to experience empathy for the psychological states of others (Cozolino, 2006). These structures enable us to perceive, imitate, resonate with, and experience empathy for the inner states of others (pre-frontal and anterior cingulate cortex). Included is the ability to bridge our *internal* experiences with the *external* expressions of others (insula and post-parietal cortex). Our brain structures also involve our ability to vicariously experience the *actual* experience of others, through the activation of mirror neurons in the temporal lobes of our cortex, whenever we observe someone else's actions that are activating the same region of their brain. So, for example, when we see someone scratch their hair, we often scratch our hair with the same motion of our hand and arm, or we notice a tendency to do so. It is the same with facial expressions. When we see a facial expression of sadness, it primes our face to make a similar expression, which in turn, primes us to feel sad.

These neurological connections don't create a rational understanding of the other person, but they do provide an intuition as to someone else's experience and how best to meet that person's - or that pupil's - needs. Our intuition about another person includes a reflective component and an emotional component. This emerging knowledge has created the field of what's known as *interpersonal neurobiology,* to describe how relationships impact the development of both the structure and functioning of the brain, creating the mind of the individual (Siegel, 2012). Not just our brains, but relationships also affect the development of our entire nervous systems extending into our hearts, lungs (breathing) and digestive system (our gut feelings) (Porges, 2011). When we use our nervous systems in this way - through our resonating connections with the experience of our pupils - we become better able to understand our pupil's current psychological state and better able to help him to settle, and then to learn. *Empathy for our pupils needs to be a central component of our educational stance toward them that will facilitate their readiness to learn.*

Why troubled pupils find empathy hard to handle

MIRIAM   *Go away. I don't want you close. I don't need you.*
PAUL   *Leave me alone. I don't want you to be nice to me.*
          It's annoying.

Our brains are designed for relationships and relationships are central to the development of our brains so that they are able to begin to learn the incredibly rich social, cultural, physical world that we live in. Yet our troubled pupils often haven't had those early experiences of relationship - based on the qualities of attachment security - that were important to the development of their brains. Not having received empathy, they don't respond well to expressions of empathy now, and they don't experience empathy for others often enough either.

Louise writes: Our vulnerable pupils had too few of the kind of open and engaged relationship experiences that would generate safety and secure attachments; this might be called emotional neglect. Or they may have had traumatic experiences that were likely to have dysregulated or disturbed the functioning of their brain regions necessary for the development of social and emotional skills. They may have seldom felt joy or happiness and so - when presented with these experiences in school - they become anxious and confused. Their brains simply haven't developed sufficiently to be able to consistently enjoy empathy, affection, or co-operation! They also may not have received sufficient comfort and support to be able to deal with vulnerable feelings from their past. When they experience their own or someone else's vulnerability in the present, their past traumas are likely to be re-activated and lead to an angry reaction, or inattentive withdrawal.

When we don't understand this, it can be really confusing, upsetting and even shocking when a pupil verbally or physically attacks us immediately after falling over or banging into something. Or when troubled pupils seem to make a beeline for us when we're feeling quite low or vulnerable ourselves, giving us an even harder time than usual. It's as if these pupils have no idea how to engage with any kind of vulnerability - theirs or ours. They seem to move into defensive mode as their default position when feeling uncomfortable in their experience of themselves or others.

Dan writes: An angry reaction or an inattentive withdrawal - will greatly impede our pupil's ability to learn. And our ability to experience empathy for these pupils in spite of their underlying vulnerability will be disrupted and impeded too.

Louise writes: Yes, it's so hard when, for no fault of our own, we are attacked. To be on the receiving end of unprovoked attacks especially when we are doing our best to care for these pupils can be truly disheartening. One Key Adult in a support group recently shared how she had been struggling: *"I'm spat at, called names and told to go away on a regular basis. If I didn't come here I don't know whether I'd be able to stick at it."* She also described how her pupil went to great lengths to describe how she would like to hurt her. All the KAs I know and work with put so much of themselves into their support roles. They go the extra mile with these pupils, but rightly ask from time to time, *"Are there any who can't be helped?"*

Dan writes: Yes, Louise and I are often asked this: can all children be reached? While the great majority of our troubled pupils are able to experience empathy *from* others and *for* others at times (especially when they feel increasingly safe with us), a very small group of children and adults seldom, if ever, experience empathy for others. These are individuals who are described as lacking a conscience, and they are certainly at risk of significant anti-social behaviours and legal problems (Tangney & Dearing, 2002). Such individuals have little empathy for the pain that other children and adults experience, even when they themselves have caused that pain in others. Without empathy, they feel little guilt or remorse when they hurt another person. However, these individuals have also been found to show high measures of shame, which they often deny through their seemingly indifferent behaviours. Such shame invariably has its roots in extensive histories of abuse and neglect, as we'll see later (Chap.13). If they are to change their functioning it's best that such change begins when they are young. If they are to change their functioning, it's crucial that they experience - and come to accept - empathy from their caregivers, therapists, and educators.

It is hard for educators to experience empathy for their pupils and not receive a reciprocal emotional response in return. As I mentioned above, empathy is designed to elicit a positive response and when our pupils don't respond positively, we tend to have difficulty continuing to experience our empathy and communicate it (I have described this reality in the parent-child relationship as 'blocked care', to account for how difficult it is to continue to meet the needs of your child for an extended period of time when your child does not appear to be responding positively to your efforts (Hughes & Baylin, 2012a). The danger when our pupils do not respond to our empathic communication is that we will withdraw emotionally and resort to simply 'doing our job'. As we pull back from developing our relationship with our pupils who do not seem to respond, they will respond even less. Our emotional withdrawal will be experienced as indifference or even dislike, interpersonal experiences that are likely to be seen as too similar to those that they have already experienced - and for some, continue to experience - at home (*and see* Chap.17).

In my work as a supervisor of psychotherapists, I am often aware of a sequence of events that occurs during the course of treatment that poses a major threat to the success of this treatment. As the therapist meets the child, becomes aware of his history and is able to see how the history has greatly impacted his life and led to a variety of symptoms, the therapist finds herself experiencing empathy for her client and finds it easy to become engaged with him and his life. The child too, may initially seem to be engaged and responsive, often out of an enjoyment of the therapist's non-judgmental attitude.

However, as the therapeutic 'issues' begin to be explored and the child becomes anxious, 'resistant', begins to disengage and there is no reduction in symptoms, the therapist often begins to have doubts about the effectiveness of the treatment. When the child begins to actively resist the therapist and to express anger and rejection toward her, there is a strong danger that the therapist will withdraw her empathy, become emotionally detached if not outwardly critical, and begin to perceive the child as being 'too disturbed to benefit' from therapy. The child's symptoms have now become directed toward the therapist and to therapy itself. These symptoms often developed in the relationships that the child had with his parents, and it is not surprising that as the relationship with the therapist become more important, that they would be activated there as well. Supervision assists the therapist in continuing to experience non-judgmental empathy for the child and his behaviours toward the therapist. What I try to provide for the therapist is my acceptance, understanding, and empathy, as I know that she will need this if her own capacity for empathy is to be replenished. She may often be able to do this for herself, but when times get really tough, when the child is really resistant, the therapist will need a supportive relationship herself to enable her empathic capacities to remain strong and available for her clients.

These same factors are likely to occur in the troubled pupil's relationship with his educators too - especially when you, as the person trying to establish a genuine relationship with him, become important to your pupil. Yet, the educator - who received much less training than the psychotherapist in developing relationships with vulnerable children - rarely has any formal, or even informal supervision, to assist her in maintaining empathy for the child. When the pupil's problems - or symptoms - become all that we can see, so that we no longer perceive the child beneath the problems, it will become extremely hard to continue to experience empathy for him.

Louise writes: Yes, schools often express this state themselves. They recognise that they have not had much access to training around this area and they are very much left to 'work it out' behind the closed doors of the classroom. Supervision is much needed. Some schools have been creative about how to meet this need - despite financial costs, and at a time when this need isn't yet recognised by those leading education policy. I know of schools which have used their own school counsellor/therapist to take on such a role, or brought in the school counsellor/ therapist from their cluster of schools. I know of ones which have asked CAMHS Therapists/psychologists in onto school sites to provide either individual time or team time through appointments, drop-ins and TACs (Team Around the Child meetings).

However, we've also found running support groups for Key Staff to be really effective too. Bringing staff together from different settings with similar training levels or experiences has many benefits. We have groups for those just starting out with developing a relationship with a troubled pupil, through to groups for those who have been involved in this work for years. We have groups for Key Adults - teaching assistants and mentors, and groups for Attachment Leads - those involved in senior management of some kind - usually SENCOs, INCOs and Assistant Heads. The benefits of these groups are substantial, making a difference not only to the staff but to the pupils in their care. These benefits can include the following:

- Normalising what can seem very bizarre, disturbed, or shocking behaviour when it sometimes occurs when we are in the midst of also working with securely attached pupils (who are usually in the majority).
- Feeling connected and establishing a sense of togetherness, as this work can make staff feel very isolated, not just because of how the pupil reacts to them, but how other members of staff react to them because of how the pupil is reacting! Upsettingly, many staff report that for them, the pupil's lack of empathy is easier to bear than their colleagues' lack of empathy.
- Having space to think. Staff report that schools are such busy places that there are no pauses built in during the school day to actually be able to process what is going on. Having protected space means that the staff are then enabled to engage in reflective practice, as opposed to reacting in an unthought through way to challenging behaviour.

- Staff feeling cared for and valued for themselves, as other members of the group acknowledge and validate their experiences alongside these troubled pupils.
- Being able to persevere despite the odds. Having fellow travellers means that more can be borne: 'what is shareable is bearable'.

Dan writes: Our vulnerable pupil's interpersonal brain has not developed as it should through open, engaged, empathic relationships with his parents. This leaves him vulnerable to moving into fight, flight, or disengaged day dreaming - none of which facilitates his ability to learn. The deficiencies in his relational brain also makes him less likely to have empathy for us, less likely to imitate us, or attend to us - deficiencies which also are likely to impair his ability to learn from us. We not only survive in caring, co-operative, empathic relationships; we learn within these relationships as well. This is what our pupils need.

Louise writes: Oh how I hope policy makers will read this and hear this message! We are *all* concerned about the outcomes of pupils at this time and so we should be: but who is making the link between relationships and their pivotal role in learning? Not many. There is a direct correlation between emotional growth and learning. We mustn't merely focus on our pupil's exploratory system but on their attachment systems first and foremost. *Both* systems need to be attended to in order for a pupil to be in a position to settle to learn. When our troubled pupils actually *experience* and *notice* safety, security and stability through relationships - watch them flourish!

We are often shocked by our troubled pupils' lack of remorse or thought for other class mates or for those who work so hard to support them. It's hard sometimes to remember that these pupils need their own opportunity to have *someone experience empathy for them*, first and foremost, in order to feel it in themselves for others.

Dan writes: Giving up on providing our pupils with these relationships when they don't respond to them is not the answer. We need to first help them to learn to respond within interactions with us, so that they can develop genuine relationships with us and others which will enable them - yes, we'll say it again - to settle to learn.

Empathy: central to any effort to educate troubled pupils

In emphasising the value of empathy in developing our relationships with and helping a troubled pupil, we'd like to make the following four points:

I   CO-REGULATION LEADS TO SELF-REGULATION

Our empathy can greatly assist a pupil in moderating his strong emotions. In an earlier chapter, we talked about the value for a child in having an adult *co-regulate* his emotions in order to assist him (the pupil) to develop the ability to *self-regulate* his emotional states (*see* p.44-5). *Empathy is central to these acts of co-regulation.* When we're able to experience the pupil's emotional state and remain regulated ourselves, this will increase *his* ability to experience his own emotions without dysregulation.

> *So, for example, Jack (aged 11) expresses anger because he was not given permission to attend a play outside school with his class, because of his defiance toward his teacher, Mr. Adams. Rather than sternly saying that Jack brought it on himself because of his misbehaviour, Mr. Adams conveyed empathy for Jack's anger and distress by saying, in a warm and animated voice:*
>
> *"You really wanted to see that play and you're really angry with me because I said that you can't go. I can understand your anger since you want to see the play so badly! It must be so disappointing to you that you can't go with your class".*

Mr. Adams conveyed understanding of Jack's anger and disappointment both through the words that he used but also by how his voice matched the rhythm and intensity of Jack's voice. Matching the non-verbal expression of an emotion often conveys empathy for that emotion and makes it more likely that Jack will be able to remain regulated in his emotion and gradually be able to reflect on it. In so doing, Jack is likely to experience Mr. Adams' empathy and be open to discussing with him how he feels about the whole situation. He is more likely to believe that Mr. Adams' refusal to allow him to go relates solely to his disruptive behaviour and not to Mr. Adams' not liking him or not caring about what he wants.

II   TRUST AND INTENTIONALITY

Our empathy assists a pupil to be able to trust our intentions. When a pupil senses that we understand - and care about - his experience - what he thinks and feels about an event - he is more likely to believe that we understand him and want what is best for him. Even if he doesn't agree with our planned action in dealing with a situation, he'll be more likely to accept our decision if he trusts that our intention is to assist him. Empathy conveys that.

For example, Julie, aged 14, wanted to participate in a class competition in mathematics that she clearly had not studied for. Ms. Casswell knew that while Juile was hoping to impress some of her peers, she wasn't ready for this particular event which would only end in failure. Given her general lack of confidence in her abilities, failure would most like lead her to withdraw from her peers and from her lessons. After class, Julie angrily accused Ms. Casswell of not thinking that she was very bright and actually wanting her to fail. Ms. Casswell replied in a gentle and firm manner:

"I am really sorry if you think that I don't have confidence in you and that I don't want you to succeed. I can understand your anger at me if you think that I am not supporting you. I am saying that you can't join the competition on Friday because I want you to succeed and I believe that you are not quite ready for it yet. I am ready to give you whatever help you need to be prepared for the competition next month. I believe that you will do well when you are ready and I hope that you come to trust me about this."

By not being defensive, Ms. Casswell helped Julie to understand that her motives came from her desire for Julie to succeed, not to fail. By acknowledging how difficult it would be for Julie if she did not trust her, Ms. Casswell helped Julie to begin to trust her and accept her guidance and support.

III   MAKING SENSE OF WHAT'S HAPPENING

Our empathy assists a pupil in increasing his ability to make sense of his behaviour and our behaviours. Empathy enables a pupil to regulate any intense emotions associated with an event and be better able to reflect on the event itself and his experience of it. Many pupils will avoid recalling and making sense of events that are associated with troubling emotions. We often hear, *"I don't want to think about it!"* for that reason. If we reply: *"Yes, that was really upsetting to you. So it would be hard to think about it. What do you think made it so upsetting?"* As the pupil experiences our empathy for the event, he will then be more likely to wonder about his experience, and to allow us to wonder with him.

IV   FACILITATING COMMUNICATION

Our empathy increases a pupil's readiness to communicate his inner life to us. Many pupils also exclaim: *"I don't want to talk about it!"* We know that the pupil is distressed; we know that he just did something that makes things difficult for himself or others, and we want to understand how he makes sense of it. If he thinks that we don't 'get it' and will simply jump to conclusions, criticise, or give advice without knowing his perspective, he's not likely to share what thoughts and feelings he has with us. Experiencing our empathy, he's more likely to experience a desire to share his distress with us rather than have to face it alone. While exploring it with us, he is likely to be actively making sense of it. This will serve as the foundation for coming up with the best plan to address the situation. It will also make him more likely to follow the plan since he was active in developing it, with us standing at his side.

Finn was angry with Ms. George because she was challenging him to make greater effort in her class. She had known that he was a good student and she was troubled that he did not seem to have much motivation to apply himself to the lessons that she gave him. Finn replied sharply that she did not know anything about why he was not doing well in her class and that he didn't care if he failed. She replied with concern in her voice:

"You are right, Finn, I don't understand why you don't seem to be doing much in my class. I'm not saying that you're lazy or a poor student and I'm sorry if you think that I see you that way. I would like to understand what's going on with you in my class so that if it's something that I said or did, we can work it out. Or if it's something else I might be able to help you with it. All that I know is that you seem to be having a hard time and I'd like to help with it".

Finn's anger immediately dissipated, and in a broken voice he spoke about two students in the class who were bullying him before and after her class. He did not see them the rest of the day and tended to dread going to her class, finding it hard to concentrate.

HELPING OUR PUPILS TO RESPOND TO EMPATHY AND TO EXPERIENCE EMPATHY FOR OTHERS - SOME KEY THOUGHTS

I   BE HOPEFUL AND OPTIMISTIC!

As education staff, we must first remember that the regions of the brain associated with social and emotional learning are the same regions that are developed through safe emotional relationships. They are regions of the brain that are very slow to become rigid, which means that they can become stronger and better organised throughout life. They continue to develop in response to new experiences, and the experiences that have the greatest impact on their development are relationships with those we trust. So it's never too late for a meaningful relationship to have a positive impact on the development of both the structure and function of these areas of the brain. Experiencing empathy *from* others enables all of us to experience empathy *for* others.

Louise writes: This is so important Dan, as many education staff can feel that they have empathy covered in a lesson plan that has been developed for a PSHE lesson or from SEAL (Social and Emotional Aspects of Learning) work. Empathy needs to be experienced. Helpful though these programmes are, we can't experience empathy solely by completing a task within a class setting. For empathy to be experienced there must be a close relationship of some kind in place. The relationship provides the context for empathy to be practised and grown.

Dan writes:

I recall a young girl, Marty, aged 11, whom I began to treat at a time when she was moving from her fourth to her fifth foster home. After six months of treatment involving her and her foster carer, her defiant and aggressive symptoms were no better and the carer indicated that Marty would have to move, yet again.

I was able to continue to treat Marty when she came to stay at her new foster home with Jill. After six months of treatment involving her and Jill, Marty's defiant and aggressive symptoms were much better and plans were in process to make this foster placement a long-term one. Both Jill and Marty were quite happy with these plans. Over the following years, they had no regrets.

What happened? Jill had a core of hope and optimism that - while wobbling at times - remained present, in spite of Marty's behaviours. Jill was able to keep an eye on Marty's symptoms and find her vulnerability, her resilience, and her determination to make a better life for herself. Jill once told me that her task was to find the 10% of Marty that contained her strengths and to focus on those so that she didn't only see the problems. Jill's optimism assumed that her empathic gaze on Marty's strengths would enable the 10% to grow to 15%, and then to 20%, and so on. And Jill was right. Jill acknowledged that at times she became discouraged. She would talk with her partner, with me, with her social worker. She would then take a deep breath, realise again that Marty needed her even if she didn't admit it, and continue to care for her.

II   CONVEY ACCEPTANCE

If we want to experience empathy for our pupil and his experience of an event, we need to truly accept what he is experiencing. We're not evaluating it, as that requires that we're detached from his experience. By accepting his experience, we're able to more fully experience the emotion embedded in it. If we can do that, he is likely to be more able to trust our response to him and his behaviour. Through our empathic acceptance, he knows that we understand what led to his behaviour and he is more likely to understand our response to it (*as we discussed more thoroughly in the earlier chapter,* Communicating Acceptance).

III   VALUE EMPATHY

Sometimes we may give lip service to empathy, and then rush on to the 'real work' of solving a problem or managing a behaviour. When we don't have confidence in the psychological benefit of truly being with a child in his distress, anger, fear, or shame, we are likely to understate the experience and devalue its importance. When we do that, the pupil often won't experience its true regulating and supportive features. When we experience the value of empathy, we become committed to giving ourselves the time to experience empathy for this particular child, communicate it to him, and then give him sufficient time to respond. We must slow down a bit and leave room for the central role of empathy in our relationships with our pupils.

IV   EXPERIENCE EMPATHY FOR OURSELVES

Sometimes we have a hard time experiencing empathy for a pupil if the emotion that he is demonstrating or the event that he is recalling activates similar emotions or memories of events in our own mind that we haven't integrated or resolved. If we have difficulty managing anger, or if our parents expressed great anger at us when we were children, then if we're near a pupil who is angry or he is recalling the expression of anger toward him, we may have difficulty remaining open and engaged with empathy while he communicates his experiences. If he's expressing his distress over having been bullied, and we were bullied ourselves when we were younger, this may be hard for us too. Let's give ourselves empathy, for our own pasts, our own struggles. Then, when our own history is activated, we will be less likely to tend towards rescuing our pupil, taking a rational problem-solving approach, or minimising what happened. While problem-solving may be indicated, it tends to be much more effective *after* we have communicated empathy for the child and his 'problem'.

V   ASSIST OUR PUPILS TO EXPERIENCE EMPATHY FOR OTHERS

Our empathy for our pupils might be considered to be successful in affecting their progress when we are able to see them as having more empathy for others - both other pupils and educators.

For years, there have been mental health and legal programmes developed for adolescents who have engaged in physical and/or sexual assaults on children or other teens, which have been based on developing the offending adolescent's empathy for his victims. These programmes often utilised group settings and involved confrontations on the impact that their behaviours had on the lives of their victims. Heart-felt remorse was often observed, along with a commitment to restitution and behavioural change.

In more recent years these programmes have evolved to include an earlier phase of treatment that involves providing empathy for the offenders for their life experiences that greatly contributed to their aggression and behaviour. The initial worry about providing empathy for the offenders is that they would experience empathy for their past as providing them with an excuse for their behaviours. This hasn't proved to be the case. The young people were still accountable for their behaviour. Now those of us providing the service - and the offenders - were able to reflect on the reasons, not excuses, for their behaviours. Knowing the reasons for their aggressive behaviours enabled them to experience empathy for themselves - for the pain that they experienced when younger, that was so similar to the pain that their victims were now experiencing. The therapist's empathy for the offender generated the offender's empathy for himself, which activated the offender's empathy for his victim. Skipping the first two phases of this sequence undermines the likelihood that the third phase would last after the completion of the programme.

Louise writes: Reflecting back on a pupil's starting point, on their early childhood, can be seen by many in school as merely excusing his behaviour, as I've mentioned above. Staff can sometimes become very agitated, assuming that we are suggesting that the pupil's history somehow 'justifies' their behaviour. This is far from the truth. I clarify to educators that we don't look back at the past to excuse behaviours. We look back at the past in order to provide a framework in which to both understand and interpret behaviours that are being acted out in the present. Quite often behaviours that we see in the 'here and now' belong to the past and not now: how would we even have any sense of this if we didn't know the pupil's early history? Many are haunted by their pasts. When we've taken the time to reflect on what the pupil has lived through, we've found it so much easier to then set up the right kinds of interventions for them. This way the past can inform our practice. If we ignore the impact of the past, we can inadvertently make things a whole lot worse! We become lost at sea (*see the Appendix for an example template of a Factfile that is now used in many schools. This is kept in a confidential filing cabinet and referred to from time to time by those closely involved with the pupil (his team)*).

Dan writes: While we are not suggesting that we educators need to be trained in the kind of treatment programmes I've described, nor that our pupils demonstrate problems as severe as those offenders, Louise and I are suggesting that the development of empathy in our pupils will best follow the same sequence. Our vulnerable pupils need to experience and accept our empathy, feel empathy for themselves, and then be able to consistently experience empathy for others.

> *Richard, aged 13, was often in trouble for his angry attitude and apparent indifference to academic expectations. While he didn't present serious behavioural problems at school, his educators did see him as being at*

risk of doing so in the future and definitely not benefiting from the school programme. One day he became angry at what another pupil, Sam, said to him and he pushed him. Sam fell down the stairs, breaking his arm. An hour later, Mr. Thomas, the Assistant Headteacher, after seeing that the other pupil's medical needs were being cared for, met with Richard in his office.

MR. THOMAS (after first calmly telling Richard about Sam's medical treatment) *So, you two got kind of angry with each other.*

RICHARD *He just kept running his mouth! If he'd just shut up none of this would have happened!*

MR. THOMAS *So, he was talking trash and that really got to you!*

RICHARD *I don't have to hear that crap!*

MR. THOMAS *What made it so hard that time?*

RICHARD *He shouldn't have been saying what he said!*

MR. THOMAS *What was that?*

RICHARD *He said that I didn't know my ass from a hole in the ground and I'd always be a loser!*

MR. THOMAS *Ah! I can understand why that would be hard to hear! Someone calling you a loser!*

RICHARD *He has no right to say that! He's not my father!*

MR. THOMAS *Not your father? What do you mean?*

RICHARD *My father calls me that all the time! I might have to take it from him but I don't have to take it from some dumb jerk at school.*

MR. THOMAS *Oh, Richard, that must be so hard to hear from your father! That would be painful!*

RICHARD   *I'm used to it.*

MR. THOMAS   *I don't know how you'd get used to your dad saying that about you. Most sons want their dad to be proud of them and those words from him probably leave you feeling that he's not.* (Richard sits quietly) *I can really understand why you exploded when Sam said that. My guess is that Sam didn't realise that calling you a loser would affect you that much. He didn't know, just like I didn't, that you've had to deal with that from your dad for so long.*

RICHARD   *Sam's a jerk.*

MR. THOMAS   *And now he has a broken arm.*

RICHARD   *I didn't mean to hurt him.*

MR. THOMAS   *I know that you didn't, Richard. And most likely he didn't know how much those words would hurt you.*

RICHARD   *Yeah, he didn't know. How long before his arm will be OK?*

MR. THOMAS   *I'm not sure, Richard. Maybe four to six weeks.*

RICHARD   *Anything that I can do to help him out?*

MR. THOMAS   *Why don't we ask him? How about if you and I meet with him tomorrow? Be good if you'd be willing to tell him that you didn't mean to hurt him and that you want to help him out now. See what he says.*

RICHARD   *That'd be good.*

MR. THOMAS   *I think so, Richard. I'm glad that you told me about what was going on with you when you pushed him. Now I understand better. My guess is you do too. You shared some hard stuff with me. I don't think that you're a loser, Richard.*

RICHARD   *Thanks.*

MR. THOMAS   *Thanks for your openness and honesty.*

Such dialogues do not often occur so quickly and easily. We can see that Mr. Thomas must have already developed a genuine relationship with Richard for this conversation to be possible. But with persistence in building our empathic relationship with our pupils, such dialogues do occur. When they feel psychologically safe with us and experience our empathy, our pupils often become more able to experience empathy for their peers and become more motivated to address their behaviours that have been harmful to their peers.

VI   USE THE LANGUAGE OF EMPATHY

Experiencing empathy for our pupils is a beginning but it will not reach our pupils if we are not able to communicate it clearly. Communications are both non-verbal and verbal:

a)   *Non-verbal*

To communicate empathy our facial expressions, voice prosody, and gestures tend to convey acceptance, interest, compassion, understanding, warmth, kindness, and gentleness. This non-verbal emotional tone safely carries the words that we use into our pupil's experience so that he remains open and engaged with us and so more receptive to our empathy. Sometimes our first responses are more animated and intense in order to match his affective expression of his intense emotions (I refer to this stage as 'loud empathy'). This conveys that we understand his anger and distress and tends to move the pupil into a less intense emotional state where quieter expressions of empathy are effective.

Sometimes too we need to tone down our non-verbal expressions of empathy when our pupils seem uncomfortable with the emotional tone we are conveying. This may be due to the pupil not wanting to become vulnerable in response to our warm and gentle expressions. When the pupil seems uncomfortable with the emotional component of our empathic communication, it's wise to have a more matter-of-fact tone, still conveying acceptance, interest and an invitation to reflect. Empathy often elicits our pupils desire to experience comfort, leading to tears. They might not be quite ready yet to become tearful.

b)   Verbal

Our words are best when they simply describe our experience of his experience, avoiding all evaluations, reassurance, or recommendations as to what he should do (though there may be a place for such comments later).

● *"You seem to be so disappointed that you were not able to finish your task"*

● *"How hard that is for you! I know that you really gave it your best!"*

● *"You look so sad! I know how much you were looking forward to that"*

● *"You really are angry over what he said! That seems to have upset you a lot!"*

● *"You seem to be feeling all alone now. Like you're carrying a lot by yourself"*

● *"I think that you are really frustrated with me now for not letting you do that"*

These kinds of comments are limited to one or two sentences during which time we observe our pupil for his response (non-verbal or verbal) to our empathy, modifying what we are saying at any time if he seems to disagree, or seems uncomfortable with what we are saying.

● *"You seem to be quite annoyed with him for that ... or maybe not annoyed, maybe just kind of frustrated and disappointed?"*

● *"You seem to be having a hard time with what I asked you to do ... no? Maybe just having a hard day generally and this is just one more thing"*

● *"How hard it is to have to tell your friend that you disagree ... Or maybe not as hard as I thought. Maybe it's just something that you'll do but would rather not have to"*

We can also make comments that are interwoven with curiosity when our pupil does not respond to our expressions of empathy through elaborating on his experience. Curiosity supports the value in our pupil communicating his experience further to us, so that we better understand what it is.

● *"You really seem to be angry over what happened! ... What do you think makes you this angry?"*

● *"You seem to be so discouraged ... have you had this experience before?"*

● *"You don't seem to want to do anything now ... Can you help me to understand what is going on?"*

● *"John, you seem to be having such a hard time handling this ... I wonder if you think that this is just one more example of things not going your way. One more ..."*

From empathy to learning

Hopefully we have shown that the language of empathy requires us to begin our engagement with vulnerable children by establishing that we are safe and our intentions are to assist our pupil with his distress, whether it is expressing itself in anger, fear, sadness, shame, or anxiety.

When we need to quickly focus on our pupil's behaviour in the interest of immediate safety, we address the behaviour only and not our assumptions about his motives, thoughts, or feelings. And then we return to establishing our empathic presence, ensuring that our relationship remains strong enough to support our pupil back into a more regulated, engaged, and reflective state.

Louise writes: Whether the pupil is in the primary phase or secondary phase - empathy matters in school. How different would our pupils' experiences be in our schools, our classes, our playgrounds, and our communities if it was deemed good practice to follow these recommendations? There is no time to waste. Isn't it time to now have empathy clearly written into all our behaviour policies in school? There are some schools I know of which have done this very thing. The turnaround has been significant. The level of inappropriate behaviour has decreased significantly. An Assistant Head from one of those schools described this to me:

We always considered ourselves to be a child-centred school staff, with lots of expertise and experience of working with pupils with a variety of complex learning, emotional and behavioural needs, and yet we struggled to make progress with certain pupils. We tried everything! We worked with CAMHS professionals, parents/carers and tried all kinds of strategies but with some children nothing seemed to work. Then, we had an adopted child who we struggled with - we couldn't grasp what the triggers were for her extreme behaviours, couldn't find a reward, sanction or approach that had any positive impact. Staff were beginning to have conflicting views about how to manage her which caused friction within the school. We then had some input and support from Louise who trained some of our staff in attachment difficulties, explaining the main theory, encouraging us to get alongside this pupil and see beneath the behaviours and start to understand the messages she was sending us.

Once we began understanding, empathising and truly believing in the pupil we were able, as a staff team, to support her Key Adult in doing the amazing job of being alongside her and translating our world of school for her.

The transformation in the school as a whole was incredible! Once we saw her grow, gain confidence and begin to self-regulate we knew that so many other children in our school who had experienced trauma could make that same leap. We then changed the way the whole school worked and designed programmes of support, timetables and staff teams according to individual need and using attachment strategies. Our school is now a very different place. It is generally calm and yet fun, children feel safe, listened to and understood. The staff team know that they are helping the young people to build towards positive adult lives beyond school.

(Clare Langhorne, Brighton & Hove, Sussex,
personal communication)

At conferences I often use the phrases *"Empathy breeds empathy"* and *'Empathy first!"* Empathy before discipline, a change of play, an instruction … empathy requires that we slow ourselves down. Empathy can't be taught through a worksheet or through the internet. Empathy needs to be experienced relationally and, most of all, emotionally, within the context of a real life relationship.

In a usual school day there are many opportunities to communicate tender, loving care. Communicate explicitly that you are 'with' the pupil in an emotional way. There will be countless creative opportunities for you to do just that. This pupil needs to know that you are at his side, that you are rooting for him and that you will do everything possible to advocate for him and support him become the person he was intended to be. Communicate explicitly that he is not on this school journey alone. There will be plenty of big asks for him along the way. He needs to know that at least one person in the school realises this, is there for him and will remain there for him when needed.

There may be times when your pupil may feel misunderstood and not known by others. When this happens he may sink into despair without you and your support. The experience of knowing that someone 'gets' him and is there for him can make all the difference on 'the road less travelled'.

We can't overdose on empathy!

Chapter 9

Be sensitive about timing

But breaking through the cocoon, the protective yet unyielding rampart
(the pupil) has relied upon for so long is a risky gamble that offers no
guarantees; a perilous venture beyond anything he has encountered before.

(Taransaud 2011, p.225)

Louise writes: Sensitive timing is essential if we want to create a genuine
relationship with troubled pupils. We need to choose the optimum times for learning
so that our efforts aren't wasted. In a thrifty age, when all our hours have to be
accounted for in terms of our productivity, we don't want and can't afford to waste
time. I'm sure we can all recount times when we didn't get this right and we then
had to set aside hours at a time to sort out the consequences.

*Dave (aged 14) is not in a good way today. He is tetchy and not settling to his
work. Last night he had contact with his dad. His KA Neil knows he needs
to finish the course objectives before the end of half term. Neil becomes
impatient with Dave, telling him he needs to get a move on or he will get left
behind. At this point Dave tells Neil to "Fuck off!" and proceeds to trash both
his work and what's in the room. "I don't care about the fucking work! OK?"*

The use of the time we do have and the timing of what we do or don't do is so important in these relationships. Time - quality time, or the lack of it - is noticed by a sensitised, troubled pupil, as he believes it communicates his worth and value. To this kind of pupil, who doesn't consider he is worth much at all because of what he experienced in his early childhood, *time* can be a lifeline. Even a moment of time used wisely can make all the difference to our pupil's school day, meaning he can find the courage required to take the risks implicit in learning, despite his low sense of self-worth.

Just imagine what might have happened in the above example if Neil had laid aside the curriculum for five to ten minutes, to spend some quality time listening to Dave? If Neil had experienced empathy for what was happening for Dave, might Dave have managed to settle down to complete some work? OK, it's possible that Dave might not have done as much as usual; but he might have had more capacity to get engaged than he had at the beginning of their time together, when he was so preoccupied with other matters. Remember the attachment system (concerned with matters to do with safety, security and stability) in each one of us will always override the exploratory system, so there is no point attempting to distract your pupil at these times.

Timings of what we do and don't do are equally important in these relationships. Something said at the right time has the power to bring hope where there might have been despair, whereas something we say at the wrong time can cause a vulnerable pupil to unravel, as with Dave in the example above. Obviously you won't always get your timings spot on as often as you'd wish to, especially when many of these pupils are so hard to read: but the more you spend time with your pupil, the more you'll become attuned to the pupil and the more likely you'll be to time it right. Time is of the essence. Time invested now saves precious time being wasted later.

Timing what we do and don't do

What might have happened in the above example if the KA, Neil, had kept his feelings of pressure to himself to discuss with a colleague, got alongside Dave, really tried to get a sense of what was happening for him emotionally, and saved his gentle challenge for another day, when Dave was more himself and upbeat? Maybe Dave would have been able to remain in the classroom? Maybe Dave wouldn't have been excluded for his extreme behaviour? Maybe he would have settled as the day went on? In this case it's clear that what was needed at that moment was nurture, as opposed to gentle challenge.

So the timings we might want to consider include things like:

When to speak
and when to remain silent
When to engage in gentle challenge
and when to engage in nurture   When to
notice something explicitly and when to decide to
overlook something   When to teach new information
and when to allow the pupil space to process what they
already know   When to continue helping the pupil practise
dependency and when to help the pupil to be independent
When to get involved and when to allow the pupil to
make mistakes and find their own way through   When
to remind the pupil of what they know and when to
give them space to work it out   When to
reassure and when to stay with the difficult,
uncomfortable feelings that the
pupil is sharing

The time it takes

Sometimes people worry that the kind of relational approach we are advocating takes too long in the school context, or even that learning how to work with pupils in this way takes too long in itself. But in our experience, the extra time we need to learn how to engage in 'sensitive timing' will be more than re-paid by the extra time we save from 'getting it right' in our engagement with our pupils. To say nothing about the extra satisfaction we will receive within our educational role.

As with empathy, we can't learn when to draw close and when to pull back simply from reading a book about it - even this one! We can really only learn the art of sensitive timing by actually practising being physically close, attentive, attuned and responsive, within the context of a real life relationship and working it out together with our pupil. There are no hard and fast rules, because, as Dan points out elsewhere, we are each unique, as are our relationships. It's also important to remember that the pupil's needs will change over time, and that we need to welcome this.

However, that being said, there are some important pointers that we do need to keep in mind when considering how to engage in sensitive timing.

Facing the unfamiliar

We need to remember something that is core to the support work we do. For much of the time, how we are and what we do will come across as quite disconcerting for the pupil - despite our good intentions. Why? Because our way of relating to them will be unfamiliar. The way you behave is going to seem quite odd to a pupil who has experienced developmental trauma and loss at the hands of someone very significant to them in their early years. As we mentioned on p.109, our troubled pupil is viewing life through an insecure attachment lens that colours how he views others, especially other people's motives and intentions.

Bella might be really agitated, drawing all over her work, completely preoccupied and kicking back and forth on her chair. You go over to get alongside because you are worried about her. First she turns her back on you and then she gets up and asks the teacher if she can go to the toilet.

The pupil may actually feel quite uncomfortable when you attempt to reach out to her when she is in distress - doing what might come 'naturally' to you. Or the pupil might even turn on you when you reach out, causing you to feel upset and rebuffed in some way. Perhaps your pupil is more familiar with adults causing increased distress rather than creating comfort. Receiving comfort from an adult might be alien to Bella. She isn't expecting that. She is anticipating further discomfort and distress in your presence, not because of her experience with you necessarily, but because of her experience with other adults, in another time and another place. We cross over the intimacy barrier with these pupils so many times in the average school day or week, unaware of our impact on them and the resulting threat they experience. In fact there is a strong correlation between the disturbance we then see in their behaviour, and the degree of threat they have perceived.

So if your pupil turns on you, your natural response may be to withdraw. Maybe you'll wonder why on earth you're bothering. You may feel annoyance, irritation and impatience because of all the time and effort you've put into getting alongside Bella and genuinely supporting her. You may find yourself saying things that you later regret, words spoken out of hurt. Maybe you'll remind Bella that you are actually giving her a lot of understanding, and that others won't, the kind of comment we've all made on occasion and cringed about afterwards.

All of us need to be really wary of this dynamic; it can occur *so* easily when we momentarily forget that the pupil's responses really are not about us. We need to remind each other that there's a clash of worlds going on, which we need to be really aware of *before* we enter this potentially toxic emotional arena; otherwise it can affect our reactions and compromise the developing relationship.

Dan writes: This exchange relates to the reciprocal nature of all of our interactions with our pupils. We need to remember that our efforts to reach out with empathy, support, and encouragement are only effective *when our pupils accept our efforts*. So our efforts in reaching out must always include additional efforts - unique for each individual pupil - to assist the pupil to accept them. And if or when the pupil rejects our efforts, then our final efforts need to be focused on remaining open and engaged ourselves, so that we're ready to try to engage with them again in the near future.

Mrs. Jensen noticed that Elaine was apathetic and distracted, whereas she had recently seemed much more animated and engaged at school. Elaine's parents had recently separated and Mrs. Jensen knew that they were meeting that week to see if they could work things out. She approached Elaine and commented that she seemed to be sad, wondering if she'd like to talk about it. Elaine snapped that she wanted to be left alone and what she was thinking was none of Mrs. Jensen's business. Since Elaine had relied on her fairly consistently during the course of the year, Mrs. Jensen became defensive and moved away from her. She then noticed Lucy watching them, and knew that Lucy often teased Elaine about being 'teacher's pet'. Mrs. Jensen realised that Elaine's response probably related to Lucy, and that it had not been the time to approach her. She later saw Elaine in the hall and suggested that they talk for a bit in an out-of-the-way office. Elaine agreed and seemed eager to receive Mrs. Jensen's support.

In this example, Mrs. Jensen was able to remain open and engaged with Elaine partly through her realisation that Elaine's rejection of her reaching out to her most likely related to Lucy's presence and the likelihood of being teased. If Mrs. Jensen didn't have confidence in her understanding of Elaine's reasons for rejecting her help, she might have been defensive and not reached out to her again. Often there are reasons in which we have less confidence. These might well include the pupil's home life and recent events with peers, that we're aware of but not in detail. It might mean that the pupil feels too vulnerable and upset about an event right at that time, but would want to talk with the teacher later. A rule of thumb is that the pupil's resistance to relate with her teacher at a given time - especially when she has related openly in the past - is more likely to involve other factors, rather than factors associated with the teacher.

The window of tolerance

Louise writes: Let's have a look at the pupil's window of tolerance, as there'll only be so much they can handle of contact with us. Whilst we do need to tune into a pupil's cues, we can't *only* be led by these signals. Ordinarily, we rely on social cues when relating to our other pupils who see the world whilst 'wearing' a relatively secure attachment lens. However, when we're supporting pupils who've experienced relational trauma and loss, we need to not only read their cues but we also need to see the world the way they do, from the perspective of insecure attachment, in order to interpret their cues accurately. So, if a pupil is rejecting you, pulling away or withdrawing, *it might not actually be what the pupil wants or needs*, despite the cue he's giving you. Things are not always the way they seem in this particular kind of support work. The pupil might actually want you to pursue him, to *not* give up, so that he can experience one person, one relationship, that actually holds him: someone staying in parallel, not too physically close, but gently communicating presence.

"Keiran, I can sense you would rather I went away and didn't care about you right now but the fact is I do care. You can push me away as much as you want but I'll still be here caring about you. What happens to you matters to me. I want you to feel OK and comfortable because I care about you."

It's hard sometimes to relate in what can feel like a counter-intuitive way, but in this type of support work we need to be what we could think of as both *intuitive* and *counter-intuitive*: we're relating to a pupil with a very different attachment lens to us, and different also to the systems we operate within in school. We can tend to stick with what we know and what usually works, but we may get really disheartened when our pupils dig their heels in. It can help if we remember that facing the unfamiliar is going to raise the possibility of anxiety, fear and shame for our pupil. The consequence is that we need to not only read obvious cues, such as whether the pupil is comfortable with proximity and distance, but we must also engage in some gentle challenge - remembering that there could well be a misinterpretation of motives and intentions going on.

Holding all this in mind, you'll be less likely to back off at the first sign of your pupil's resistance! Some education support staff have gone off to support someone else as soon as the avoidant pupil has communicated they don't want help. Understandable, but, if you do this, you could be leaving your pupil stuck, colluding in a way with his world-view which says, *"So it's true, the adults can't be trusted, they shouldn't be allowed close and I should never let them into my vulnerability"*. As adults, we must gently challenge these misassumptions! That understanding might have been true with respect to someone else, in another place, at another time, but it's not true in the 'here and now' in this relationship. We can be trusted. We can respect and empathise with vulnerability .

At the same time, there's a balance between respecting what feels comfortable or tolerable for the pupil, what he might find uncomfortable, and what might feel intolerable to him - at the moment. We need to be mindful of the pupil's window of tolerance but always be seeking to extend it, not in a manipulative or forceful way, but in a way that matches his growing trust and development. Often we'll need to say this out loud, as we've described in other chapters. Constant commentary is so helpful when working with troubled pupils as otherwise, our pupils won't be able to work out what we're up to, and may become suspicious.

As one Key Adult said, *"Keep talking, keep explaining, keep describing, keep making connections"*. Yes: this work demands a lot of patience. But the benefits are enormous!

Debbie worked with a vulnerable pupil, Raymond, for three years. He was so, so avoidant of her help and support for the first 18 months but she kept on going. She remained consistent in her approaches. I remember her saying once, "This is so difficult, it's not like working with other pupils. I don't get anything back from working with Raymond. It's really hard talking to the back of his head. I have no idea what's going in."

However in an interview with her around the time when Raymond was off on his way to college, Debbie stated how this had been a life-changing support case for her. She described how there had been a significant shift and that now Raymond was even able to even talk about his lack of eye contact and his resistance! She said she was very fond of him and the warmth with which she spoke about Raymond proved that she had managed to break through his cocoon of defences to have a genuine relationship with him. She was sad that she was having to say goodbye, but she was really excited for him at the same time, as she knew he was ready to fly off to new pastures.

Debbie smiled as she shared some of Raymond's hopes and dreams. She shared how she was especially moved by the way he now wanted to help others like him who struggled. He wanted to make a difference like she had. Debbie has since been working part-time so that she could train to be a school counsellor. The work influenced her and enabled her to see the significant impact working with a pupil in this way could make.

The dance of attachment

To promote healthy attachment we need to find a balance of togetherness and separateness. A coming and going. Turn taking. Following and leading. It doesn't really matter which happens first, but they both need to happen. Both are required.

This can challenge how we currently 'do school', since, at the moment, we will usually view a pupil not following our instructions 'first time of asking' as exhibiting non-compliance, rather than as an indicator of his or her distrust of grown-ups, or of the pupil not being able to manage the intensity of intimacy in a relationship. We need to allow ourselves to be OK with sometimes letting the pupil 'go first'. For example, if a pupil says no, he doesn't want to answer the five questions in Numeracy, he wants to play with the Numicon, the KA might say *"OK, let's play with the Numicon first."* She would really engage with the Numicon so that he felt she was genuinely alongside him. After five minutes, she would then state that it was now her turn: she wanted to work together with him on the five questions in numeracy. If he protested, she would too!

"What? It's my turn. We played Numicon. Now it's my turn to decide what we do. That's how this works!'"

Dan writes: Pupils who have experienced developmental trauma tend to relate with adults and peers with a strong need to try to control the interactions, control what happens. While this is understandable, given their histories, we know intuitively that we cannot simply allow the pupil to decide at all times what he will do. So our tendency is then often to say, *"No, I will decide"*. We tend to try to assert control. This results in a battle for control, a 'power struggle'. When that occurs, when one wins, both lose, as the relationship has been damaged.

The dance of attachment - what some call the dance of attunement - doesn't involve control battles. Rather it involves the adult joining with the child with sensitivity - being 'in synch' - walking together for a bit and then leading the child in the next step. If he resists, then gently challenging him, as Louise has stated above, letting him know with empathy that we recognise how hard or uncomfortable it might be for him to accept the lead of the adult.

Louise writes: Supporting a pupil to engage in this 'dance of attachment' means we too may have to feel uncomfortable for a while, as new growth occurs. Growing pains hurt! Gradually, over time, our aim is to ease them into the dance so that we are in step together, attuned. At the beginning of the work, our steps will be clumsy, but over time they will begin to synchronise, and when they do it will be hard to not reveal how you experience a connection that you had never thought possible! Don't be embarrassed about showing the joy you feel, and the sense of wonder: this support work will engage you at your deepest level of being human.

The fear around

So during the first phase of the work, the pupil is likely to experience intimacy as quite intense, and find your support and care as intrusive and controlling. But even though we know that us taking the lead as the grown-ups is the healthiest way to engage with children and young people, we need to tread carefully and mindfully - timing is key. Knowing when to back off (to give your pupil a break from the intensity of intimacy - *see* p.34 for cues) is just as important as knowing how to get close.

Knowing when to swap in with another person as your back-up can also relieve a build-up of this intensity from time to time. Whilst the pupil does need the experience of practising relative dependency, they also need space to 'recover' from the demands it makes on them. Expecting them to sustain the intimacy of having us close to them over a long period would be a bit like asking ourselves to run a 10k when we've only just taken up jogging!

So let's create pauses at regular intervals during the school day to allow for this recovery, especially if you've been allocated over ten hours support time with your pupil. We must take both gentle and strong steps: gentle steps that communicate our empathy and acceptance, strong steps that communicate our curiosity and playfulness.

Dan writes: What you are saying, Louise, reminds me of what an adoptive mum said to her eight year old daughter whom I was working with. The mother had just shown care for her adopted child's struggles, and her daughter became anxious about the gentle support that she was receiving. The mum said, *"Don't worry, honey, what I am doing isn't called love. It is simply what mums do for their daughters"*. Taken alone, that comment makes one wonder; whereas in fact, it reflects the mum's sensitive response to her daughter's anxiety over signs of love. It is sad that love from a mum would frighten a daughter, but it is understandable, given her history, and is a sign of sensitive care that the mum was able to help her daughter accept love by giving it another name: simply something that *"mum's do for their daughters"*.

Louise writes: Let your pupil know loud and clear that you are alongside and you're not going anywhere: *and* that you realise that this is hard, annoying and uncomfortable for them. Many of the pupils we support have managed to muster a grin or a giggle when we have playfully sussed them out this way! This is why it's so crucial that you don't take things personally, or else you won't have the capacity to relate in this way.

Please realise that we're not encouraging disrespect (in fact we'll explore this in our chapter about discipline). We're not merely simply overlooking certain behaviours. Instead, we're giving these pupils more space and more time in order to learn how to allow us to take the lead when we need to, and in order to practise following our lead.

The challenge

Everything is a balance. We need to work hard at learning our pupil so that we can dance the right steps at the right time; this takes time and practice, just as in learning any kind of dance. I (LB) am a Salsa dancer. The best dances are when both the man and the woman are in tune with one another. Whilst the man is supposed to lead, in Salsa, the woman might indicate that she wants to engage in some additional, more complex steps. At these times the man must wait and watch, noticing the right moment to come close again to lead the next part of the sequence. This only works well when both partners take on active and complementary roles. If, as you can see in many dance classes across the UK, both try to lead at the same time, then the dance is a mess and both partners want to walk away in frustration. I often smile to myself when dance teachers remind me to be led, as my feisty leader instinct comes all too readily into play!

Dan writes: I love your analogy! It reminds me of comments made by Susan Johnson, the developer of an important leading model of couples therapy, Emotionally

Focused Therapy (EFT).   Sue states that in her efforts to improve the couple's relationship with each other she is reminded of tango dancing.   In fact, Sue is a student of the tango, and at an International Conference in EFT she had two professional tango dancers perform for the participants to demonstrate their sensitive, attuned, movements. Sue then joined one of the dancers and showed her increasing ability to perform the tango herself.   The very synchronised movements of the partners in this dance are quite similar to the highly attuned psychological moves of a sensitive teacher or KA with her troubled pupil.   She takes a step forward and her next step is determined by which one of the many possible steps her pupil then takes in response to her.

Talking through the difficult stuff

Louise writes: What kind of thing do we mean by 'difficult'? We suggest that the list can include times when a pupil has:

* hurt someone physically or verbally
* got lazy and is not doing much work
* damaged something
* taken food
* been disrespectful
* not turned up to classes
* lied about something that has impacted others

Just as with gentle challenges in other areas, when it comes to raising difficult matters that must be talked about, we need to choose our time wisely. Saying that doesn't mean that we are advocating avoiding discussing difficult problematic areas and topics, but simply that there are can be a spectrum of difficulty, and we need to be sensitive to what should be addressed when, where and by whom.

I do find myself getting very concerned in schools that very important issues are sometimes raised at the worst possible times. When I enquire about why this is happening, the explanations I am given includes that there are not enough staff, there is no other time and that the pupils we're referring to in this book *"... can't keep having 'special treatment"*. My concern is that mis-timing of such discussion can precipitate ineffective and bad practice.

Dan writes: As I see it, every student should have 'special treatment', if by special treatment we mean personalised educational programming and efforts to maximise his or her chances of success. If I'm fairly sure that a standard programme will not meet with success for a given pupil, then it seems the only reasonable thing to do is fine-tune a programme to have a better chance of being successful. If, to be successful, one pupil needs a programme that requires extra resources, then we need to find a way to give him the extra resources. If we don't, let's be honest and not blame the pupil for our failure to give him the resources that we know he needs to be successful. Time and thoughtful timing are such resources.

Louise writes: When asked, pupils state that they would rather we talked to them:

- away from their peers
- with someone/those they trust
- as if they were still liked and valued - where it was clear that the relationship was still intact
- in an open, non-judging way
- using pictures, puppets or role play to take the intensity down
- in a calm and considered way

- where they were given space and opportunity to talk too
- where they were offered ideas for reparation, if appropriate
- as if you were going to be alongside them in this, together, to help them work it out

In order to make sure all this happens, we're going to have to set aside some planned time together with our pupil, rather than merely reacting on the hoof.

Dan writes: If we want our pupils to listen to what we say in an open and engaged manner (when we can truly have an influence on them) we need to maximise our pupil's sense of safety. The neuropsychologist Steven Porges is very clear that children - and all of us for that matter - listen better to the human voice when we are feeling safe. So if we want to tell a pupil something that he will not forget, we might think of waiting until he appears relaxed and receptive, rather than telling him immediately after an event which has left him angry and tense.

Louise writes: Yes, some pupils really are at risk of being 'punished' and/or missing out because of this: let's remind ourselves that mis-timing difficult conversations doesn't match the inclusion policies we've signed up to within our schools.

If the pupil has retreated into shame and fear and is functioning from the primal fight/flight/freeze part of his brain, this is not the time to try to address difficult issues with him. He simply won't be able to engage in a reflective manner at these times, and if we persist, the situation may quickly degenerate into something even more worrying. Unfortunately, I've heard of staff knowingly engaging in inappropriate timing *in order to catch the pupil out* - as if they have had enough of them, and want them out of their school. They seem almost happy to pre-empt an exclusion. Thankfully these members of education staff are in a tiny minority: we can only speculate as to the kind of stress, impoverished support systems and feelings of insecurity which must have led them to thinking that this kind of manipulative - and most importantly, unethical - measure was acceptable. If we hear about such behaviour, we need to seriously think what kind of support such staff might need, and act promptly to address the issues with them.

When choosing our timing we also need to be mindful that some pupils might *become* anxious in order to avoid 'the conversation'. This is quite a powerful and 'useful' defensive strategy when experiencing stress, albeit an unconscious one - we need to remember that it's not deliberate. Remember too that these pupils get stressed very easily. Some ideas to support your pupil with difficult conversations include:

- Engaging in a sensory break first. Sensory breaks quieten down stress levels, freeing up pupils to engage their thinking brain.
- Talking whilst completing a task together. This reduces the intimacy intensity, as focusing on a task means intermittent eye contact rather than full eye contact
- Talking whilst engaging in an activity they enjoy, to relax the pupil.
- Stating that you can see they are nervous about talking right now.
- Stating *"Let's press the pause button and come back to this later"*. Then give the pupil some choice as to when and where the conversation will happen, within reasonable boundaries (that you might need to state). Though you may have to be careful with this question with some pupils, as they can get so anxious about the anticipated interaction that you've lost them before you've begun!
- Writing to one another, rather than talking.

Dan writes: Louise, I am aware of parents who will have these needed 'conversations' with their children over the phone, with the parent on one phone in the kitchen and the child on a mobile phone in the living room or bedroom. Often children will talk on the phone, safe that his parents will not see him as they talk.

When they're experiencing shame, children (and all of us) tend to want to hide from the eyes of the other person. Children often won't talk while sitting at the table or on a sofa together, but they may do if there is a safe distance between them and the adult: in the school context, a pupil may talk if he is in his favourite hiding place. Many parents report that their children talk most with them when they are in a car, without eye contact and with the relaxing rhythmic motion of the driving. Driving with your pupil may not be an option, but going for a walk with him, looking straight ahead, might work almost as well.

Louise writes: In one secondary school I know, a pupil writes letters to his Key Adult in a notebook called 'Letter to Miss', and the adult writes responses.

Managing your own timing

Make sure you're in a calm, reflective place yourself. Be aware of your own sense of self, your needs, hopes and fears. For a potentially difficult conversation, it's going to be best not to choose a time when you're exhausted and feeling at a low ebb.

When both the pupil and the adult have the capacity for reflective dialoguing, adaption and recovery is possible. When adaption and recovery becomes possible the pupil is more likely to be able to take on new learning, new growth, new development: the possibilities are endless. Sensitive timings have such a powerful impact. They can sometimes determine whether or not a pupil will be in a position to experience the permanency that is needed in both their school context and their home placement in order to fully recover from everything that they have had to survive in their short lives up till now. Let's take this corporate responsibility seriously.

Chapter 10

Gently challenge perceptions (wondering together)

Dan writes:

- Were you ever in the middle of expressing frustration with your partner for having forgotten to put away the garden rake before it rained, when you suddenly recalled that actually you were the guilty one?
- Did you ever scold a pupil for something and later discover that another pupil had done it?
- Did you ever think less of a friend for not acknowledging your success, when you actually had failed to send the email that you were going to send to tell him?

I have misperceived - many, many times over the years.

Our troubled pupils misperceive - many, many times too. Our perceptions are not objective reality, though we often act as if they were. Our perceptions grow out of our histories and include assumptions and selective perceptions (we notice what goes wrong and forget what went right) that often are quite a bit off target from what another person may perceive with another perspective and another personal history. Our troubled pupils perceive with a perspective that is often highly influenced by rejections, losses, a lack of support, and indifference. Their histories often create assumptions of indifference or antagonism that lead them to be hypervigilant and defensive, when from our perspective, there was no need for such a stance.

Our troubled pupil's misperceptions most likely extend from their interactions with us and their assumptions about our motives, to their interactions with their peers and their motives. Let's focus on these a bit, notice them, and rather than react to them defensively, consider ways to respond to them so that our pupils might begin to perceive a safer school environment in which to relate to others and take advantage of their opportunities to learn.

Gently challenging our pupil's perceptions of us

As you develop your relationship with your pupil, you will quickly encounter a challenge that can undermine your best efforts. His perception of the motives behind your behaviour toward him may well be embedded in negative assumptions - assumptions that to him are as obvious as the colour of paint on the classroom wall. Examples abound:

"You said "Yes" because:

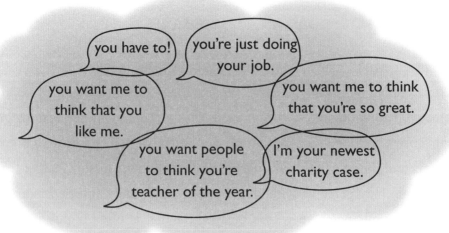

"You said "No" because:

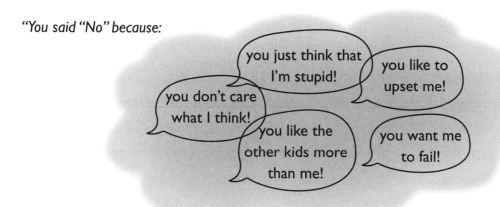

We need to wonder where these assumptions come from. The likelihood is that they come from a history in which caregivers had these or similar motives while interacting with this particular child or adolescent. When he was being hit, laughed at, ignored for hours or days, not fed, threatened, or called names, his assumptions about the motives of his caregivers - that their intentions toward him were bad - were easy to make.

But why does he make those assumptions about you when you've never acted that way toward him? The reason is that his brain and its billions of neurological connections are conservative - as is mine, as is yours. For his survival, his brain perceives things in a manner that will make it unlikely that he will overlook any acts of potential maltreatment. With his history of maltreatment, his neurological connections prime him to be prepared for similar acts - with similar motives - from those responsible for his care now.

Louise writes: In effect, Dan, you are reminding us that this pupil is in survival mode. He is watching his back - on the alert for danger. As education staff, we don't see ourselves as threats, but we are to him. How can he know what we might do next? He'll attempt to anticipate because he's needed to in the past, in order to protect himself. In some cases, he's needed to be on the lookout in order to even stay alive.

Dan writes: When there is ambiguity, he will perceive negative intentions on our part. When we frustrate him by saying *"No"*, he'll assume the worst possible motive. He has developed an 'internal working model of others' which is based on how he made sense of his life when he was being habitually mistreated. This model is his template as to how to make sense of his interactions with others now. We are relating with him against a backdrop of hurtful intentions and broken promises from his primary attachment figures.

Louise writes: This troubled pupil relates to us as if we were someone else. His responses are more fitting for another person, in another situation, at another time. This is why we don't need to take how he treats us personally, even when it really feels like it is personal. Your pupil is not relating to you in the 'here and now'. He is, in effect, locked in the past.

Dan writes: So why does the vulnerable pupil make those negative assumptions about positive interactions? His position in response to *"No"* and to discipline is understandable: but how can he perceive our friendliness and support as being negative?

First, it's likely that his caregivers sometimes treated him well, for various reasons of their own, often having little to do with him. But he learned that just because he was treated well once, he couldn't trust that the maltreatment would not re-occur.

Second, and most likely even more significant, is his 'inner working model of self' that I mentioned above. When he was maltreated in the past, our pupil worked hard to make sense of why this happened. When a young child is being repeatedly mistreated by his parents, he always - yes, always - also makes sense of it as meaning that he is bad and/or unlovable. His shame becomes pervasive. He firmly believes that he does not deserve to be treated well. So when *we* treat him well, he becomes confused, puzzled, and sceptical. Fairly quickly, he concludes that we are tricking him, we are mistaken: and eventually, when we discover how bad he really is, we will stop treating him well, or we are only doing our job and really do not mean the nice things we say or do.

Louise writes: I know of an art teacher who was so impressed with a piece of artwork from a vulnerable pupil that she praised her in front of her peers, describing her as really gifted and her work as having many remarkable qualities. To her shock, the pupil swore at her and proceeded to rip up everything she had done, saying it was crap. This is so hard for education staff to understand, especially when we've been encouraged to praise pupils. We know that many guidelines for teachers have been based on the assumption that all pupils have received good enough, sensitive, attuned care in their early years. But we also now know that the thinking, practice and the guidelines all need to be updated. We're going to have to use different interventions for our troubled pupils.

Dan writes: Yes, we must, if we - and they - are to be successful. Our task is to challenge our pupil's perceptions of our motives with regard to both our limit setting and directives and also with respect to our positive interest and friendliness toward him. If your pupil could accept and trust your positive behaviours toward him, it would make it easier for him to temper his reactions toward your limiting behaviours. But he can't. To him, the limit setting makes the positive less trustworthy, rather than the positive making the limit setting less negative to him. And his negative inner working model, of both self and other, presents us with all the challenge that we need in our efforts to form a relationship with him that might lead him toward hope and positive self-discovery.

Louise writes: This is so significant, because in the main at the moment, behaviourist principles and interventions are used in our schools. Whilst these can be effective for pupils with a relatively secure attachment lens, the opposite is true as Dan says for those with an insecure attachment lens. These pupils are going to need stepping stones first before they will be in a position to use the external controls we so readily use in our schools as a way of managing behaviour.

As one young person so poignantly stated, *"There were teachers there to monitor our behaviour but there wasn't anyone to take care of us."*

Accepting does not mean agreeing

Dan writes: When Louise and I speak of 'gentle challenges', we have not strayed far from our need to rely on PACE (pp.79-91). Here, our intention to work with playfulness is not likely to involve much laughter (since our pupil is likely to be feeling threatened and would experience laughter as belittling him) but rather us maintaining a light optimism in the background, a sense that we can journey together toward a new way of experiencing safety within a relationship. We don't challenge our pupil's perception directly, as that would be evaluating a central aspect of his experience of himself. We need to first accept his perception as his true experience of our inner life. If he experiences us as being mean to him and we argue that we are not being mean, but rather have other motives - helping him to develop important new habits - he will only be more convinced that he is right. Accepting his perception of us does not indicate that we agree with his perception. Accepting his perception of us simply opens the way toward exploring it and creating the possibility that it might change.

Louise writes: I know that this will feel really unfamiliar to many staff. To stay with something that is quite negative seems to contradict everything that feels right inside us; and yet, as you say Dan, we can't minimise, distract, avoid or rescue these pupils away from their perception. We have to start from where they are. This is of course how we are taught to teach curriculum, so we just have to import our skills base! We start from their starting point, notice it, acknowledge it and then we can move onto the next stage - but only then. There are no fast tracks!

Dan writes: Not if we want to avoid going *off* the tracks, Louise. We must remember that within the safety of acceptance, we will be able to communicate non-judgmental curiosity about our pupil's perception, while at the same time expressing empathy for his experience. The interplay of our curiosity and empathy, communicated without defensiveness or the monotone voice of a lecture, may create an openness on his part to the possibility that our motives might be different from what he habitually imagines. Our motives might even be positive. So for example, we might respond along the following lines:

- *"If you think that I think that you're stupid, of course you'd be angry with me! That would be so upsetting if you had a teacher who thinks that you're stupid. And you do believe that! I am very sorry if I said or did something that made you think that I see you as being stupid. Could you help me to understand what makes you think that I see you as being stupid?"*

- *"How hard it would be if you think that I don't like you! That wouldn't be right! How is a pupil supposed to feel good and learn if his teacher does not like him! I'm sorry that you see me that way! Are there ever times when you think that maybe I do like you? Can you help me to understand better what makes you think that?"*

Allowing new perceptions

When we are able to help our pupil to safety begin to explore his perceptions of our intentions, we are likely to help him to entertain *uncertainties* about their origins and their accuracy regarding our motives. We might then help him to realise that perceptions are not necessarily objective realities. They are heavily influenced by assumptions - by the meanings that we give to the actions of ourselves and others - which are in turn influenced by our histories. This is true for all of us. When this happens, without defensiveness on our part or the child's, he might then be open to allowing new perceptions of our motives toward him.

Louise writes: Whenever there is the possibility of misinterpretation, I've also found that it's helpful for education staff to think through what might be triggered and to *pre-empt* the possibility of misinterpretation by stating our motives and intentions at the time. Such moments might include:

● *"Whenever we sit down to do Maths you say "No, no, no, no!" Let's get our "No's" out the way now, and then let's have a go at practising making mistakes, as that's how we learn Maths!"*

● *"Whenever I leave the room, know that I will always come back. I may just have to do a job or two but I'll never be gone for long."*

● *"When I talk to another pupil you haven't dropped from my mind. I'm always connected to you even when I'm not looking at you or talking to you. You are important to me. As if I'd forget you!"*

- *"When we go back into class, I will need to raise my voice to Tom as he was being really naughty earlier and he needs some firmness. Please know that you are safe and OK, and so is Tom."*

- *"When I go into assembly and my face doesn't look all friendly and warm, please remember that I am still feeling friendly inside. I'm just showing everyone through my face that I'm waiting for them all to sit up and quieten down so that I can talk to everyone. I will show them my smile again once I can start talking."*

- *"When the fire alarm goes off it will sound for a few minutes so that we can practice lining up outside. We are doing this to help us all get quicker at lining up. It is not to frighten you."*

It is important that we show sensitive care in our interactions as these can keep anxiety levels low in school. If the anxiety levels are low, then your pupil will be more able to be freed up to settle to learn.

However, being proactive and pre-emptive isn't always possible. A helpful intervention I've found when the misinterpretation has already occurred is to 'freeze the frame'.

When Melissa winced after I reached for a book off a shelf near her desk I noticed this out loud. I said "Melissa, I noticed that when I went for a book you moved away from me like this. (I mirror back to her what I saw.) It was as if you thought I was about to hurt you in that moment. Please know that I will never hit you. We take safety very seriously in our school. None of the teachers here would ever hit you. If you ever see me reaching like that again, please know that I'm just trying to get something that is high up, like a book".

It's important that we give opportunity for the misperception - as in this example - to be gently challenged. Otherwise these clashes of interpretation build up during the day and can lead to what I call the 'pressure cooker effect', whereby that pupil can begin to unravel as the stress gets too much.

What Dan has been describing so well gives me a lot of hope for our pupils, who can sometimes seem so entrenched in their ways. To think we are capable of actually widening their vision by engaging with these principles in our relationships with them is so inspiring. And in those moments when a new realisation dawns for the pupil we're working with, those of us doing this work often find ourselves deeply moved. Many Key Adults I work with would testify to this. I've seen evidence time and time again of pupils moving into a new, more secure way of relating to and experiencing themselves, others and their worlds. It is truly awesome, especially when you know their starting point. Such moments can include:

☆   the first time a pupil trusts you

☆   the first time a pupil follows your lead

☆   the first time they accept your compliment

☆   the first time they smile

☆   the first time they accept help

☆   the first time they come to you with a problem

☆   the first time they experience stress without falling apart

☆   the first time they accept they have made a mistake

☆　the first time they take the initiative and apologise

☆　the first time they give sustained eye contact

What a shame we don't acknowledge or celebrate these significant areas of progress within school league tables! Surely a good school is one that engages in this kind of work, as well as the academic? School is the context to support pupils to become all they were intended to be so that they can function well in the world, and make a genuine contribution.

Gently challenging their perceptions of others

Not only do these pupils have distorted perceptions of us and how and why we relate to them the way we do but they also have faulty perceptions of others too - their peers, their parents/carers, members of the community and other education staff. As I mentioned earlier there are countless opportunities for clashes in school due to these different lens being used.

- The pupil who rushes to the front of the queue every day at lunchtime because he doesn't trust that the adults have ensured that there is enough food to go around.
- The pupil who hits out at any pupil who brushes past him in the corridor as he assumes they must be about to attack him in some way.
- The pupil who suddenly becomes very aggressive when an adult gives him full eye contact because he assumes the worst.
- The pupil so anxious about getting all her work right because she feels she needs to keep adults happy in order to keep herself safe from harm.

We have a responsibility to not only gently challenge how our pupils interpret us and our intentions, but also how they interpret other people who come their way. We need our Key Adults to act as 'translators', supporting our pupils to make sense of why people do what they do, as so often troubled pupils will get the wrong end of the stick. The clashes are inevitable if the vulnerable pupil is interpreting everything through the filter of an insecure lens and the other person is interpreting everything through a secure lens. We can't just leave them to get on with it. I know of tragic cases that have ended up in exclusion because of these misperceptions. If only someone had stood in the gap, providing a human bridge into the world of secure attachment. One way of doing this is to use the 'Hand of Options' which I described on p.134, which gives a visual, tactile cue and enables the pupil to think about possibilities for other people's motives and intentions which he has probably never even considered before.

So we must hold in mind possible alternative interpretations using what we know about both -

a) the pupil's background history

and

b) the pupil's internal working model, which has developed as a
   result of that history

We can provide the pupil with a relationship which can confirm or challenge everything that's happened before - so let's gently provide them with the necessary translation to understand our motivation for actions. Only then can these pupils start to learn security in our care.

When Rohema experienced the Maths teacher hating her, stating decisively that she was never going back to his class, the Key Adult firstly communicated empathy (as Dan has so beautifully described above) and then she held out her hand indicating her thumb, suggesting that the teacher hating Rohema was only one possible interpretation. She encouraged Rohema to think up some other possibilities as to what might be going on. She encouraged Rohema's curiosity. The Key Adult also became curious herself, wondering out loud with Rohema about what might have been happening.

In this case it became clear that because the Maths teacher had a neutral face and spoke sternly to the class about their noise levels, identifying Rohema and some others who were laughing loudly, Rohema had immediately assumed he must hate her. His motives weren't hate. He was merely trying to teach his prepared lesson and hoping that the class would be quiet enough to be able to hear his instructions and engage in the next task. This is not uncommon, especially in secondary.

Rohema will not necessarily adapt her assumption when she meets another neutral face who speaks sternly to her and her class, but with repetition of this process, Rohema is beginning to question her own assumptions. She has also become quite curious about herself and why she does what she does. Sometimes when her Key Adult wonders aloud with her she fills up with tears, as she is beginning to have the unfamiliar experience of another person 'getting her'.

Dan writes: Yes, Louise, we cannot forget Rohema, and the many like her. They are not truly 'misbehaving' as much as they are 'misperceiving'. If Rohema's perception had been accurate - that her math teacher definitely hates her, then we would be less likely to be worried about her behaviour, and more likely to worry about her teacher's feeling of hatred for her. If her perception was accurate, the problem would lie within her teacher, not within Rohema herself.

Finally, we should say that in gently challenging our pupil's perceptions we are likely to be gently challenging our own. Quick to judge and react to our pupil's misbehaviour, we often judge because we misperceive our pupil's motives and overlook the context of his personal history. If we are able to remain 'not-knowing' about our pupil's motives we are likely to inhibit our first reaction, develop a perception of him that includes his defensive and most likely negative perception of our motives, and then respond to his behaviour and the misperceptions that directed it in a more humane, sensitive, and ultimately, more effective manner.

Chapter 11

Be creative

Dan writes: Because each of us - each pupil and each educator - is unique, each relationship between pupil and educator must also be unique. Given that, given the 'one of a kind' nature of being a person, we need to be creative if we are to attain our fullest potential as a person who teaches. Educational texts, curricula, workbooks, outlines, and check lists need to serve as our guides, not our rules. Our primary strength is what we bring to the pupil and to the relationship we make with them, as a unique person with our own strengths, interests, personality, perceptions, history, and aptitudes.

Using our selves - creatively - in making our relationships

Creativity involves developing something new, learning about and perceiving something in a new way, as well as being able to combine two different bits of information and seeing something unique emerge. Being creative can be viewed as beginning with the ability to stay in an open and engaged state of mind, while facilitating a similar state in our pupil. We bring our thoughts, feelings, imagination, and past experiences to our pupil, and elicit similar features from his inner life. Together, we explore whatever our joint attention is focused on; we become excited about it, and deepen our appreciation for it. In this joint creative stance, the new learning comes to us both. As we teach, we also learn. As our pupil learns, he also teaches. If we had just presented him what we read in a textbook, he might have retained some information, but neither of us would have experienced the meaningful learning that arises from this joint, open exploration.

In being creative, we bring our unique interests, knowledge, skills, and manner of relating to the pupil. At the same time, we are open to his unique interests, knowledge, skills, and manner of relating. He has something to offer us as well. When he senses this - that we are offering a true interwoven journey, he is much more likely to become engaged with us in this joint project. In being creative, we make learning - and the relationship - personal. When our pupil senses that *he holds unique meaning to us* - that we are open to what he brings to the process of learning - he will be more likely to be open to our knowledge, experience, and abilities, allowing them to influence him.

You might believe that you're not creative and so must rely on a textbook. With this kind of doubt in mind, we need to look more deeply into ourselves. What, for example, are your interests, skills, hobbies, collections, favourite holiday places, adventures, fantasies, favourite music, movies, plays, sports? How about your genealogy? What have you discovered about your pupil's life, interests, wishes, goals, abilities, culture and the life of his parents or carers? Are there any fascinating areas of convergence? Or, at some time, have you both had fantasies about exploring the north pole, winning the marathon, inventing a personal helicopter, holding an audience rapt with your singing? If so, where can you lead these wandering ideas so that you can develop a joint project that holds your minds and hearts and creates a new dimension to your relationship?

Still struggling? How about if you sit down with your pupil and each write down or draw the first five things that come into your minds. Then compare what you've both done and see if you can develop a theme that holds both of your interest and develops your mental skills. Maybe you could write a work of fiction together, or draw a cartoon story.

Louise writes: Dan, I think in the education world we can become so overwhelmed with new standards, agendas, tests and expectations, that we easily lose a sense of the best tool for learning - ourselves. We can also quickly lose sight not only of ourselves but of the pupil's humanity too, due to the extraordinary pressures on us at this particular time in education. Let's remind ourselves of what makes us human, as whatever it is can make an invaluable contribution to someone else!

I know of a Key Adult who loves poetry and music, writing his own poetry and owning his own extensive, eclectic mix of albums. The young pupil he supports struggles to communicate, but he shares his Key Adult's love of poetry and music; this has deepened their working relationship in school, facilitating many intelligent and profound pieces of work together. This Key Adult and vulnerable pupil have found their own language in which to communicate. This would never have happened if the Key Adult had only worked within the restrictions of textbooks and the usual school systems. During this process, the pupil's use of language and confidence has been greatly developed and the Key Adult's own writings have been inspired. Within a meaningful relationship there are all kinds of learning possibilities.

Dan writes: Maybe if, as all-knowing teachers, we are still not able to distinguish a daffodil from a rose, we could admit that to our pupil, and commit to teaching each other the 25 most common flowers in our region of the world, and then plan a trip to a spring flower show together. Is there something wrong with learning with our pupil? Are we being selfish if in teaching someone else, we're receiving some benefit ourselves? Actually, no. When we benefit from an interaction with our pupil, he benefits as well. He, and his relationship with us, has brought something to us and our lives are richer as a result. There is nothing more empowering than having a positive influence on a significant person in your life. When an infant is not able to elicit joy, delight, and new discoveries within the mind and heart of his parent, that infant suffers, and is not likely to attain his full potential. One of the gifts that we give our student is to appreciate and be touched by the gifts that he and our relationship with him brings to us.

Louise writes: I believe Dan has touched on something very important here. Sometimes as education staff we don't feel it's appropriate to reveal our own lack of knowledge. The thought of exposing vulnerability would be horrifying to some! What Dan seems to be inviting us to do is to be more human, to actually model our own process of learning in the presence of the pupil.

The reality is that we're all learning. There's so much still to learn whatever our age, experience and training. I've discovered in my work that vulnerable pupils seem to warm to those who are honest. Those who are real. Those who aren't fazed by 'not knowing'. Those who are open about who they are seem to be are the ones who work best with troubled pupils. The way in which we communicate within the relationship we make with our pupils can also extend the use of our own creativity.

Communicating creatively: some interventions

ROLE PLAY

Some very effective work has been done with troubled pupils when education support staff have facilitated and joined in role play with them, testing out not only present dynamics but alternative ways of relating in schools. Using real life scenarios as they come up brings role play alive, offering space and practice time to test out possible scripts and non-verbal cues. Pupils can find themselves suddenly becoming aware of a lot more than they had previously realised by using this very helpful tool.

CONTAINING DOUBLING

In some of my support work we use *containing doubling*, a technique Dan developed. This is an effective way of supporting vulnerable pupils when they are 'lost for words'. We will say *"May I have a go at being you for a minute?"* Then we put a hand on the pupil's shoulder (if they are comfortable with this) and we have a go at being them - expressing what might be difficult to put into words. We have used this in reunions and reparation pieces of work, as part of repairing relationships in schools (*and see* Chap.13)

For example, when a pupil, Craig, clammed up with shame after his meltdown in Maths, his Key Adult took over in the reunion afterwards, and spoke as if he were Craig:

> *"Sir, I'm really mixed up at the moment. I don't know whether I'm coming or going. Things get too much for me sometimes and then I just lose it. I don't mean to cause anyone any harm. I don't really know yet how to manage all my overwhelming feelings and so they just all come tumbling out in one go. I scare myself sometimes as to what is going on inside. I guess I'm trying to help you understand. It is hard being me sometimes."*

Dan writes: Over the years when I have spoken for a child in psychotherapy (through doubling, as Louise mentions above), I have often noticed how relieved children were to know that I understood confusing or difficult aspects of their inner lives. I also notice how animated they often become in giving greater expression to those features of their inner lives that they previously hadn't known the words for. When you try to express what the child or young person is experiencing like this, you're giving your pupil the gift of your mind (and words) to help them to notice aspects of their own minds more clearly, which they are then able to communicate about more clearly.

What makes it possible for us to do this, to enter into what the pupil might be thinking or feeling? By remaining open and engaged with the child when we explore aspects of his life with him. This enables the areas of your brain that are designed for experiencing empathy for others, for having an intuitive sense of their experience, to begin to resonate with that experience, and then be able to understand it better from the child's perspective. This is a creative, intuitive process, not one that relies solely on cognitive analysis and reasoning. From a neuroscience perspective, this process involves the integration of the pre-frontal and anterior cingulate cortex, the insula, as well as the mirror neurons that also involve the temporal lobes. *You'll be able to have confidence in this act of doubling when you sense that your mind is becoming synchronised with the mind of the child.* You'll be able to resonate with him within a reciprocal dance.

However, we cannot take for granted that our doubling will always be correct. Guard against giving the child words that don't match his inner life. Notice his response - non-verbal and verbal - to your guesses about his experience; if he is puzzled by your guess or shows that he doesn't agree, then change your guess until he says that you have got it right. In my experience, creative people who are open and sensitive to the experiences of the children they are engaged with are the most successful at doubling. Those who have been trained to rely heavily on rationality or on statistics or lists of 'common characteristic' over various types of children tend to be much less successful in doubling in a helpful way. In my view, professionals from this kind of background tend to be searching for the answers as to what a child *should* be thinking and feeling, rather then being open to discovering what this unique child is actually experiencing at this moment, which is what we need to do so we can truly help him to 'find his words'.

Louise writes: As well as role play and the use of containing doubling, there are several other ways of being that can really enhance our relationships with these pupils in schools. Let's think outside the box. Let's get creative!

The use of metaphor

Rather than only using ordinary, direct methods of communication, we can experiment with the use of metaphor, a powerful medium to communicate with troubled pupils whatever their age.

> *After showing Amy different pictures of water - a still duck pond, a gurgling brook, a moving river, a whirlpool, a stormy sea - Reya, Amy's KA, asked her which represented how she felt most of the time when she was in school.*

Story telling

We're all fascinated by story! In fact stories surround us not only through the obvious medium of books, but in our photographs, conversations, memories, lives, music and films. We are in effect the characters of our own stories that are emerging as our lives unfold. Let's use this love for the powerful medium of stories within our work in schools.

Let's find stories already written and published through the spoken word, books, films and music that address the issues that our pupils are struggling with. David Taransaud's book *You Think I'm Evil* (2011) gives many examples of how we can use film and music which might challenge our usual way of thinking about how we work. There are some ideas at the back of our book to start you off but there are always new titles, so keep your own list updated. Stories can bring down anxiety and shame levels by reminding us that we're not alone, that we belong to a community who share similar feelings, passions, sorrows, grief. Normalising our experiences can not only restore our sense of calm and well-being, but also give us a platform from which to make new discoveries, to develop our insight, to develop alternative ways of being and doing. Stories unlock us. Your troubled pupil will need you to introduce him to stories throughout his education journey! Yes, even when he is an adolescent.

Let's encourage our pupils to create their own stories using all kinds of media: miniatures, puppets, sand, water, paper and pen, technology, paint, collage, cameras, instruments, their voices … the list could go on! Encourage the creation of music, role play, dramas, films, cartoons, magazines and books. Any kind of playful process will encourage creativity. Within creativity our worlds open up. New possibilities emerge. New opportunities start to be noticed. Hope is restored. Many school counsellors and therapists have already been using creative approaches within their therapy sessions in schools. Education support staff can do so too, so that our pupils are encouraged to make meaning of their lives so far, and to create new meanings for the future. Storymaking doesn't need to be restricted to the therapy room, English, Art or Media lessons. Storymaking can be encouraged across the curriculum and outside the curriculum.

As education support staff, we can have a go at re-telling our pupils' stories as we join them on their life journeys - re-telling a chapter here and a chapter there. We can assist our pupils in making sense of and remembering what's happening right now in the school context, so that the pupil can start to integrate his own story, his own narrative. Commentate on what you observe, what you notice. Make connections. Be a memory bank for your pupil. It's in the re-telling that explicit memory can be stored in the pupil's brain - that is, a memory that has been made sense of, processed and integrated into the pupil's narrative of their life. It is also in this process that a coherent sense of self, other people and the world can be created, an important feature of resilience, which can then be accessed when our pupils most need it.

If our pupils are not given any support to develop their explicit memory, their unprocessed experiences will be 'floating about', unstored, and likely to pop up at any time in their minds during the day or whilst dreaming at night. In this way our pupils can find themselves 'lost', at sea, overwhelmed and haunted by the traumatic ghosts of the past. Let's get alongside them as they create the future chapters of their lives, which can take very different paths from what's happened before. *Oh the Places We Will Go* is a great story by Dr. Zeuss (2003) and reminds us of the stories we're all part of, which we can influence at every point along the way. Our pupils need to know that their lives so far are not the whole story. It's not over yet!

Dan writes: Yes, I agree. The human being has been described as a story-telling mammal. We have a drive to create meanings in the events of our lives and we organise these meanings into stories. I have often noticed over the years that when I've helped a child to make a new story - one without shame and hopelessness - about the stressful events of his life, the power of that stress to undermine his functioning is greatly reduced. The child then has the ability to act in healthier, more adaptive, ways, organising his behaviour around new stories that enable him to take real advantage of his opportunities.

I was asked to see an eight year old girl, Grace, who had been adopted several months earlier but had not yet spoken one word to her adoptive parents. Previously, she had lived with a foster carer to whom she had been securely attached. As Grace played quietly in my office I spoke with her adoptive mother about Grace's life story, as I had understood it after speaking with her social worker. As I spoke about her life since her adoption, Grace screamed, "You stole me!" My animated response conveyed my new understanding about the meaning that Grace had given to her loss of her foster carer, as well as her refusal to speak to the person who 'stole' her.

As her story changed in her mind - she hadn't been stolen from her foster carer - she began to cry, and exclaimed, "I was bad!" Now she was creating a new story to explain why her foster carer had sent her away. My continuing animation helped Grace to develop a more complex story about foster care - you taking care of yourself - home and adoption - your growing up home. She began crying with grief over the loss of her foster carer, and Grace's mother began to gently cuddle her. Grace gradually calmed and began to talk quietly with her mother about the toys in my office and having lunch. Over the next few weeks she began to create a new story, one that was based on her developing attachment with her adoptive parents, including their readiness to help her with her grief as well as the anxieties and emerging joys of her new life. Her developing story would lead her into a more hopeful and empowering future.

Puppetry

Louise writes: So telling stories with and for children is extremely powerful. I've also found really animated responses from troubled pupils of all ages when faced with a puppet! There are some fabulous ones available. Puppets can take on all kinds of personas to support a vulnerable pupil in exploring themselves and others, one step removed. Being one step removed means that more challenging and deeper work is possible. Being one step removed means that anxiety, fear and shame can be kept well at bay, freeing up the pupil to engage in their ability to reflect on what's happening, rather than retreating into fight/flight/freeze responses (Levine 1997). At present I have three favourite puppets that have come in handy within my own attachment support work out in schools. I will introduce you to them so that you have a sense of how puppets might be used with troubled pupils.

There is Tolstoy the Tortoise who has an avoidant attachment style, hiding away, retreating at the first sign of challenge or conflict. He prefers to cope on his own, keeping others at a distance. We consider together how we can support Tolstoy to come out of his shell as we realise that he is missing out on so much by remaining inside, rather than venturing out. Comfortable, familiar - and restricted. Together we think of how we can encourage him to explore, to take the risks required in learning so that together we can open up his world so that it is even richer.

There is Sid the Snake, who has an ambivalent attachment style. He doesn't venture far for fear of being lost from someone else's mind. He clings, holding onto all he treats as dear (Sid can actually be wrapped around my 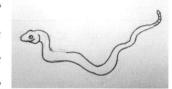 *neck as he is very long and coils). Together with our pupil we can consider ways to support Sid to risk separation, to test out whether his secure base will remain or not. Together we start realising that evidence needs to be noted and remembered as it can be when someone stays, remains, doing what they say and saying what they mean: then we can risk trusting and our trust can be built. We can then explore together which people are trustworthy, when to engage in trust and where to trust. Learning all about trust and what it should look like is a life lesson that isn't often addressed fully in school (explored further in Chap.12: Following and Leading).*

Then finally there is Rufus, the Reptile! Well, he's a tricky character. He is hard to work out. One minute he's charming and allows close proximity, and the next - well, anything can happen! Yes, he presents with the disorganised/

reactive attachment style. Together we work out what it feels like to relate to someone like him and we consider that he might sometimes feel quite lonely and upset because of others' reactions to him. Together we come up with a plan to support him to feel more accepted and to help his peers accept him. Together we introduce him to the world of secure attachment where things don't have to be as scary as they have been, where there is the opportunity of being relaxed - letting go of his usual state of high alert for longer than ever he would have thought possible!

So these puppets are just some of the many that could be used. Let your imagination lead you! In my work out in schools, we also recommend using small beanies (learning friends) with younger children to settle them physically into their learning by allowing them to fiddle with the beanie when the class expectation is to focus and concentrate. We've found creatively using learning friends effective for this. These learning friends can also be doubled up as imaginary friends who come alongside the pupil - giving them ideas when puzzled, stuck or feeling a bit wobbly or stressed. We, as the education support staff, can step in creatively, encouraging imaginary thought such as, wondering what Tilly the small Tiger wants to contribute today.

Being creative with resistance

Dan writes: A few final thoughts on the use of creativity when our pupils are resistant with us. Rather than entering power struggles, you might often find it more helpful to go along with your pupil's resistance, so that you can experience his behaviour as simply being another way for you to become engaged with him.

For example, when your pupil says *"No, I'm not going to do that!"* you might respond in one or more of the following ways, each one accepting the *"No"* and developing it or using it to relate in another way.

"Thanks for being honest with me that you don't want to do it. Pupils working with me get a lot more out of being together when they are honest and don't just go along with something simply because I ask them to. Are you honest with your friends too ... other teachers ... your parents? How did you learn to be so honest? Does it often take courage?"

When pupil, Abdul, says "No", the educator turns to a poster of Babar the Elephant on the wall and asks Babar why he thinks Abdul said "No". Babar replies: "Well, John, maybe because you suggested it in a grumpy way. Try being a little more enthusiastic and Abdul might just be interested in doing it."

When the pupil says "No", the educator looks out the window and talks (out loud) to himself: "I wonder what's up today for Jennie. She often is fine about doing that activity. Maybe it was how I asked her. Maybe she's just not feeling like working on that today. Maybe she's not feeling like doing much of anything today. Maybe she'll tell me if I wonder about it. That's it, why don't I just find out if she'll tell me. Oh, Jennie, I was wondering why. . . "

When the pupil, Jennie, says "No" the educator pretends that she is another pupil, putting on a jumper, using a different voice and walk and saying, "May I do it since Jennie does not want to?" Then the educator sits down in a pupil's seat and starts working on it with enthusiasm, asking Jennie for a bit of help at times or wondering why she's not in the mood to do it.

None of these ideas in this chapter will work with all pupils or all the time. They must not be used with sarcasm. But if done in a light-hearted manner, they tend to diffuse an emerging power-struggle and enable you to remain engaged with your pupil. When you are able to remain engaged, many good things might happen. Without engagement, there is likely to be little safety for either pupil or educator, as well as little opportunity to learn or to develop and maintain your relationship.

Chapter 12

Practise following and leading

Dan writes: If life were simple, we would stand by our troubled pupils, following their desires and tendencies with our minds. Over time, we'd discover that our presence was able to influence their choices and even their wishes, and find that our pupils were developing in very healthy ways. Some of us hope that this is the most accurate summary of the most effective educational framework. We are following our pupils' lead, and they are successful.

Or - if life were simple - we would lead our troubled pupils into better choices, goals, and habits, by initiating activities or discussions that they listened to and ideas that they followed. Over time, we'd discover that our directives would influence our pupils to develop in very healthy ways. Some of us embrace this alternative educational framework, as being the most effective. Our pupils are following our lead, and they are successful.

But life is not simple. Our troubled pupils need us to be sensitive and responsive to their wishes and initiatives, and they also need us to lead them in a way that will make it easier for them to follow us. They need us to find an approach that will help them learn a way of life that is more successful and satisfying than the one that they are inclined to take.

When we speak of following and leading (from the perspective of both the educator and the pupil) we will be revisiting somewhat our comments made in Chapter 9 regarding the need for sensitive timing and the importance of the reciprocal dance of attachment, the synchronised interactions that remind some of us of a tango dance. For the most part, 'sensitive timing' refers to the overall context in which we interact with our pupil (is it the 'right time'?). In speaking of following and leading, we are referring more to the actual interactions between educator and pupil - how the pupil's immediate response to our initiatives or our responses to his initiatives enable us to best know what is the next step.

If you see your pupil arguing with a friend of his, you might lead him into a discussion about it, and he might be very willing to follow you into the dialogue. If he has been arguing with a friend, he might approach you and lead the discussion, with you following. With co-operation around exploring the theme, either following or leading is effective. A problem emerges if you believe that you need to address an issue with your pupil, you try to lead the discussion, and he refuses to follow you into the discussion. On that occasion, you might well consider following his resistance to your lead by saying something like:

"John, you don't seem to want to talk about this now. What makes it hard for you to do so? Is there a better way for you that we might handle this?"

Louise writes: Like many other situations out in the wider community, school requires pupils to follow the lead of those in authority. In the school context, these are the teachers and the support staff. Education staff usually lead. Secure pupils follow, most of the time. However, troubled pupils often have real difficulty relinquishing control to the education staff who oversee their support, insisting on taking the lead most of the time themselves, panicking if they feel they are being made to let go of control. Troubled pupils tend to operate out of pseudo-independence, by which I mean they have learned through their early experiences that adults cannot be trusted, that adults bring pain and loss. So our pupils believe they need to do all they can to hide away any vulnerability they have - despite the cost. They don't trust the adults. They don't want to follow the lead of adults. So the pupil leads. That's the way it is, as this is the safest option - or so it seems to them. Our pupils are hard wired for survival. They expect the worst, because of what has happened to them previously. They aren't just doing what they do in order to make our lives difficult. They are doing what they do in order to survive.

This habitual response or way of managing is more familiar for them, and it feels the safer option. It's too risky for their sense of self, their sense of others and their sense of their world to allow us to lead them or control them - as they perceive it. They haven't had enough experiences yet of being able to trust grown-ups. So letting us be in charge is a very big ask for them. Imagine if you were holding on tight, out of fear, and someone told you to let go and trust, or even worse, punished you for not letting go and trusting. Would you be able to manage? Would you be able to relinquish that control? Yet the fact that 'following' is such an incredible challenge for these troubled pupils is usually overlooked and misunderstood in schools. We often continue with what you have described above, Dan, and we so need an alternative way of relating to our pupils in order to support them well. We can't just continue on as if they are just pupils who need to learn that they cannot take control or be manipulative. As we have stated already, looking beyond behaviour can reveal so much more than we originally thought. Looking beyond behaviour gives us the keys to sensitively and gently 'unlock' these pupils so they can move on from these insecure ways of relating.

Dan writes: Yes, we do need an alternative way of relating, a way based on reciprocity and co-operation. Since following and leading with one person implies leading and following from the other person in the interaction, we will speak of following and leading with regard to the actions of both. Remember the analogies of the salsa and tango dancing in Chapter 9. Our goal with our pupils is to make leading and following integrated into one successful dialogue and interaction.

This reciprocal interaction involving following and leading is easier said than done. Many times over the years, with my friends, colleagues, children, and clients, I have had an exciting and interesting idea that I assumed that the other person would like as much as I did, and that he or she would quite willingly follow my lead. But many times the other person did not. His experience or her thought led them into another course of action that didn't quite fit with my own. I'd like to say that I was responsive to their ideas, and happily worked to develop a consensus that valued and incorporated both perspectives. I have to say that many times I did not. Rather I held onto my original idea quite strongly. Rather than trying to understand the other perspective and find ways that it added to my own, I focused more on finding weaknesses in the other person's view so that I could convince him or her that my idea was better.

Following and leading means that we step back from proving that our position is the correct one. It means being committed to understanding both positions and then seeking a common path that meets the needs and wishes of both.

In this chapter, we will first describe the educators' need to follow and lead our pupils, and then consider how to assist our pupils in following and leading in their relationships with their educators, and with peers.

Following and leading: education staff

We are going to explore following and leading in describing the actions of the teacher or Key Adult as they set about initiating and developing the relationship with a troubled pupil. In the first instance, we need to follow our pupil so that we can begin our engagement with him *where he is in the present*, as well as to help him to experience our interest in him, as well as drawing on our understanding of his life. Subsequently, we'll need to lead our pupil in order to assist him to develop experiences, knowledge, and ways of relating with others that were not part of his difficult history and early upbringing.

Following

When you follow a troubled pupil with your mind so that you become aware of his inner life - his thoughts, feelings, wishes, intentions, memories, perceptions, values, and judgments - he is likely to experience you as being someone who wants to know him and wants to discover what his strengths, dreams, and challenges are. When you discover what is important to him and understand why it is important, you are less likely to direct him in a manner that devalues his sense of who he is. When you follow him before trying to lead him, he will be more likely to have some confidence that your directives come from your knowledge of him and your wish to assist him in his life's choices, rather than coming from an attitude of *"I know what is best for you and you need to do what I say."* If you don't come to know your pupil first, he will rightfully question how you know what is best for him when you don't know who he is. If you do not first follow a child with your mind, he will think and feel:

- You are interested in controlling him rather than getting to know him in order to guide him
- You judge his behaviour before taking the time to know what place the behaviour plays in his life
- You evaluate him and his inner life rather than focusing on his behaviour
- Your judgments and directives are made in an authoritarian, rather than a collaborative way

- You are not interested in getting to know him, only in him doing what you say
- While you believe that he should accept your influence on his judgments, you show no interest in allowing him to influence your judgment
- If he disagrees with you, he is either wrong or foolish

Louise writes: This simple act of following the pupil first has such a profound effect on vulnerable pupils - I've seen it time and time again. Our pupils don't seem able to believe that it's possible for someone to care that much, that someone is actually taking the time it takes to truly get alongside them.

> *One pupil I know told me that for a long time school had been rubbish. It had been a place she dreaded each day and her behaviour had reflected this. After a year of her Key Adult and team getting alongside her in the way Dan has described, she told me that she now rated school as eight out of ten, and that she couldn't believe the transformation. She put it down to her team. She said it was good to know there was someone there, someone who really knew her, someone she could count on.*

Dan writes: That's a lovely story, Louise. Following our pupil's mind with our own is a sign of respect and care. If we intend to take a place in her life where we can guide her in her development, we need to 'get it right'. We're not going to present her with a 'cookbook' that tells her what she must do to succeed. Instead, we are going to get to know her. We need to find out what is unique about her before we are able to design a course of educational study and programming that best meets her needs.

What do I mean by 'following her with your mind'? We need to know both her strengths and her challenges. As well as her wishes and her fears. Her interests and her dreams. We need to know a bit of her life outside of school in order to best know what resources and stresses she carries with her as she faces her school day. All of these things we'll find mostly by listening to her, truly listening, in order to understand her experience. We'll also find them by noticing her - her vocal and facial expressions and body movements, what she is carrying and what she is attending to. Our minds - while noticing and listening - are focused on being aware of her, rather than evaluating her. She is more likely to welcome a relationship with her educators when she trusts we want to get to know her more than we want to evaluate her behaviour.

Of course some pupils are easier to get to know than are others. The following might present challenges in our efforts to understand them:

- The pupil who does not talk much to educators or to peers about anything
- The pupil who will talk when things are going well but refuses to discuss any mistakes or problems
- The pupil who has unusual habits or behaviours
- The pupil who belongs to a different culture or community that we do not understand well
- The pupil who wants to be left alone, who does not want aid or guidance
- The pupil who seems to take pleasure in annoying or defying educators

How might we best approach these pupils? By leading them into conversation or interaction with us and then following their response to our lead. Often we worry that we are being intrusive if we initiate conversations and ask questions with pupils who seem to want to be 'left alone'. I don't believe that such initiatives are intrusive if we are aware of when our pupil pulls back from our initiative, if we accept their hesitation or refusal to engage, and convey gentle curiosity and empathy about their not joining us in the interaction. If we keep those responses in mind, our initiatives are *invitations*, not intrusions. We are showing an active interest in them, with the intent to get to know them, not to evaluate and change them. For example, we might say to the non-communicative pupil:

KA   *You seem to have had a hard time during lunch with Kate and Jane. They were pretty rough with you.*

PUPIL   (Silence in response)

KA   *I thought about coming over and telling them to stop it but wasn't sure if you'd want that.*

PUPIL   (more silence)

KA   *Just want you to know that I noticed, and I want to help out if I can, but I don't want to make it worse. Give it a thought. I have a few minutes after the next class. I'll stop by again and ask you what might be best, as you see it.*

KA   *I noticed that you were really involved in that assignment that I gave in History.   What was it that so fascinated you?*

PUPIL   *Nothing. Just ordinary stuff.*

KA   *I don't think that I've seen you so focused before in History. Something seemed to really hold your attention.*

PUPIL   *I don't know.*

KA   *Would you tell me which of the questions you wrote about?*

PUPIL   *I never even heard about the druids! They did so many things well and that was so long ago! I was wondering what we'd be like now if they still had a big influence on what we believed and what people thought was important!*

KA   *What a great question! Do you have any first thoughts about that?*

As we come to know her, as our minds follow her mind along the journey that it is taking, we will have a better sense of the obstacles and resources ahead that we need to know in order to be more effective as her guide.

Leading

As we follow our pupil with our mind, we are positioning ourselves to be able to provide the best possible educational programme for him. We are able to find the best match between our knowledge, interests, experience, and educational practices and his unique educational needs. We are in the best position to know how to approach his educational needs so that he will allow us to influence his motivation and behaviour. It doesn't do our pupil much good if we know him but do not try to guide him.

Louise writes: Sometimes, in my experience, I've found that education staff may over-compensate the nurture side of support and not provide the boundaries and direction that our pupils desperately need too. These pupils don't need 'marshmallow care'. They need us to be both gentle with our strength and strong with our gentleness in order to guide them through. They need us to stay centred, giving them a balance of experiences of being followed and of being led.

Dan writes: Yes, if we have confidence that we do have something to contribute to our pupil's development, then we have to find a way to support him to believe that we can make a positive difference to him. We have to convince our pupil that while we understand and value where he is in his life and what is important to him, we want to share our knowledge with him in order to increase his opportunity to attain his goals - even those goals that he might only be vaguely aware of at the moment.

And coming to know him and wanting what is best for him, we don't have a 'take it or leave it' attitude. We're going to show him our desire to work with him - and to work hard with him - so that he can attain the educational goals that we have developed together. Yes, he needs to know that we will fuss, push, and challenge him because we truly care for his future and we know that we're able to assist him in achieving these goals. He is so much more than 'our job'. He is a person we have come to know, to worry about, and to do whatever it takes to make his journey more successful.

We may be confident that we know what our pupil needs. But perhaps we don't know how to increase his willingness to co-operate with us in addressing his needs. As our troubled pupil most likely has not benefited in the past when he relied on adults (who used or were indifferent to him), he most likely isn't ready to easily co-operate with our efforts to assist him now. So, what to do?

Initially we may think that all we can do is present what is available to enable our pupil to learn what he needs to learn, and if he rejects that, well, that's his choice. We might even feel it's appropriate to walk away and tell our pupil to let us know if he changes his mind. However, I fear that in taking that stance we wouldn't be providing him with an educational plan that best addresses his educational needs. In fact, *if he habitually doesn't co-operate with adults, then the first stages of our pupil's individualised plan is to elicit and maintain his co-operation with his educators.* If he doesn't co-operate with adults, then he needs to learn the value of co-operation! It seems of little value to provide him with an individualised educational plan that covers Steps 3 to 6, if Steps 1 and 2 involve his greatest challenge - being able to co-operate with and rely on his educator's guidance.

So there will be creative tension between your following and your leading your pupil. To attain that balance where you and your pupil are co-operating on attaining your joint goals for him, you will need to get to know his habits and dreams, show him what is available to enhance them, present other possible paths that might provide him with more satisfaction in his life, and then gently challenge him with inconsistencies, missed opportunities, and any unrealistic plans that he might have.

And then - follow his response to your gentle challenges. If he resists, becomes defensive and angry, withdraws and seems indifferent, stop your efforts to lead him with your agenda and get to know his resistance. Accept it and try to make sense of it. Does he fear your motives? Does he believe that you think that his goals and efforts are wrong and foolish? Does he lack confidence that he can attain the goals that you are suggesting for him? Does he worry that he will lose too much if he changes course, gives up what he knows and is comfortable with, and follows you into unknown territory? Does he think that as he begins to work with you, you will realise that he is hopeless and so you will give up on him?

KA   *What's going on? You've seemed really angry with me today.*

PUPIL (CLYDE) *You don't know - I'm not telling you.*

KA   *I thought so. As you see it, I messed up. Could you give me a clue?*

CLYDE   *You're the one who is supposed to know things. But you don't understand anything.*

KA   *I'm sorry that I don't.*

CLYDE   *Yeah, right! Like I'm going to believe that!*

KA   *Would you help me to understand?*

CLYDE   *You always seem to have time for the 'good kids'. But I guess that I'm not one of them.*

KA   *If I did something to make you think that I have favourites in this class and you're not one of them, I'm really sorry. Whatever I did that led you to think that - I know that I didn't do it for a reason like that.*

CLYDE   *Well then why - when you asked if anyone needed any help - and both Jake and me put our hands up, you helped Jake and forgot about me? Guess you thought, "Stupid old Clyde, not worth the bother, he won't get it anyway."*

KA   *Ah! I did mess up! You did put your hand up too and I had planned to take care of Jake and then go over to you. Our time was almost up and I never got to you! I'm so sorry, Clyde! I should have told you that I was out of time then and worked out a way to help you later. Please believe me, Clyde, you are not a bother to me and I am glad when you ask for help. I am sorry and I do hope that you'll give me another chance.*

CLYDE   *Forget about it.*

KA   *No, Clyde, I will not forget what happened. You deserved better than that and I'm committed to being sure that it doesn't happen like that again.*

Let's be patient with our pupil in his fears and doubts about himself and about us; let's develop and experience empathy for how hard this process of new learning is for him, and let him know that we know how hard it is to believe that trust will develop. Sit with him in the joint awareness of how big a challenge all this is for him.

And then … lead him again. Challenge him again. And follow his response to your second challenge. Again, with patience and understanding. Sit with him again. And challenge him again.

Yes, be aware of how difficult this process is for him and accept his resistance. At the same time, after getting to know him by following him with your mind, and having confidence that your knowledge has something to offer him in attaining educational goals that will add value to his life, you mustn't give up when he says in his actions that he wants you to give up. He may resist you again and again. Accept his resistance each time. If you don't give up, he may be frightened by your efforts on his behalf and he might even be annoyed by them. But he will not give up either.

Louise writes: Yes, we must engage in this kind of dance. There will be times when the easiest thing to do would be to give in, to allow him to take the lead because we feel exasperated. Sometimes being patient yet again, and again, and again, can just seem like too much hard work. But that is what this work is all about. We need to engage actively in this process, knowing that we are aiming to develop a rhythm, a reciprocity to the dance. And that *it's the not giving up* that is making the difference, maybe even more than what we say or how we say it.

> *I will never forget Otis. He was a pupil I got alongside who constantly attempted to push me away with his regular insults and rages. On his last day, I handed him some paintbrushes and a roller as a little gift, as I knew he was hoping to be a decorator. He took them, bemused! One day to my surprise he came back to visit me. He asked if he could have a private word with me. Looking down and blushing slightly he struck up courage to say, "Miss thank you so much for not giving up on me. Out of everyone here you believed in me. You even liked me. Thanks Miss." I grinned from ear to ear, as you can imagine. "Of course I liked you Otis. How could I not have done? You have made me smile so many times. Like today."*

Following and leading: moment to moment

Dan writes: When you are able to integrate following and leading in your day-to-day activity with your pupil, the resulting interactions will come to resemble a reciprocal conversation when you are sharing experiences, perspectives, ideas, and plans with a friend, each contributing to the dialogue, each influencing the thoughts and perspectives of the other. While your pupil is not your friend - the focus of the dialogue is on his life and educational goals - the characteristics of the dialogue that are the most effective in maintaining his interest and motivation contain the same reciprocal quality. The following dialogue is another example of what we are suggesting:

> *Sue is a 14 year old pupil with poor attendance, effort, and achievement over the past three to four years, coinciding with increasing problems and stress within her family. Mrs. B works daily with Sue individually, with the goal of providing her with educational support so as to increase her motivation and success.*

SUE	*Before you say anything, I want you to know that I didn't write that paper that you asked me to do on Friday.*
MRS. B	*Did you have a lot going on over the weekend?*
SUE	*Yeah!*
MRS. B	*The way you said that, "Yeah!", Sue, I'm not sure what it means.*
SUE:	*'Yeah' is 'yeah'! What don't you understand?*
MRS. B	*Well, from the way that you said it, my guess is either that you had a hard weekend or you didn't really feel like writing the paper.*
SUE	*What difference does it make! I didn't do that rubbish paper. OK? God!*
MRS. B	*Now I'm more confused. Are you angry with me for asking?*

SUE   *Why, why why! You want to know everything!*

MRS. B   *I want to know you better, Sue. So I can support your work here, not make it more difficult for you.*

SUE   *Well you are making it more difficult! Can't you just leave it alone?*

MRS. B   *I'm sorry Sue if it seems that I'm too nosy about your life. I have no right to know anything that you don't want me to know. I'm sorry if you don't feel that I respect that.*

SUE   *Why don't we just stop talking about it?*

MRS. B   *Fair enough. Would you be OK with my helping you to get a start on the paper during our time together today?*

SUE   *You're still talking about that stupid paper!*

MRS. B   *But not about why you didn't do it over the weekend. I'm not upset that you didn't do it. I'm just suggesting that I help you get started with it now.*

SUE   *I'm not going to write any stupid paper.*

MRS. B   *Because ... ?*

SUE   *Because I'm no good at it! Are you happy now?*

MRS. B   *Oh, Sue. I didn't realise that you thought that you were not good at writing the paper. That's hard, to try to do something if you think that you can't do it.*

SUE   *I can't! You know I can't! Why don't you just admit it instead of pretending that I can! You won't hurt me if you just tell the truth! It's better than lying about it.*

MRS. B   (in an animated voice, matching Sue) *You believe that I don't think that you can write! I'm sorry, Sue, truly sorry if I said anything to lead you to think that's what I*

believe about your writing. I am sorry if I gave you that
impression.

SUE   *Maybe you didn't say it but I know that's what you believe!*

MRS. B   *How do you know that Sue?*

SUE   *That's what my dad said!*

MRS. B   *Your dad?*

SUE   *He said you were just filling my head with nonsense because*
you had to. He said that it was your job. He said that I
write like crap and any teacher would know that.

MRS. B   *Oh, Sue! Your dad said that you write like crap! How hard*
that must have been to hear him say that ... how hard.

SUE   (beginning to be tearful) *Why act so surprised? I know*
that you agree with him but just can't say it.

MRS. B   (gently) *Sue, you're in a lot of pain. Please tell me what*
happened?

SUE   (after a pause) *I left the paper on the table by the chair*
where I was writing and went into dinner. He came in a
minute later holding the paper and laughing. He stood
there and started reading it in front of my mum and brothers
and sister. I tried to get it away from him but he pushed
me away. I ran out of the kitchen but I could hear him
continue to read it to them. He read it like it was the silliest,
stupidest, story ever written. They were all laughing! Mum
told him to stop it but he kept going on about it. Then he
came into the living room and threw it at me. That's when
he said that it was crap and he said that you would say the
same thing if you read it and were honest with me.

MRS. B   *Oh, Sue, how hard that must have been! I'm very sorry that you had to go through that! I'm sorry that your father said those things to you and made fun of your paper in front of the family. And I'm sorry that he said that about me. He is wrong.*

SUE   *How do you know that? You haven't read it.*

MRS. B   *Because I know you, Sue. And I know what you can do. Would you trust me to read it, Sue? Would you trust me to read it with you now?*

SUE   (she sits for a while thinking, then reaches into her backpack and pulls out the paper, giving it to Mrs. B. without looking at her)

MRS. B   (she carefully reads the four page paper while Sue looks out the window) *Sue, there are so many parts of it that I love. You speak from your heart and I understand what you are saying about your experience. Thank you.*

SUE   *How do I know that you mean it?*

MRS. B   *Look into my eyes and listen to my voice and I'll say it again. And I will keep saying it until you believe me when I say that I love what you have done.*

SUE   *OK, you win. Now what do we do?*

MRS. B   *Now we read your story again together and you tell me about it.*

SUE   *Great - not.*

Louise writes: During this experience Sue is learning something significant. She is learning a *relative dependency* that is born out of trust. We know that this is what is required in order to support this pupil move into healthy *interdependence*. As Sue experiences these types of interactions on a repeated basis, the stronger she will become. Dan, how about if I now take the lead in exploring this further in our next section, where we focus on the pupil's perspective.

Following and leading: the pupil

We are now going to explore following and leading from the pupil's perspective. We need to support our pupils to follow so that they can be dependent on us, rely on us and trust us. We need to support our pupils to lead so that they can become increasingly independent in a healthy way. Eventually we're aiming for our pupils to be interdependent - to move between following and leading at appropriate times.

Some education staff are suspicious of creating dependencies in school and yet we expect troubled pupils to be ready for an advanced stage of relating - that of following our lead when they haven't even got past first base yet. We tend to focus on supporting *all* pupils to be independent regardless of their background or starting point. For pupils with a relatively secure attachment system, it is appropriate for them to start developing independence. However, for those who have experienced disrupted care the opposite needs attention. We need to support these pupils to have opportunities to become stronger in dependence *and* independence, *and* to know the difference between the two, so that they can use each style of relating with the appropriate people, in the appropriate contexts and at the appropriate times. Whilst we've briefly discussed these ideas earlier, let's be sure we're clear about the differences in their definitions so that we know where we are heading with our pupils.

Healthy dependency - is when a pupil is able to rely upon a member of staff for help.

> *For example, the pupil who seeks proximity at times of need, when they don't understand something, when they need help, when they fall over, when they are unhappy, when they are confused ...*

Healthy independence - is when a pupil is able to be self-sufficient in order to achieve their own aims and to meet their own needs - when appropriate and right to do so - according to the age and understanding of the pupil in question.

> *For example, the pupil who gets themselves organised and starts up a task on their own, the pupil who notices that there is a problem that needs solving and goes about solving it, the pupil who organises a team to tackle the technology task, the pupil who routinely waters the plants ...*

Interdependence - this is when a pupil is capable of fluidly moving between different and appropriate states of dependence on, and independence from, the other people in his world.

> *For example, the pupil who is able to move almost seamlessly from being the Team Captain of the Netball Team to asking for help in Maths from her tutor, the pupil who is able to go to the medical room for assistance and is able to then go into Textiles and set up a project for the group of peers on her table.*

The pupils we are concerned about really struggle with all three of these styles of relating. Even their independence can be felt to be domineering and intrusive - usually alienating the pupil from their peers. Of course your troubled pupil is going to need your help in navigating his way through this minefield. Let's start by thinking through what might lie behind these difficulties.

Earlier, Dan was curious about why our pupils might do what they do in response to reflective questions. As we wonder about this, we realise that things are not always the way they seem. I've found that when I start to wonder aloud in this way, distrust usually surfaces. Distrust is often behind many of the responses I come across in school and yet this is rarely talked about amongst staff, never mind directly with pupils. Yet distrust needs to be explored. Distrust is …

> The confident expectation that another's individual motives, intentions and behaviours are sinister and harmful to one's own interests. In interdependent relationships, this often entails a sense of fear and anticipation of discomfort or danger. Distrust normally prompts us to take steps that reduce our vulnerability in an attempt to protect our interest.
>
> (Lewicki et al, 2003)

Dan writes: I'd just like to add that in healthy homes, trust develops during the first year of the infant's life when the parent sets few limits and issues few directives that might frustrate the infant. Then when her child begins to crawl and for sometime afterwards, the parent sets many limits as she begins the process of healthy socialisation for her toddler. Though these limits are frustrating to the toddler, the toddler trusts the motives of his parent: he knows that the parent is limiting him because the parent is doing what she thinks is best for her child. Contrast that with a highly troubled family, where the infant's needs are not met routinely and well and the child never develops a sense of trust in the parent's care for the infant. Then, when this infant becomes a toddler and socialisation begins in earnest, the toddler has a core sense of distrust of his parent's motives. If his parent is deliberately frustrating him, he assumes that the parent is doing it for selfish motives or that she deliberately wants him to be unhappy, does not care what he wants, is not interested in him or similar motives. It is not hard to imagine that this child, upon entering school, will assume similar motives for his teacher's limitations on his behaviours and expectations for him to do what he does not want to do.

Louise writes: In our relationships with our pupils, they show us distrust in so many ways.

Kevin is getting himself into all kinds of complex difficulties with some young adults he has met outside the school gate. He is worried about seeing them. However he doesn't seek help from you.

Martha continues writing even though she is really confused about what she is meant to be doing. She doesn't put her hand up. She does not seek proximity with you.

Byrony has a nasty fall in the playground. There is blood pouring down her leg. She will not allow any adults around her to comfort her or attend to her leg. She screams hysterically, stating repeatedly that she is the one to put the bandage on - no one else!

What we need these pupils to do is to trust us, our motives and our intentions so that they can experience a relative dependency as Dan was describing above. So they'll need opportunity to practice what so many of us take for granted: to practice trust at its most basic level. Trust is ... 'a firm belief in the reliability of truth or strength etc of a person or thing ... or a confident expectation (The Oxford Compact Dictionary, 1996). As Dan points out, we must never forget that these troubled pupils are terrified of relying on someone, being convinced that they will be let down.

Let's think about how trust presents itself in the school context. Those pupils who can trust are able to make the most of the countless opportunities in school.

You'll know a pupil trusts you when he:

☆   Follows your lead

☆   Relinquishes control and can participate in reciprocal decision-making

☆   Assumes the best

☆   Is able to wait, delaying gratification

☆   Allows the grown-ups to deal with things

☆   Comes under your authority

☆   Is able to share you with others

☆   Is able to share friends

☆   Asks you for help or support

☆   Gives you eye contact

Now that we know what we're looking for, let's start to consider what such trust might need in order to grow, so that we can facilitate the right kind of environment. Then we'll consider what kind of additional interventions we might use in order to support our troubled pupil to practice trust, moving onwards on his developmental journey from dependence through to interdependence. And let's recognise that facilitating an environment of trust requires us to:

COMMUNICATE EMPATHY   **BE FAIR**

stay calm   SAY WHAT WE MEAN

create   be consistent

safety   HOPE   *create*

R E M A I N   *pauses*   do what we

DEMONSTRATE   say we are

keep our word **SENSITIVE CARE**   ADVOCATE   going to do

INTERVENTIONS TO SUPPORT TROUBLED PUPILS TO PRACTISE TRUST

● Notice out loud any evidence that would back up the principle that you and other grown-ups in school can be trusted. Make the connections for the pupil.

In primary when a pupil falls off a wall, the MDSAs take the pupil into the medical room to clean him up. I would commentate on what happened when it was witnessed by the pupil I was supporting. "Did you see that? That pupil was climbing on the wall and lost his balance and fell. The MDSA rushed over immediately and led him inside. We take safety very seriously in our school. That is an example of an adult caring for a pupil who is hurt."

In secondary, when a pupil is having a full blown argument in the corridors with other year nines, the HOY(9) comes over immediately, stops the girls and asks them all to fill in their versions of what has happened. He then gets them together in his office to facilitate mediation. I would commentate on what happened when it was witnessed by the pupil I was supporting. "Did you see that? The pupil was really upset. There was obviously a big disagreement going on and the girls weren't able to sort it themselves. The HOY(9) spotted they needed help and took over. That's what we do in our school. We take safety seriously. The HOY(9) will want all those girls to feel OK with one another so that they can feel OK about being in our school. It's important that they all feel comfortable and feel heard."

● Notice out loud any indications, however small, that your pupil is starting to trust grown-ups:

"I noticed you putting your hand up today to ask for help. That shows that you are getting stronger at trusting."

"I noticed you were able to give your form tutor some eye contact today in registration. That shows that your trust is getting stronger."

"I noticed you went and knocked on the Head of Science's door yesterday because you hadn't understood the homework requirements. Your trust must be getting stronger!"

● Show them how you are going to remember them or remember something you have said you will do for them. This will communicate their importance to you.

● Get involved if the pupil experiences any difficulties.

● Remember his hobbies and interests, his birthday, any special anniversaries, any known triggers, any known vulnerabilities or strengths. Being known supports trust.

● Remember them at times when they may need additional support.

Up to now we haven't been explicit about these areas of vulnerability within pupil's individual development plans but we must include them if we're to give our pupils what they need in order to succeed at school. For these troubled pupils to develop healthy interdependent relationships out in school and in the wider communities, different styles of relating need to be practised. Let's finish by considering how we might help pupils to practise the three styles I described above.

Interventions to support healthy dependence

- Trust games: see if your pupil is up for allowing you to help him keep his balance on an object. See if he is up for being blindfolded around an assault course with you giving him directions. Naturally, don't force him if he isn't, as some pupils really don't like their eyes being covered.

- Theraplay activities: please visit the *Theraplay* book (Booth & Jernberg, 2010) or website (www.theraplay.org) to find all kinds of fun activities that can be used together, whatever age.

Interventions to support healthy independence

- Giving an area of responsibility: find something that the pupil can do that will give him both a sense of belonging and a sense of purpose within the school community. He can be on a rota. He needs to experience you trusting him. For example watering the plants, feeding the chickens, supporting the school office, giving out the books …

- Peer support: give him opportunity to get alongside a younger pupil to teach them something he is stronger at. For example - reading, chess, playground games, numeracy support, skateboarding, computer games …

● Setting the pupil short tasks to do on his own with a visual timer: ensure that he has regular opportunity to try something that is achievable on his own from time to time. Let him know how long he has managed. For example if he manages just five minutes, let him know he managed five minutes. If he manages half an hour, let him know.

Interventions to support healthy interdependence

● Turn taking: encourage explicit turn taking, for example by using a musical instrument: *"We will follow your lead, and then it's time to follow mine"*. Mix and match.

● Theraplay activities: please visit the *Theraplay* book or website (as above) to find all kinds of fun activities that can be used together, whatever age.

● *Follow the Leader* (Bombèr, 2007 p.237).

In all of this, do remember that you'll need to start where your pupil is at and then gradually support him to move into new learning, new development. He shouldn't remain stuck because you haven't included any challenge. He shouldn't be rushed on because you've made your expectations too challenging. Let's all learn to wait, watch and wonder. Where is your pupil in all of this? Where are the gaps? Time and time again, we need to practice dependency with our pupils - as a pre-requisite to healthy interdependence. Let's not rush this stage, but honour each pupil's developmental pace. Together we can support our pupils into new ways of relating no longer based on distrust, but on trust. *And let's be trust-worthy.*

Dan writes: When we follow our pupil's leads we are showing our desire to know him and to facilitate his ability to take the initiative in pursuing his interests and contributing to the class. We are showing our readiness to support his developing independence, his decision-making, and his capacity to bring his gifts, skills and strengths into his work and his relationships. When we show clear enjoyment of the success of his initiatives as well as his struggles to get it right, he develops a sense that we truly do want what he wants to accomplish, to give him the opportunity to present his contributions and develop a sense of pride in his effort and in his success. With our motives so clear and so positive, then later when we say, 'no' and direct him into areas that he is not interested in to do things that he does not want to do, he is much more likely to trust our motives. He may disagree with what we think is best for him but he does begin to believe that we are nevertheless motivated by what we think is best. Then when he shows his disagreement with our decision and we accept that, we will be conveying that our relationship is bigger than disagreements and that we do not limit our liking him to only the times that he agrees with us. We simply disagree: no-one is right and no-one is wrong. Following and leading. Nothing builds trust so reliably as this process. Within it we are able to influence and be influenced by each other.

We want our children to respect our authority - and rightfully so. However, we need to know and to not forget, that they are likely to respect our authority once they trust our authority. If we focus on building trust, then respect, deep, reciprocal respect, will more easily follow.

Help repair relationships

You'll get mixed up, of course, as you already know ... So be sure when you step. Step with care and great tact and remember that Life's a Great Balancing act.   (Dr. Zeuss, 2003)

Emotional collapse
Louise writes:

Ben (ten) was fidgeting at his table in the middle of the classroom when his teacher told him to stop and to listen to what she was saying. Ben continued, seeming oblivious. She repeated herself: "BEN!" and put his name under the sad face on the board. Ben's fidgeting increased in vigour. "Right, that's it Ben - two warnings" as she wrote his name again on the board. "If you ..." Before she could finish her sentence, Ben went berserk, turning over his desk, flying off around the room screaming hysterically, landing in a heap outside the door, sobbing uncontrollably.

As we get further into relationship with our troubled pupils, it's easy to notice how they collapse emotionally when they feel overwhelmed or stressed. It doesn't take much for them to quickly unravel; even minor stressors can trigger this response. We should never underestimate the number of potential stressors in the school context.   Here's a list of a few low level stressors that might be affecting the pupil you work with:

ARRIVING LATE TO CLASS

not having the right uniform on

FEELING   DIFFERENT

NOT UNDERSTANDING A TASK

not being able to sit still

FINDING   IT HARD TO WAIT

misunderstanding something you said

someone brushing past him

not feeling remembered or known

someone looking at him

not having the right equipment/kit

We couldn't possibly list all the big asks or challenges that happen in school, but there are many during even an ordinary school day (*you can see more in* Bombèr 2011, p.29).

A pupil's emotional collapse will be especially noticeable at times of interpersonal clashes. School is a breeding ground for the misinterpretation of motives and intentions. We know that troubled pupils tend to have very poor social understanding and can lack empathy (Luke, 2012). And so misinterpretation is commonplace.

During these particularly stressful interactions, shame - a constant antagonist to many troubled pupils, is likely to rear its ugly head. You can recognise this by noticing behaviours that are indicative of what Dan Hughes and Kim Golding have called the *shield against shame* (Golding & Hughes, 2012). This is an effective defence that is used to protect these pupils from the overwhelming impact of shame. It's overwhelming, as they have experienced more than their fair share already, due to the early toxic experiences they lived through, and how they interpreted what happened to them (*"This awful thing must be happening because I'm bad", see* p.197). The shield against shame tends to come into play almost immediately within the pupil's over-reactive mix of emotions. The pupil's reaction is likely to include any or all of the following: denial, minimising, blaming and raging, all by way of self-protection. Being on the receiving end of this mix can be an intense experience which can make it hard for us as adults to think anymore: we lose our reflective capacity. And so do our pupils.

The 'fall out' of this happening can be considerable. You may well have noticed that if pupils from 'good enough' backgrounds experience a slight stressor, they can appear uncomfortable, but they don't unravel like troubled pupils seem to. For the first group of pupils, recovery time is relatively short. For our troubled pupils however, recovery can sometimes take hours, days, weeks, months … Shame seems to severely compromise their capacity to think clearly and to problem solve, and the effects may be long-lasting.

Many of our pupils simply don't know how to bring resolution when what happens begins to escalate to this kind of situation. Whilst we might be attempting to actively think about how to restore calm, the pupil is likely to be becoming increasingly agitated, sinking deeper and deeper into the sense of hopelessness so integral to shame. The situation can go from bad to worse very, very quickly. Sometimes your pupil may be beside himself with profound feelings of despair and rage, in a state of feeling overwhelmed, with no means of escape. Here's what it's like.

Your pupil feels sick, hot, clammy, frozen, scared ... vulnerable. The situation has become a blur as his primal responses kick in, and his internal panic button now firmly pressed as his brain stem becomes fully activated into fight, flight or freeze. Some of the people nearby will withdraw from him, confused and bewildered. Some of his peers may find his reactions funny, giving them another opportunity to point the finger and confirm that he is different and weird. Others become scared, and look at him with fear in their eyes. Seeing their fear and feeling his own takes your pupil down a spiralling tunnel of terror. What if he is a monster, after all? Everyone was lying with their compliments and smiles. They were tricking him. As if it's all been deliberate. He realises that now. The mistake that mum called him. The one that 'should never have been born'. And yet he was born. And here he is. In this place. This place of seemingly no return.

If someone like you dares to get alongside, someone with caring eyes and a kind voice, the panic might, just might, start to subside. In a heap his body trembles in the after-shock of panic - as if he has been traumatised, all over again.

Inside your pupil's psyche, shame is 'shouting' that he is an accident - a mistake. This is not a message that can be easily ignored. Experiences in the 'here and now' can confirm everything that has happened in the past, that was too horrific to contemplate, that had lain buried - only to unwittingly surface under stress in the school context. The build-up of that internal pressure is evident to see in some of the outbursts you will have witnessed, and he will have experienced, from the inside.

One of the triggers for these particular pupils to get rattled very quickly is any mistattunement from us, however slight. As we'll be discussing attunement and misattunement quite a lot in this chapter, it's worth clarifying what Dan and I mean by this.

Attunement is when two individuals are moving in synchrony together with matched feelings, wishes, desires, experiences and goals. The dance is a joy to watch, as the movements of each partner with the other is smooth and fluid.

> *"We are SO together. Our relationship just worked really well. I will not forget this time together and I look forward to more."*

Misattunement, on the other hand, is when two people are out of synch, not getting, understanding or sharing in each other's feelings, wishes, desires, experiences or goals. The dance doesn't work. In fact the two bang into each other or fall apart. There will be clashes, tension, or distancing.

> *"We are SO far apart. There is only misunderstanding and discomfort between us. I can't remember ever feeling good with you and I won't want to try again".*

A simple example would be the teacher who is so keen to get everyone out of the class for lunch that she misses the delight and engagement of the pupil who is staring intently at a book of insects, hurrying him on. An attuned response might have been to have stooped down to his level to share in the book, even for a couple of moments, to share in his delight and to have been curious about the insects on the page he was looking at.

For pupils who have experienced toxic experiences in their early lives, who are already filled up with an overdose of shame; little doses of shaming from those in authority, slight stressors or misattunement can take them over the edge into a state of being overwhelmed. We see big, over-the-top reactions, either through acting out behaviours or shut down/cut off behaviours.

Dan writes: I'd like to add another comment about the precarious nature of our pupils' relationships.

Having been hurt badly in family relationships, troubled pupils tend to find all their relationships very difficult to navigate. While they often say they have friends and that their friends are the only ones that they trust, these friendships are often short lasting, conditional, and are maintained by avoiding noticing or addressing problems that are present in the relationship. In addition, as they begin to develop a relationship with us and the relationship begins to assume importance, they often become more sensitive to perceived slights, disagreements, or expectations. With any increased emotional meaning given to a relationship with an educator, there is a similar increase in seeing reasons for not trusting this adult. It is safer to reject the educator first than to experience the rejection which is seen as being certain to happen.

Louise writes: So, all this being said, deep breath: how are we going to use the relationship we've been developing with our pupil to help at times like this? To repair a situation that's gone badly wrong? This chapter is about helping us to make the most of the moments in our relationships with our pupils when we can facilitate repair, to show them that our relationships are stronger than whatever comes along to disrupt them. We'll be taking time to think about what's really going on behind shame for a vulnerable pupil, and then think about how understanding the healthy developmental movement of shame into guilt can help us find a framework on which to base our interventions in school. And we'll then consider what we as staff might need to manage these 'fall outs' most effectively.

What we all need to remember is that it's not the incidents of unravelling in themselves that matter so much, although as your work continues you'll notice there are less and less of them. What happens *after* the incident is what matters most.

The presence of shame

Evidence of high levels of shame can imply that troubled pupils are stuck developmentally, that they haven't experienced adequate levels of empathy - yet. Our work with them will help them move on, so that their story up to now isn't the final version. But we mustn't overlook or ignore the powerful negative impact of shame on the individual. The following definitions are the best descriptions Dan and I have discovered: both communicate well what some of us observe in our classrooms day in and day out as education staff when working alongside troubled pupils.

> Shame is the powerful, painful emotion that combines feelings of unworthiness, inadequacy and powerlessness, and a deep sense of discomfort and self-disgust. (Taransaud, 2011)

> Shame is an affective expression that violates interpersonal trust and internal security. (Kaufman, 1996)

Dan writes: Shame is an emotion associated with one's sense of self, whereas guilt is an emotion associated with one's behaviour. When our pupil is embedded in pervasive shame, he won't face any of his misbehaviours because he won't experience them as a poor choice, error in judgment, or something careless. Rather the behaviours simply represent to the pupil an example of his unworthy, inadequate, bad self: and so they are denied. When confronted with his behaviour, the pupil reacts with rage - an emotion that is highly correlated with the underlying presence of shame. Telling your pupil lost in shame that you are angry with his behaviour, not with him, will elicit disbelief. He will be convinced that his teacher is being paid to say that and is a liar and/or a fool.

Louise writes: If a pupil moves into shame he can become preoccupied with it to the detriment of anyone or anything else. This is when we'll see the shield against shame being 'used', as we mentioned above. We'll probably see the pupil experiencing intense discomfort in himself - enough to distance himself from it in whatever way he can.

If our pupil experiences guilt, we'll notice something different happening. Not only does the pupil seem to experience discomfort in himself but he also seems to feel discomfort on behalf of others too. That discomfort for both himself and the other person may lead him into taking actions that repair whatever has gone wrong. This sense of another person means that our pupil is starting to have the capacity for empathy. To experience empathy in the first place implies that he must have had the experience of another person having empathy for him. We learn empathy through receiving it. Shame gets in the way.

If a pupil hasn't been able to go through the normal developmental process from shame into guilt, because of either having had an overdose of shame from someone significant and/or as a consequence of not having experienced sufficient repeated opportunities of both reparation and re-union following breaks in attunement, then he's at serious risk of experiencing toxic shame. This will lead to him feeling overwhelmed and hopeless, and of being triggered into additional experiences of shame later on.

So, in other words: not having had someone warm and receptive to his needs at difficult times in his early life will now mean that our pupil is hugely vulnerable to having a distorted view of himself and of his impact upon others and his world. It will feel too overwhelming to acknowledge what's going on, when things go wrong: if he were to do this, it would feel as if that would be further evidence that he is indeed just as bad as he originally thought. Unconsciously shielding himself against shame, he can keep these overwhelming feelings that cause so much pain and grief at bay, at least for a while. Many of our vulnerable pupils are in this place and they really need our support.

> *"I didn't do nothing. What do you have me for? Oh great I get it. You think*
> *I'm a thief. Well if that is how you think about me, I'm not interested."*

By the way, the defences work so effectively that we can actually start to question our own observations even if the evidence is all there! Our pupil's shield can convince us otherwise, making us doubt our judgments!

> *"You always blame me. You just don't like me. You would do anything*
> *to catch me out. To prove your point. I know you don't really like me.*
> *It's obvious!"*

Shame can become a familiar territory - to be expected and prepared for. A look, a word, tone of voice, pace of voice, gender, an atmosphere, particular body language or actions taken: all these have the potential to trigger something unexpected and over-reactive because of the powerful effects of the internal shame the pupil is already experiencing. The pupil focuses on relieving the uncomfortable and deeply painful feelings that may seem to be about the present situation, but are actually being experienced because of his existing level of toxic shame, created by past events. It can feel to the pupil that if he were to stay with these feelings, that his already fragile sense of self would become even more vulnerable. Some sense of relief and necessary protection comes about in response to the present situation by denial, minimising, blaming or raging, as we mentioned above. However all these defences come with a cost to both the pupil using them and to those involved in the interaction.

Other options, such as being honest, having integrity and revealing vulnerability are harder, especially alone. A pupil or indeed an adult experiencing this depth of shame needs the support of another person: but this is the road less travelled, because shame makes us want to hide away, and knocks out any capacity to think about taking an unbearable step into the unknown with someone else. And yet, that's the step that remains necessary for adaption and recovery.

Later on in the pupil's life, a significant other person, such as a Key Adult or a teacher, might come along and have all kinds of good intentions, for example to facilitate better understanding, to further connection by expressing feelings, to benefit the pupil's well-being or create opportunity for following up their interests and motivations and so on. However, our often innocent intentions can be so very easily misinterpreted by a pupil who is filled up with internal toxic shame, and on guard. To the highly sensitive pupil, the world is a battlefield. Hypervigilance to the nth degree is commonplace. The intense emotional energy required to keep this degree of alertness and the part of the brain necessary for this level of vigilance active means that the possibility of even using limited reflective capacity is severely compromised. This is exhausting for all those involved.

High levels of shame are likely to be toxic not only to the pupil but to those on the receiving end of interactions instigated and fuelled by shame. Shame is likely to be triggered over and over again until internal toxic shame is acknowledged, worked with, reduced, and then integrated into a coherent, personal narrative.

The way forward

There is a way forward, but it will take an ordinary kind of school with some ordinary members of staff facilitating the 'extraordinary', through their sensitive time and care. The capacity for healing will increase in its momentum when the pupil is in a school which provides a safe and secure relational context, which can facilitate repetitive experiences of unconditional patience, love, respect and understanding through its staff members.

When we use the word 'love' we mean having grounded care and affection towards the well-being of this pupil. Love describes something more meaningful and permanent than 'like', which could seem to be or experienced as transitory in its affections. These pupils will not be moved by superficiality, but are moved by genuine, long-lasting connection. A genuine relationship where both parties *matter to the other* is what is necessary.

Knowing that someone remains at the pupil's side, no matter what, has a profound impact that we shouldn't under-estimate. Qualifications and status are irrelevant. What matters is the member of staff's character, value system, their own attachment history and their commitment to the pupil.

However, it must be stressed that because we are all fallible as human beings, no one person can relieve the profound effects of the trauma of shame. The pupil themselves has to also come to a place of acceptance: this will only come about through the grieving process of all that could have been, and wasn't. Shame implies profound loss. This is deeply painful. However, denial of this reality just brings further suffering.

Dean (15) is asked whether he would like to spend some time together
with the new mentor Leon who also loves football. Dean is told that Leon
would love to get alongside him to be there for him when things get tough.
"Things aren't tough. I'm fine. I don't need nobody. Why is everyone
interfering in my life? Just fuck off and leave me be. Give me some space.
I'll be a lot happier with you lot off my case". Dean slumps off pulling up
his hoodie. He continues to be isolated and unhappy.

Until the recovery process is well underway, shame is very much like a time bomb
with the real possibility of the unique, fragile beauty that is at the core of each
precious human being who is exposed to it being damaged. This damage can be
psychological and sometimes physical in more extreme cases.

Linda (14) uses her pencil sharpener to cut into her arm in the school
toilets. If she could only get rid of the bad inside of her, but it won't go
away. She senses some relief as she watches the blood trickle onto the
floor, but stares into the distance feeling empty and a deep sense of sadness.

Unleashed internal shame can have serious consequences for everyone involved.
We need to take action to help our pupils tame and quieten shame's terrifying voice,
which actually belongs to another time and another place.

The process of building relationship with us

I've noticed in my work out in schools that as they begin to take the risk of building
relationship with us, troubled pupils often have very high expectations, assuming it
is possible for us to provide them with 100% attunement all the time - as if making
up for lost time! During this part of the process, I feel an important message for

them to learn is that all humans mess up from time to time and that we don't always get it right and can't be available all the time; yet, most importantly, we can still be trusted. It seems that the more the pupil has been hurt, the higher their expectations. I think it's quite important for education staff to let these pupils know very explicitly that they (the staff) are *dependable* but that sometimes they might not be *available*. This doesn't mean that these staff are out to harm the pupil - just that they are human with some traits that they are still practising and getting stronger at too.

Attention to sensitive care around these times matters. If we 'notice out loud' what is going on, we may also be able to disempower the intensity of the rage that is so easily aroused. This rage is intense, as it encompasses the feelings associated with the grief of what the pupil didn't experience in his early family life, as well as the overwhelming pain around how he now views himself. As education staff, I think we are often so focused on the benefits of what we are offering in our support work that we often overlook the fact that it provides constant reminders of what these pupils didn't have, or don't have.

Dan writes: I would go a step further too. Not just that we might sometimes be unavailable, but also that sometimes we might let them down - doing or saying something that they may be offended by. It might be wise to request up front that your pupils tell you at any time they feel that you said or did something that hurt them in any way. We can state our commitment to be there for them and indicate that there is a good chance that any hurt that we cause would be unintentional, accidental, or a misunderstanding.

The rejection inherent in transition

Louise writes: Feelings of rejection may run especially high at the times that are already challenging, for example, when term is drawing close to the end, and when our troubled pupils are preparing for a big transition, such as their move to secondary provision. In fact it's well known that our specialist behavioural provisions receive the most referrals at these flash points. Often we're too tired ourselves to have the patience to realise what our troubled pupils might be attempting to communicate with us, and so we merely punish them. Actually, these times give us significant opportunity to create pauses - freeing up space in order to support our pupils to process what is coming up for them in their relationships. Yet schools tend to become manic at the end of term, building up pace and the number of transitions, rather than slowing down in order to allow pupils to manage all the feelings inherent to change.

Dan writes: Yes, yes, yes, Louise. The most vulnerable, troubled pupils are the ones who have the greatest difficulty with transitions, and the larger the transition, the larger the difficulty. This is such an important point that I would recommend that educators who work directly with troubled pupils keep a list of transitions for each pupil. As it approaches, sit with the pupil and reflect on it. Recall a bit of the past and comment on the future. Acknowledge that those changes can be tricky or stressful, acknowledge that you also find it a bit unsettling to have changes in routine, people, and places. Especially address your relationship with the pupil, whether or not it will be changing. If it's going to be ending, acknowledge ways you have come to know your pupil and changes that you have seen. Acknowledge that you will miss your frequent contact, and, if it is realistic, how you will be maintaining contact or keeping yourself informed about the pupil through contact with his new educators. Consider giving your pupil a momento of your work together. If your relationship is not ending, you might exchange something small that you will return to each other when you get together again. Count the days until you'll be together again and ask your pupil to guess the first thing that you're going to ask him when you see him (or something else that will convey the idea that you will be holding him in your mind during your time apart).

The reunion

Louise writes: When something has gone wrong, and the pupil seems steeped in shame, we need to remain close by, connected and engaged. So, for example, when a pupil has smashed up a pane of glass in the door frame when he made a mistake in front of his peers, and then rushes out of class mortified, his KA will be close behind to catch up with him. Not to give him a lecture but in the very first instance, to communicate care and concern. The KA knows that he is feeling terrible already and doesn't need to feel any worse. He actually needs someone to get alongside, to make sense of what happened and to explicitly communicate what needs to happen next. This implies some type of bridge-building back into relationship. This is called the reunion.

Usually at times of difficulty such as the examples I've given, staff tend to withdraw or to isolate the pupil, using different kinds of relational withdrawal, including time out or seclusions/exclusions. When the pupil most needs a member of staff to be close, he is abandoned. Though we don't intend harm, the messages inherent in this practice collude with the pupil's assumptions about other people and themselves: that adults reject and cause harm and that he, the pupil, is without value or worth.

Instead we need to think through how we can remain alongside our pupils at such challenging times. We need to think about factors such as the level of staff care, the availability of back-up staff to swap in, and strategies and tools to facilitate safety, security and stability.

Staff care

If staff are experiencing enough care themselves, their own care-giving capacity will be enhanced (*see* Chap.17). They will have the emotional resources they need to navigate their way through even the most distressing of incidents. If a Key Adult feels valued, appreciated and supported by those around her, she will take up her place and remain alongside the pupil. However, if staff care has been compromised in some way, then our capacities may be lower, and unwittingly, we may well aggravate an already stressful interaction.

Swap-ins

If there are enough staff on the ground, there will be the flexibility of swapping in at times of intensity. This allows the Key Adult or back-up adult to relax from the stress of the situation, and get back their ability to think clearly, to fully utilise their own reflective capacity. This is always important but critical in this context, especially as the pupil isn't in a position to access theirs. It doesn't necessarily have to be for long - just enough time to think again.

> *For example, when Tody called Ms.Taylor 'an old fart' and then started to mock her, she said "No - enough" and the code "Swap in". Tody knew this meant that Ms.Taylor was not going to tolerate such disrespect and that she needed a short time out in order to press the pause button in this horrible interaction. If she had stayed both her and Toby knew things would have escalated. Tody looked a bit taken aback nonetheless, but the situation soon de-escalated when Ms.Carr greeted him with a smile and said "I don't know what has just happened but I reckon you both need a break right now. I'm guessing that Ms.Taylor probably needs a sorry card too as something has happened that means that she had to take time out". (see The Respect Plan, written about more fully in Bombèr, 2011, p.198)*

Strategies and tools

There are various strategies and tools which can strengthen connection between us and our pupil at times such as these: for example: anchors of safety, using a safe space, time in, taking sensory breaks together ...

We need to maintain our connection with the pupil. We need to protect our own ability to think, and help our pupil to restore theirs. We need to be wary of the powerful, unconscious dynamics that will be around at times of heightened stress that may be luring us to create distance and even rejection: that would be to collude with an all too familiar internal working model within the pupil. Doing all this will sometimes require us to have a stubbornness to remain connected against all the odds! We will discuss connection further in subsequent chapters.

Dan writes: I would add that when there has been a break in the relationship, regardless of the cause, it's the responsibility of the educator *and not the pupil*, to initiate relationship repair. That makes it clear to the pupil that no matter what the conflict or behaviour was that led to the break, the relationship is more important than the event. The commitment to the pupil and the relationship is as strong as ever.

As soon as the educator is confident in being able to be open and engaged again with the pupil, the educator initiates the reunion. It is often valuable to describe the event in a relaxed, conversational voice:

> *"You and I seemed to be really focused on that puzzle and then I saw the time was short and said that we wouldn't get it done. And I think you really wanted to finish it and you yelled "No!" I don't think I realised how much you were enjoying it, and rather than letting you know I understood how disappointed that you were, I just got kinda stern and raised my voice a bit too. And I think that you might have felt that I didn't care that you were upset, maybe even that I just wanted to get rid of you. Whatever. . . you got more angry and then I got angry and you knocked over the*

puzzle and ran out of the room.   Then I was not pleased that you weren't there to help me to pick it up.   Was that what you recall?   How are you feeling now?   Still angry?   I'm not, but I want to be sure how you are.   My guess is that we both were disappointed because we really were enjoying ourselves together and it ended like that: both angry and not feeling close."

Describing a past event, without evaluating it, without any efforts - at least then - to develop better coping skills in the future, is usually a strong way to successfully initiate a reunion.   It communicates that in all relationships, these things happen, and in your relationship with your pupil, these things are not a threat to it … they just happen sometimes.

Reparation

Louise writes: Because at school we assume that all pupils can think about what's happening and what they are doing and that they will therefore know what to do, we sometimes leave them without the necessary tools and strategies to build bridges.   We are quick to threaten them, to spell things out as we see them, but we are not so quick to help them as they continue to sink into their pit of despair.   We often interpret this sinking as the necessary consequence of guilt: but again, how far from the truth might we be?   This isn't guilt.   This is shame, and shame is toxic to both the pupils and others.

If our pupil needs us to provide the way out, then what can we do?   Well, firstly, we need to be physically and emotionally present: reparation is not something our pupil can manage alone.   Secondly, we need to use various tools and strategies together such as role play, mending, paying back time and the Respect Plan.   Rather than asking our pupil what he could do to put things right, give a few possibilities and ask him to pick one, or give a few possibilities and ask him to think up some more. Here are some possible suggestions.

Ripping up his work	*We could suggest we sellotaped it back together again*
Trashing a classroom	*We could suggest we put everything back where it belonged*
Swearing at a peer	*We could suggest making a sorry card*
Falling out with his best friend	*We could suggest facilitating mediation between them*

As we discussed in Chapter 7, after some kind of outburst, we need to be mindful of not questioning or interrogating - even though this is the approach we are more familiar within schools. There is no point using this approach since firstly, our pupils don't have sufficient connection-making capacity to provide the answers, and secondly, it may tip these pupils into toxic shame. If this happens, nothing will be learned as the pupil's fight/flight/freeze reactions will be activated in defence. Remember that the development of the pre-frontal cortex has been compromised because of relational trauma and loss. This means that the pupil's thinking capacity is impaired. So certainly to begin with we will have to do a lot of the thinking work ourselves.

So instead, we need to engage with our pupil with curiosity, whilst maintaining our own state of calm. Curiosity is very different to mere questioning and interrogation. The pupil will know we are genuinely curious when the member of education staff speaks from a place of openness and absence of judgment. This kind of relational way of being will support the pupil to allow us to come alongside him, for him to draw close and to experience our positive motivation to help him with the break or conflict. This will in turn reduce the shame, and will support the pupil to experience guilt and accept the need for and value of reparation.

Dan writes: I wonder if our challenge is to stand by our pupil with empathy while helping him to openly explore his relationship with his friend or another educator, so that he can make sense of the perceived rejection or conflict within the context of the whole relationship. From there we might help him to be aware of a sense of loss resulting from the conflict, and to explore the value of finding a way to restore connection. If he acknowledges a wish for a way forward in the relationship we might then wonder what possibilities for that come to mind.

> *John is angry with his friend Stan because Stan did not invite him to a trip that he took with his family, though he had invited another friend. When John expressed anger about it Stan became angry in response and said that he could invite whoever he wanted. They had not talked in the two days since then.*

We might begin with empathy to convey our understanding about John's distress over the conflict, since they had been friends for so long.

> *"How hard this must be! You've been so close to him for so long! You weren't expecting this!"*

Empathy might be followed by curiosity about how John made sense of what his friend had done. If possible, the educator might raise the question about other possible reasons for Stan's behaviour, to reduce the certainty or intensity of the perceived rejection.

"It seems to you that he is spending less time with you then before - and maybe doesn't care as much about the relationship as he once did. If that's the case, I can certainly see why it would be very hard to take."

Acceptance of the distress associated with the conflict might be followed with a broader focus on the history of the relationship and the sense of loss that will follow if the relationship is not healed.

"And you haven't talked for the past two days! And he has been a good friend for so long! It is so hard to make sense of this. And with you both getting angry with each other it is probably even harder now to find a way resolve this."

Empathy might follow over how hard it might be to try to resolve the problem by initiating a discussion with Stan. Along with recognising how hard it might be to try to resolve it, you might suggest that it would be very sad if the relationship ended without trying to repair it.

"After that anger, it would be hard for either of you to take the first step to repair your relationship. You probably each would want the other one to take the first step now. Your friendship with him was so important! If you both want to stay good friends, I guess it would be sad that your relationship broke because both of you didn't try to work it out."

After acknowledging the difficulty you might wonder if there was any possible way of trying to resolve the problem.

"If, without getting angry, you told him that you were upset that he did not invite you and asked him what it was about, do you think he would tell you? Would you believe him? Would you want me to go with you if you decide to talk with him about this? Would that help?"

Moving on developmentally

Louise writes: Once our pupil has had sufficient, repetitive experiences of reunions and reparation through empathic responses he will start to move on from shame to guilt. Guilt is the next developmental stage. It implies that the pupil has made a mistake, rather than him *being* a mistake. He will start to become aware that as well as feeling discomfort himself, that the other person can feel too. He will start to develop a theory of mind, a sense of otherness. This opens up a range of possibilities. Having had experience now of healthy reparation, he is more likely to be able to keep thinking, to engage his reflective capacity and choose a suitable way back into relationship: he has learned through experience with us. This is where we want our pupils to be. They are then less likely to over-react and engage in what can become very disturbed interactions and behaviours. They start to enter into the secure context that we are offering them. This in turn will then free them up to engage their exploratory system which has been lying dormant whilst they were caught up in so much anxiety and trauma. And then they can really settle into learning.

It's easy to recognise that our pupils need a lot of practice in experiencing togetherness. Knowing that together, being honest with each other about what's happening, we can put things right. These pupils will be too familiar with having to deal with stress all alone and will know the feelings of being overwhelmed associated with this. Our job is to slowly introduce them to the possibility of relationship actually being advantageous! And satisfying, for both people involved!

Now is the time for relating differently. Together it is possible to gently challenge our pupils into new ways of being, doing and relating. Trauma and loss doesn't need to be a life sentence. Internal shame doesn't need to be triggered. Shame can be quietened, tamed and converted into a healthy, productive sense of guilt that has the potential to kiss a hurting world and to make a difference.

> *'Together we can figure this out.*
> *Together we can find a way through*
> *Together we can build the necessary bridges*
> *Together we can have another go ...*
>
> *... so much is possible - together'.*

Chapter 14

Promote integration

'Dance me through the panic until I am gathered safely in ...

(Leonard Cohen, *Dance me to the end of love*,

1984, Sony Music Entertainment Inc)

Fragmentation
Louise writes:

Danny is a terror for his adoptive mum as she struggles to get him to school but once he spots Ms. Hilda in the playground he becomes an angel, smiling and giggling - almost charming! Feeling overwhelmed, his mum walks over to Ms. Hilda and says "Danny is a nightmare. I don't think I can cope. He is running me into the ground. He's so controlling and manipulative. He is quite difficult to like at the moment." Danny hides himself behind Ms. Hilda - as if his mum is an abuser.

It is easy to see how school could get a very distorted picture of Danny. There is so much more going on here than meets the eye. Danny is displaying a complex mix of adaptive behaviour, which he needed to develop to survive a toxic home in his early life: his maladaptive behaviour towards his adoptive mum: and, at school, 'charming behaviour', which hides his more difficult-to-love parts. I am aware that instances like this are quite common, as are the reverse, the school being privy to the 'nightmare parts' and home being privy to the lovely, adorable parts of any given child! These complex dynamics can occur either way round, in either context.

In order to survive the overwhelming stress and pain of not being wanted, of being scorned, rejected, neglected or abused, many of our vulnerable pupils will have needed to distance themselves from themselves and their experiences, or from aspects of themselves and aspects of their experience. How could a pupil have built an holistic, healthy, appropriate view of himself if he received the kind of distorted picture the experiences above will have conveyed, intentionally or non-intentionally? You may not even be aware of your pupil creating distance, compartmentalising parts of himself; you may only be aware of the part/s that you have come to know through your relationship with him, in the specific context of school. Some of his parts may be being expressed, but others may be being kept from you, to keep him feeling safe.

Sometimes our pupils reveal particular parts of themselves to some people in school, and other parts to others. Such compartmentalisation or fragmentation within the same context (that of school) may create a divisive effect, 'splitting' opinion and attitude in the people around them - and can be quite confusing to those involved. Elsewhere I've defined splitting as follows:

> … an (unconscious) defence mechanism that is used against anxiety inside an individual, in relationships and in organisational situations. A 'Jeckyl & Hyde' dynamic can develop, in which oneself, someone else, or a situation, is seen as all good or all bad. It is difficult to acknowledge both the good and bad that is present in oneself or other people.
>
> (Bombèr 2007, p.300).

Sometimes the pupil will dissociate *(see below)* and actually not be consciously aware of different parts or personnas which actually belong to them, parts or personas which other people might be relating to.

> *For example the pupil who is usually warm, engaging and funny. But then at other times, it's as if we are relating to someone else, his twin, as he can seem cold, distant and aggressive. Completely opposite to what we know of him.*

or

> *The pupil who is one minute involved in navigating his way in and out of computer applications may suddenly become like a dog, getting on all fours, barking, growling and sniffing about.*

I and my colleagues have particularly noticed this amongst pupils who are intelligent and creative. The brain engages in dissociation as a very clever defence: and what a sophisticated and helpful mechanism it is for those who are highly complex and sensitive to what they have experienced.

However, when the pupil is then in a safe context, this defence of separation between aspects of the self can obviously compromise them. In fact the mind finds it hard to keep up the high level of compartmentalisation as the years go by: there's always a pull towards integration. Some of the walls dividing the parts/personas can start to crumble over time, and this can be distressing for the person, and potentially problematic in school.

> The price of focusing and attending in class may be too high, as it switches off the system that detects danger, therefore potentially leaving one more vulnerable.
> (Bhreathnach, 2012)

Dissociation and dissociative responses

Dissociation describes how pupils may respond if they feel overwhelmed in some way. It enables them to switch off temporarily from what's going on around them. This is something we all do sometimes. For example, I might be driving along thinking about something that happened at work, and then find I'm heading towards the station rather than where I'm meant to be going - home! Or I might day-dream out of the window at home and not hear my husband call me for dinner!

However, when a pupil who has experienced relational trauma and loss dissociates, we notice other things, such as when he is stressed he freezes to the spot and remains motionless for long periods of time: or when he is stressed he sits and stares, oblivious that he is cold and shivering, needing a jumper: or when he has no recollection of something that just happened, even though he was present. The behaviour is not a complete guarantee that the pupil is dissociating, but it may be an indication - what we need to look out for is repeated patterns of such behaviour.

Our pupils may be dissociating from all or parts of their sense of self, or they may dissociate from the external world. It's an adaptive and protective response that was needed to survive trauma and loss in their early lives. However, it becomes very unhelpful when circumstances change for the better. The tendency to disassociate may have become a habit that's hard to turn off.

In terms of the sense of self, being compartmentalised or fragmented as I've been describing can lead to social difficulties and mental health difficulties. In terms of the external world, it can mean that children can miss out on chunks of school, which can affect their ability to make the most of everything we're trying to offer them in education.

Integration

This is an important developmental process. A child is moving towards integration when he starts to have a holistic sense of himself across relationships, time and space. So we need to be very mindful of the defence of compartmentalising when we are drawing up plans for troubled pupils in our schools - provision mapping. We don't want to fragment the pupil further by directing him to many discrete pieces of support work, or by giving him too many adults to relate to. In fact the statutory guidance for designated teachers (2009) actually recommends working in a joined-up way in order to minimise disruption to a pupil's education. Nor do we want to reinforce compartmentalisation through giving our pupil highly stressful expectations that are likely to create failure, anxiety, and shame which he will feel forced to separate off. There are many benefits from integrated support. In order to support this integration we need to consider what we can do to *downsize our pupil's world*, to truly know him and to explicitly reflect back to him all the parts that make him who he is.

Downsizing the pupil's world - transitions

Let's really recognise the vast number of transitions involved in school life, especially when we're making a relationship with a troubled pupil who is internally fragmented. Unfortunately troubled pupils tend to have far more complicated timetables than everyone else, due to all the different kinds of the support going in! This can kind of defeat the overriding purpose of support work - to move these pupils on into adaption and recovery. Our pupils can find it very hard to transfer what they learn in one context or with one person to another. They need us to do the integrating on their behalf for a while, until such time as they're able to do it for themselves.

With this in mind, let's keep transitions to a minimum and the number of staff closely involved to just a few - four at most. Obviously in secondary there can be as many as 12 subject teachers involved in teaching, but let's reduce the number that get involved in nurture, support and gentle challenge by referring on to the pupil's team. By making the pupil's world smaller, we are supporting them to integrate. They won't need this type of support forever, but for a period of time, this attention and boundary can be really beneficial. Slowly the boundaries can be extended out, but not before the pupil has had sufficient time to experience integration.

Being known

Many of these pupils have a very narrow and distorted view of themselves. Because of their experiences, they may well believe themselves to be bad or even evil in some cases. We need to gently challenge this over time. We can only do this through the vehicle of a close relationship.

These particular pupils need us to set aside time, quality time, in order to get alongside them and to truly know them as whole pupils, not just part of them. With this in mind, what I'm about to say might sound contradictory: but in order for these pupils to fully integrate they first need to know the individual parts that make them who they are. Who are they? What are the parts that are visible and therefore seen? What are the parts that are hidden and unseen? We don't need to go digging around, and in fact, Dan and I don't advise this at all. As the relationship deepens and safety increases, their different parts will naturally come to the surface for you to see and know.

Gradually over time we can notice out loud the parts that we see and encourage our pupils to notice too. As we bring the pupil's different parts into their awareness, they start to discover that there is more to them than they ever first realised!

The use of parts language with troubled pupils

During a 1:1, start visually representing these parts as you discover them together. With the younger pupils we make life size drawings of them to do this, which they love! With older pupils we use giant jigsaw templates to pictorially represent that we are all a combination of parts.

It is important that parts are only identified when linked to some kind of evidence. Some staff might be tempted to use parts language as a vehicle to build a pupil's self-esteem: but anyone who's worked around these particular pupils will know that they are very wary of 'sweet talk' and may just think you are tricking them or manipulating them if you do this without linking it to evidence. So for example, we'd be on safe ground noticing their humorous part as they were making their friends laugh so much on Monday. Or their pizza loving part, as they say they always ask their dad for pizza on Friday nights! But it would be wishful thinking to merely state that they are special or great when we haven't anything specific to contribute to help the pupil connect with this. They need connectors in order to make sense of who they are, as an increasingly integrated individual.

We tend to start off with naming the parts that they are happy to share, moving into the more tricky parts over time. However, we need to ensure that we never polarise the parts, by stating what we think is appropriate/inappropriate, bad/good, helpful/unhelpful, as these pupils are already prone to holding very polarised views, seeing situations, things, themselves, other people, as all bad or all good. We see our support role as integrating their parts on their behalf, until they are ready to do so themselves. For example their pizza loving part might be next to their spitting part. Their hard working part might be next to their punching part. We acknowledge and accept all the parts that are present in this window of time.

Dan writes: Let's also remind ourselves that as we discover and welcome these parts of our pupils we are doing so with the same attitude of PACE, showing the pupil that each part is accepted, with non-judgmental curiosity, empathy, and, where possible, playfulness.

Louise writes: We ensure the pupils in our care realise that whilst we might never get rid of some of our parts, they themselves can determine how big and strong a part can become, or how small and weak a part can become. We encourage them to interact with the visual images we have created together with arrows, letting us know which ones they want to expand and which ones they want to reduce. We explain how giving opportunity for a part to be practised increases its size! This work can be empowering for the pupil. Being known in this way restores their confidence not only in the adults around them, but also in themselves.

Dan writes: We can also explore with our pupils the origins of their various parts, so that they become aware that their parts developed in an effort to best serve them, to meet the stresses and challenges that they were facing at the time. Thus, none of the parts are 'bad'; rather they have, or had, a purpose which most likely was to help the child to feel, or be, safe. We might then add that before we try to reduce a part, we must be certain that our pupil will still be safe with that part becoming less influential. In fact, he might be made more safe by developing other parts before reducing this one, since his world has changed quite a bit since the time that it originally developed.

Louise writes: Yes, this is so helpful: we don't want to ever under-estimate the value of why certain parts were needed: each has served some purpose in the pupil's life to date. I think we should also remind ourselves that educational staff don't need to become therapists and to go into unchartered territory. We're not asking anyone to leave the boundaries of their roles behind. We're merely asking staff to notice, to acknowledge and to journey together with these pupils. We don't need to be experts to show empathy.

Once a pupil realises there are more parts to them, their options start to open up. They start to realise that despite them feeling despair, things are not always the way they seem. Despite feeling bad through and through, or like an accident, or evil, our pupils will start to realise that they are in fact a combination of parts and that this is the reality, and moreover, true for all of us. Despite feeling that they are trapped in their past where there were no choices available - they begin to realise that this has all been a distortion. Remember we learn who we are through the eyes and the mind of another person.

A member of staff getting alongside a pupil in school in this way is so much more helpful than I think we ever first realised. For too long we have been intimidated by the grand concepts of 'mental health': yet all the tools we need for adaption and recovery are well within our grasp - within everything that makes us human, and within everything that goes towards creating great relationships. Yes, there will be a few pupils who may need additional specialist help from outside school, but let's give ourselves permission to get involved to a greater degree than we have done to date. Those of us who are involved on a day-to-day basis can facilitate integration more easily and more naturally than someone seeing their client once a week. The consistency of our everyday presence is our greatest strength.

Dan writes: One additional thought here: looking at how we address pupils when we relate with them around their successes or their failures. Too often our voice tone, manner, facial expression, gestures, and posture are dramatically different when our pupil is doing well than when he is doing something that we might need to correct. Our non-verbal expression when he is doing well suggests that we experience him as being worthwhile. But when we are correcting the pupil for a particular behaviour, our non-verbal expression may be communicating that we experience him as not trying hard enough, being lazy, selfish, and undesirable to be near.

If we truly want to facilitate integration, we need to be fairly similar in how we relate with our pupils, regardless of their behaviours. In therapy I work hard to maintain a similar conversational tone regardless of the content we are exploring or the behaviour that my young client is showing. I do address misbehaviour, but I do so with the same qualities of playfulness, acceptance, curiosity, and empathy that I demonstrate when I am focusing on areas of success and pride.

Hope for the future

Louise writes: School holds countless possibilities for raising healthy awareness of the potential for integration in our pupils. Healthy self-awareness is the stepping stone towards healthy self-control. Healthy self-awareness means that not only is the pupil in a position to make healthy choices, but that he will also start to have the tools he needs in order to interpret others in a more realistic way too. He'll have a way of relating that is more about what's happening in the present, rather than being so tainted by the past.

Supporting a pupil to understand who they are is invaluable. They can then be released into realising their true identity. Once this happens the opportunities are never-ending! Their vision is extended, their prospects and future open up. Hope becomes either a possibility for the first time, or is restored.

I worked with a young pupil called Imogen who was so fragile and broken when I first started working with her. She didn't seem to have any sense of what she liked or disliked and was too anxious to make even the simplest of choices. Over a period of three years I saw her open up and blossom like a rose. In fact she loved roses and so I brought them in for her whenever I could to smell, touch and draw! She took a photo of one to remind herself of how she was emerging into something beautiful - as she experienced the care and attention she had always dreamed of. Just like the rose opens up in relation to the warmth of the sun, Imogen grew into a confident young woman in relation to those around her giving her the support she needed. She was even picked to be a head of house in school, which I could never have dreamed possible when I first started working with her!

Many pupils have gone on to achieve a huge amount in their lives because at least one person wanted and made a real relationship with them. With Imogen, I was able to show her that I genuinely cared, that to me she was *worth* getting to know and being alongside. Our supportive care in school can make a truly significant difference.

When out and about presenting all over the UK I am often privy to personal testimonies of those who have been through the most extraordinarily adverse of circumstances. Often these people are heading up the conference or in a senior position within education. I ask what made the difference when their expected outcomes would have been poor. They always say that there were one or two teachers out there who cared, who demonstrated their care and value of them. I ask if their teachers would realise what they had contributed, and these people say, probably not.

I'd like to add that if anything happens in the pupil's circumstances that might make us doubt the impact that our relationships have had (for example, if they suddenly get moved away because of placement breakdown or exclusion), please remember that our relationships with each individual child or young person is a parting gift for our pupils. Nothing can get in the way of what has been experienced to date. They are memories that are stored away safely. The experience of relationship will never be forgotten: genuine relationships never are. All kinds of factors can interfere with our support work, but let's keep this in mind as we persevere alongside our troubled pupils.

Dan writes: Well said, Louise!! Too often we forget that the gift of ourselves - as a Key Adult or mentor or teacher or therapist or social worker - provides our pupils with the experiences that they need to heal, integrate, and develop well, that are far more beneficial than are those that result from our particular technique or the latest educational programme.

Chapter 15

Strengthen resilience

Louise writes:

When Craig was in year eight, he would smile, seemingly OK, compliant, engaging in tasks teachers asked of him. But he froze, becoming speechless if at any time he was approached directly, turning his back, avoiding eye contact, putting his hand up to hide his face. This happened regularly. His stress system was over-active; understandably, with all that he had lived through in his early years. However, now in year ten, his KA, Rachael, describes Craig (with a smile on her face) as more 'him'. She says he has really opened up and seems so much more confident nowadays. She says that today, you can even see this in the way he holds himself - he seems so much taller, both physically and emotionally. He gives eye contact now.

He has even noticed the change himself. "I didn't used to be able to give eye contact or talk much but now I can. I've got much better at it". Rachael describes how Craig bounces along to see her now and is keen to initiate conversation, whereas before he would have avoided having any contact with her. This KA gently perservered, despite Craig's resistance, using empathy, humour and playfulness, and Craig's resilience strengthened.

Petra, in year seven, was constantly in the Head of Year's room, with behaviour slips from teachers. She seemed to always have rude and disrespectful outbursts in class. When Petra was anxious this was her default position. It kept staff at a distance, which is what she wanted. She felt so vulnerable and didn't want to feel that way. However when Carrie, was assigned as Petra's KA, things changed big time. Carrie took a real interest in Petra - in what made her tick and what stressed her out.

If you were to observe Petra now in year nine you would find her so much calmer. Carrie describes her as a lovely student who is really doing well. She describes how Petra seems so much more robust now within herself and is more aware of her capacities. Petra had experienced herself as fragile, and as a victim. Carrie describes how Petra is now able to spot her stress triggers and can calm herself. Her scenes are less likely these days as she understands her faulty alarm system and how it works. She tends to tame it herself nowadays, with frequent sensory breaks. Throughout their time together, Carrie always noticed out loud anything that she spotted that seemed a strength for Petra, anything that seemed healthy and appropriate. Realising she had a lot more going for her than she thought originally, Petra has grown into her true self. Petra's resilience was tended to regularly and of course it - and she grew.

Pupils who have low resilience don't seem to move on much in their development. They seem to remain stuck. The staff around them can end up feeling frustrated and then seem to give up on them: a vicious cycle gets perpetuated.

The question we therefore need to ask ourselves is what made the difference for Craig and Petra? Why such a shift? Did all their difficulties just disappear, or was their evidence of adaption and even recovery due to the increasing strength of their resilience? If so *what* strengthened their resilience?

Recently, resilience has become a hot topic at conferences on working with troubled pupils, resulting in many different definitions of what we might mean by this concept. A definition Dan and I like is from Gilligan (2001), who states that resilience is '*a set of qualities that help a person to withstand many of the negative effects of adversity ... bearing in mind what has happened to them, a resilient child does better than he ought to do*' (p.5). Most practitioners and researchers seem to believe that resilience is affected by both nature and nurture.

We believe that the level of resilience in a pupil isn't static, that it can change dependent on the people and circumstances surrounding him. We believe that as education staff we can have a profound impact on whether and how a pupil develops resilience. We're well placed in our schools to make a real contribution, but we don't always make the most of all the opportunities available to us in school. Our aim in this chapter is to encourage educative practice that strengthens resilience for each and every vulnerable pupil in our care.

From our own experience, as well as that of others, we've compiled a list of the twelve qualities we see as most linked to the development of resilience, and which seem to dramatically influence a pupil's outcomes. The resilience factors we want to highlight are:

☆ Having at least one secure attachment
☆ Being able to trust
☆ Having good self-esteem
☆ Being able to face and learn from mistakes
☆ Being able to manage conflicts and repair relationships
☆ Having a faith or a sense of morality
☆ Having a belief in one's own efficacy

☆   Being able to take the initiative

☆   Having meaningful roles

☆   Being able to be autonomous

☆   Having a sense of identity

☆   Having a sense of humour

We're sure you'll recognise from what you've read of this book so far that we want to give attention to all these qualities: we know that the ideas and practice we're sharing here help our pupils' resilience grow. We've found it helpful to have this list in a place where we can refer to it on a regular basis. Even better if we can commit it to memory! We do need to justify why we do what we do within our school systems, especially at this time, within this financial climate: we need to be so clear about our aims and objectives in education support work. So it's crucial to keep in mind the capacities we're aiming to help our troubled pupil develop.

In this chapter we're going to consider our pupil's capacity for greatness - to be all that he was intended to be originally if he hadn't experienced extraordinary stress *and* everything he has learnt because of having lived through extraordinary circumstances. We'll reflect on how much we can make a difference through our genuine relationships with our pupils: how by engaging in repetitive reflective dialoguing, connections can be made consciously, as the pupil's own sense of himself develops, and more deeply, at a brain level. We'll consider how to honour the pupil's existing strengths and capabilities. Finally, we will think through how to encourage further growth and most importantly, how this can be sustained.

Let's also remember that it's important for staff to look after and develop their own state of resilience in order to do this work well (*please also see* Chap.15 *on staff care*, Bombèr 2011).

Toni loves all kinds of physical fitness and is really supple and strong. She ensures she goes to the gym two or three times a week and ensures she uses this ability in her work too. At the moment she runs a Zumba group for pupils at lunch time and heads up the staff run every fortnight on Thursdays after school.

The capacity for greatness!

Every troubled pupil has strengths and capabilities, regardless of what they've been through. Every troubled pupil is valuable and has something to contribute. We may need to search for their particular treasure (which can sometimes be well hidden) but it will always prove well worth the search. Our job is to get alongside our pupil to discover together what his contribution might be. Many of those whom we support show a strong aptitude for the creative arts. Some write prolifically. Some become amazing sports people. Some pioneer new ideas and concepts. Some may become all kinds of talented leaders and end up governing us! Let's not think that their lives will necessarily be bleak because of their experiences. Some of our greatest world leaders have been through the greatest adversity. Ken Robinson writes and speaks extensively about us needing to facilitate the growth of whatever it is that lies within each of us that is our own unique contribution or gift to the world (Robinson 2010). So as you're getting to know your pupil, think about what makes him or her truly unique. Once we know what these gifts are we can nurture them, whatever they might be.

Liza (11) loves painting. She is really struggling with year six work at the moment as the gap widens in terms of her learning pace. She missed out on a lot during the difficult years when she was on the receiving end of all kinds of horrors through significant abuse and neglect. She is trying so hard but still has a lot of developmental tasks and abilities to catch up on. However her KA, Lindy gives her opportunity to paint each day. Liza's competency is really valued this way, meaning that she has an increased level of hopeful energy to apply herself to the struggle of catching up on her learning in other areas.

Martin (15) loves outdoor pursuits. His KA, Bruce, didn't know much about this kind of thing as he's a person who is usually a lot more sedentary in his own hobbies. But he researched the area, and found some clubs and courses that Martin could join in with.

We need to go the extra mile and sometimes research areas that we aren't that familiar with, in order to show appreciation for what we're learning about our pupil.

Dan writes: And some of our pupils will have skills which - while less dramatic - are nevertheless equally important in our complex society. They may have the ability to become excellent homemakers, productive employees, valued and trusted friends and companions, loving and committed parents. But they may never attain these important skills without the opportunity to develop their resilience in school.

Louise writes: Sometimes we try and fit these pupils into our own mind sets, into our own created systems. Instead, we need to be adapting our practices in order to nurture everything that makes these pupils who they are so that they can be free to be all they were intended to be - first time round. Let's be flexible rather than feeling restrained by school systems. School systems are tools intended to guide us - not to imprison us or to hamper necessary growth or creativity for individual pupils. Let's free each other up to do whatever it takes in order to strengthen resilience in our pupil - however outside the box it might seem.

For example, Martin (above) *now has access to 1:1 personal training sessions at the local gym: he loves being challenged physically and needs an enhanced curriculum, as life is still really tough for him right now.*

Reflective dialoguing

What we need to be encouraging in our schools is what Dan and I think of as *reflective dialoguing,* which is a slightly formal expression for a particular way of being with our troubled pupils. It includes watching, waiting and wondering. Bringing out into the open that which is usually left unsaid. Providing commentaries. Making links. As educators, we need to encourage each other to give our pupils feedback in a way that builds them up, giving them a healthy sense of who they are. We need to remember the fragility of the lives in our hands. These pupils will be affected by how we see them and how we think about them, because they learn who they are through the eyes and minds of other people. Yes - what a responsibility. But what an honour. Let's take it seriously.

Honour the pupil's strengths and capabilities

Remember that we're trying to find a balance between support and gentle challenge. Sometimes, getting the balance right, in the interests of enabling our pupil to develop their resilience, can present us with genuine dilemmas, as we hope the next section illustrates.

So to begin with, when a pupil is allocated to us, take the time to check out any previous records and to talk with those who know him well. Then, most importantly, do take the time to truly get to know him. What does he seem to have most pleasure doing? What is it that he would like to try? We need to ensure that our vulnerable pupils have continuing opportunity to develop in these areas, especially in the school context. Sometimes this might mean allowing an enhanced curriculum, as with Martin, above.

I've been really concerned when I've heard of pupils' activities being withdrawn as a consequence of their inappropriate behaviours - to 'teach them a lesson'. So, for example, a pupil I'm aware of was stopped from taking part in an important cricket match because he kept running away from home. Sometimes there are only one or two areas in which the pupil seems to be functioning. Let's not take away the very activity that might be helping our pupil to keep going. He might already be living on the edge of despair, and this could be the final straw.

Imagine if you were going through a particularly difficult time, maybe after a bereavement, for example, and the only thing that brightened your week was going out to your book club, or seeing a particular mate at the pub on Friday night after work. Then imagine if someone took that away because they said that you had been irritable all week and had taken it out on the cat, dog and kids. What would that be like for you? How would you feel? What would you feel like doing? Our pupils are no different.

We really need to be mindful of the impact of our choices on our pupil's well-being. Let's put an end to the practice of withdrawing something the pupil enjoys and is good at: they need encouragement to develop in these areas, in order to grow strong and healthy. Check out our reparation and discipline chapters for what to do instead, when things go wrong.

Dan writes: I'd like to underline what you have just said, Louise. We need to give pupils what they need for their development, not what they have earned. Some opportunities and activities need to be unconditional for certain pupils, rather than being something that they need to earn. These activities may well be the only things that are keeping them afloat with some motivation and hope for a chance for a better life.

Louise writes: Yes, let's always keep development at the forefront of our minds. We've often been distracted from this by other agendas, but the developmental need of troubled pupils is core to our support work in school.

Encourage growth

Those of us involved in support work in schools always need to be open to the possibility of growth: let's ensure that we allow room for this. Our role is to be a human bridge into something more, not to be the finishing point. Our pupils don't need our pity. They need a careful balance of compassion, nurture and gentle challenge. Gentle challenge into new areas of growth, as we discussed in Chapter 10. So let's be alert to the signals and cues of the growth spurts and adaptions our pupil is making so that we don't stand in the way of his growth but instead, make the space he needs to grow. I call this wriggle space, and it's essential for the growth of resilience.

> *Key Adult Maggie inadvertently remained too close for too long to the pupil in her care, not allowing Simon the wriggle space he needed. He was observed becoming more and more agitated as he longed for some independence now, some healthy independence. Her colleague gently challenged her to give him some opportunity to practice his growing independence from time to time and wow, how this pupil responded! It was as if he started to fly! The content of his writing developed to such an extent that he emerged as someone who was well capable of competing in BBC Radio 2's short stories competition!*

I really want us to think about this, as some well-meaning adults can and do stand in the way. For example, people with rescuer tendencies find it hard to let go - we've probably all held on a bit too long at times. This is why it's so important that we develop a healthy self-awareness and good accountability ourselves, so that we can watch our 'shadows'- the parts of ourselves that we try and hide or don't acknowledge. We need to check in regularly with ourselves as to why we're doing what we're doing. A good question to ask ourselves about the choices we make is *"Whose needs are being met?"* In the school context, we're employed to meet the needs of the pupil. All our educational support work must always be in their best interest - not ours.

Dan writes: This is an important point, and Louise's question doesn't have an easy answer. It highlights a key dilemma and challenge we all have to face in our work. Let's think about the example Louise gave above about a child who was not allowed to participate in an important cricket match because he kept running away from home (or we could substitute because he did not do his homework or because he got into fights after school hours). When are we 'rescuing' the pupil (from understanding that actions have consequences), by *not* taking away his participation in cricket (as the KA Maggie might have been tempted to do), and when are we providing the pupil with something that he needs for his development, by allowing him to play (as KA Bruce from p.290 might have wanted to advocate for Martin, who so needs physical challenge)? These are difficult decisions, and most likely the answers lie in the unique needs of the particular pupil, the self-awareness that Louise mentions above, and consultation with other educators.

Louise writes: Yes, I think we should always reflect upon a *pupil's needs* in every instance. Dan and I believe that developmental and attachment needs are paramount and so should always take a priority over everything else. The tasks needed to fulfil these needs must always continue. I also believe that any consequences given must be

a) directly related to whatever the difficulty is

and

b) as immediate as possible, as with a much younger child.

Our troubled pupils find it hard enough as it is to remain connected with other people after difficulties and to make sense of or make connections with what has happened. So, make the connections easier, so that your pupil can actually make sense of and learn from his experiences - good or bad.

Thus, in the case described earlier about the boy who kept running away from home - wouldn't it have been more appropriate to have increased the supervision around him for a time, until he was strong enough to take the responsibility of managing his own time and whereabouts by himself? He needed to get stronger at keeping himself safe. That to me would have been a far more appropriate consequence than him missing his cricket.

Over time, we can allow our pupils more and more space to develop. Relative dependency within their relationship to us to begin with, and from that secure base, we can expect developmental movement on into healthy interdependence.

Strengthen new areas of growth

When we notice growth in the pupil we're working with, let's draw attention to it. To do this, we'll have to create pauses, as we discussed in other chapters. Strengthening new learning means that growth can be reinforced. Notice out loud: *"I've noticed that you can now..."* Don't leave it at that! Link statements such as these to further opportunities and possibilities for growth. *"I wonder if you could now ... "* - *"If you can do that let's see if you are now up for ... "*.

At the same time, it is so very important that we are thoughtful in our timings with all this. It is not always appropriate to jump in enthusiastically the moment a tiny bud of growth is emerging, immediately saying - *"Great, what's next?"* The bud of growth needs to be allowed, enjoyed, feel confident and welcomed for itself, *without* the pupil having to then think of the next thing straightaway. As adults, we need to savour and trust this emergence, rather than rushing our pupils on. There is a developmental pace that must be honoured. We may need to be patient sometimes and wait. Yes, even when the clock is ticking and we have hundreds of demands on us. Development can't be fast-tracked, despite the current fast pace in school life right now. We just need to keep our focus on maintaining the balance between support and gentle challenge.

Let's be aware of the following possibilities:

•   There are some pupils out there who have never been allowed to grow at their own pace but have always had to rush to keep up with others' agendas, who have never been allowed to savour the positive outcomes of their growth but always been pushed to get on with the next goal.

•   There are some pupils out there who may need to suggest for themselves what the next step is, and may *hate* being seen to be making progress with relationships.

•   There are some pupils who may need to know that someone is holding them in mind, and *hate* to be seen to be making progress in terms of their own independent thinking and action.

Let's therefore make gentle connections on their behalf. *"When you do this, this shows me that you are getting stronger at trusting the grown-ups/at making decisions. What do you think?"* Any connections we make on our pupil's behalf can help increase their self-awareness and confidence. Growing self-awareness means more possibilities and increased self-control.

We can set up 'Jars of Strength' for some of our primary pupils (*see* p.138). In these jars we post small notes of anything we notice that the pupil can do. Over time they can see their jars filling up. This visual cue serves as a helpful reminder as to how strong they are becoming.

This was especially beneficial recently for a young pupil, Nathan, who was preparing for transition to secondary and who felt so daunted by the move that he kept collapsing emotionally. Nathan's Key Adult Jen reminded him of how far he'd come. In effect, Jen had became Nathan's memory bank. She also started drawing explicit attention to what Nathan was capable of, to help challenge his sense that he was really fragile. It was as if he'd got stuck with his previous experience of himself: he couldn't actually see or remember the changes he'd made.

As the Key Adult got closer to Nathan within their relationship, and offered him both empathy and gentle challenge, it was as if a light bulb came on inside him. He started to update his experience of himself. He was even heard saying one day, "Did I do that?" with a smile on his face.

Books and portfolios of success are used in very much the same way - as visual reminders. Please note that we're not suggesting this as part of any kind of reward system. We're just reminding these pupils of their successes to date, that's all. They tend to forget!

Brief eye contact and light, warm touch can also reinforce and strengthen positive and life-affirming messages, by engaging the deeper sensory receptors in the brain. This will then strengthen the likelihood that more growth or adaption will happen.

Dan writes: A final note, Louise, on the kind of adversity that demands our pupil build resilience if he is to develop and be successful. At times, the challenges our pupils face are dramatic and involve abuse, loss of parents, home and/or culture, as well as severe disabilities of different kinds, and disease. At other times, they involve the daily experiences of not being valued, talked with, enjoyed, or understood. Some pupils do not have a trusting adult to rely on from whom to accept comfort, guidance, and support.

If they mistrust the adults in their lives they develop an alternative plan for survival. This plan involves various actions and goals that they do by themselves and for themselves. These may include efforts to control others and the events of their lives, while avoiding anything in the present that might be threatening. Not trusting that adults will do what is best for them, these pupils often relate with others by (unconsciously) trying to manipulate, deceive, or intimidate them. Mistrusting adults, they avoid interactions that might help them to realise that the adults in the present might be different from those of their past. Remaining defensive with educators or other adults they might find they could rely on, they are not open to their assistance when in distress. As a result they have their own survival skills, which, as children, are likely to be insufficient to prevent the emergence of many behavioural problems.

Whether it is described as a significant stress, challenge, ordeal, or trauma, it is more likely to be contained and to have less impact on our pupil's life *if it is shared and supported by one trustworthy adult.* The adult's emotional and cognitive strengths far surpass those of the child and may well be sufficient to help the child to resolve and integrate the stressful event. With such support, the stressful event may actually lead to the development of the strength needed to better face similar events in the future. Much of the motivation for this book has been to offer ways to assist pupils in moving from mistrust to trust for the educators who enter their lives. With trust comes a safe relationship that is the basis of new learning about self and other. From such a relationship comes resilience.

There is one additional result that comes from the pupil having a relationship with one educator who helps him through his difficulties. That pupil is now likely to have the confidence to trust other adults in the future, who will be motived to help him further along his journey, in part because of the resilience that he displays. When children develop resilience through relying on one adult in their lives, this resilience includes the readiness and ability to select and turn to other trustworthy adults and friends in the future.

Louise writes: So it's really important that we ensure troubled pupils have adults whom they have permission to relate to on this level, within the school environment. Relationships provide the stepping stones for adaption and recovery so that our pupils can settle to learn, to be able to make the most of all the educative opportunities that come their way.

Chapter 16

Holding the boundaries: re-thinking discipline

Dan writes: Since this is a book about the central importance of the relationship between us and our pupils, one might think that we would ignore discussing discipline as if it were not important. We might hide it in a footnote with the caution that we need to minimise discipline, as if we thought we had to prevent if from causing harm to the relationship that we want to develop.

Louise and I are doing neither. Since 'discipline' derives from the Latin word for teaching, and since this is a book for educational staff who must teach pupils, we need to describe its important role in our relationships with them. In fact, we've been interweaving comments about holding boundaries and limits into many of the previous chapters which have focused on the different aspects of creating reciprocal relationships with our pupils. We intend this chapter as a summary of those comments.

As adults, as teachers, we often evaluate our pupil's behaviours and determine whether a given behaviour is likely to be of benefit to his development, or a hindrance. We habitually judge that working independently, sharing, assisting others, developing interests and skills, and communicating with us, are behaviours that we want to encourage, that we want to' teach'. At the same time we are likely to consider lying, stealing, cheating, fighting, ignoring assignments, and avoiding challenges as behaviours that we'd hope to discourage. In acts of discipline, we hope to influence pupils to act in certain ways and to not act in other ways. The question is how to make discipline effective, eliciting our pupil's co-operation as well as his effort to develop habits that will have merit for his ongoing life.

In this chapter we are going to focus on the context in which discipline has an important role in providing safety for our pupils, ensures that the structure necessary for attaining our educational goals is present, and assists our pupils in achieving these goals through managing the stress and the frustrations inherent in meeting our expectations and limits on their behaviour. It's hard for all of us to do things that we don't 'feel like' doing. Discipline's function is to assist pupils with that task - doing what they do not feel like doing - while still maintaining our relationships with them and encouraging the development of their own interests and initiatives. The following six suggestions are provided with the hope that they will facilitate success with all of these aims.

I   ESTABLISH YOUR RELATIONSHIP

- Establish a strong relationship with your pupil, one that is based on your mutual interests, trust, respect and a desire to communicate. As you come to know and like your pupil, he is likely to come to know and like you as well.

- Communicate your liking for your pupil, your trust in him and your commitment to him.

- Gently challenge his distrust of your motives. Recognise that it will only be when he trusts you that he will accept you are genuinely acting in his best interests, not your own.

II   ONLY EVALUATE BEHAVIOUR

- Evaluate only your pupil's behaviour, not his wishes, nor his feelings, his thoughts, intentions, perceptions, memories, values or interests. Your pupil will be much more receptive to your suggestions or directives if they only involve his behaviour. He will become defensive if he senses you are evaluating his inner life - his self.

- Recognise that our best way of influencing is not through evaluation but rather modelling, sharing and wondering (without judgment) about the implications of certain thoughts, feelings and plans.

Louise writes: During teacher training, many of us were encouraged to focus on differentiating between behaviour and the personhood of a pupil, but I can't remember anyone ever being this explicit about how that could be communicated. Quite often we were given instructions, but not always the practical tools to realise them. This is so much clearer.

III   REMEMBER THE IMPORTANCE OF RECIPROCAL RELATIONSHIP
Dan writes:

- Build a strong reciprocal relationship with your pupil, rather than one based on dominance and submission.

- Remember that compliance does not imply learning: the original behaviour may well return. Optimum learning won't come about through power, control and authority. Feeling valued, understood and believed is a far better place from which to learn from mistakes. Use your authority within the context of the reciprocal relationship to look for the best interests of all.

- Communication involving discipline works best when it begins with us asking our pupil about his thoughts, feelings, motives and so on, whatever has led him to behave as he did, rather than starting by us immediately telling him that the behaviour is not acceptable.

- Provide safety to facilitate discussion, by remaining open and engaged.
- Convey empathy for your pupil's interpretation of the event.
- Once he knows you understand his perspective, and, over time, trusts that he can safely express his own reasons for his behaviour as he comes to understand them himself, your pupil will become
  - ☆ more receptive to your perspective
  - ☆ more open to considering alternative behaviours to attaining the same goal
  - ☆ more likely to embrace, or at least accept, your ideas and alternatives.

IV   RESPECT

- Aim to build a relationship based on authentic respect which is mutual, rather than one which is one-directional. Our kind of discipline involves understanding the pupil's perspective as much as communicating our own perspective. With this attitude, discipline often creates consensus, rather than obedience.
- Even when consensus is not attained, and you need to make a directive that must be followed, your pupil is more likely to do so if he feels that he has been heard and that you understand why it is hard for him to do what you are asking, or why he disagrees with you.

Louise writes: Throughout the book I've been suggesting that in these kinds of conversations, using the phase *"I know this is a big ask for you"* can be so, so helpful. This phrase acknowledges how hard doing something different really is, and the cost inherent in that. If you truly understand the cost, your pupil may find the risk easier to bear. The phrase also gently gives the pupil permission to venture into the unknown, to give the system of school, the relatively secure system, a go. To test out the evidence. To see whether what we say really does bring a better outcome. How will our pupils know what results a new behaviour will bring, unless they take these tentative steps? Our relationship can provide the security, stability and safety necessary to take these steps, and, in the process, to build new and healthier neural pathways.

V   OPENNESS AND ENGAGEMENT

Dan writes:

- Any conversation you want or need to have that is focused on issues of discipline will tend to be the most effective when you come from an open and engaged stance, rather than one of anger and defensiveness.
- From this stance, you are likely to notice the emergence of more satisfactory relationships for you and your pupil.
- If you are having difficulty maintaining this stance, this is likely to be a sign that you yourself need to find support.

Louise writes: What we're encouraging is beyond mere calm; it's the open and engaged state we've referred to many times, so easy to speak about, so challenging often to maintain. This raises questions around our own self-awareness as education staff. Those of us who are developing mindfulness of what is going on inside us at body, heart and mind levels in the 'here and now' are enhancing the likelihood that we'll be able to inhibit our responses when they are more reactive than constructive.

Mr. Spark could easily lose the plot by shouting at the class and using sarcasm, as yet again he feels he has been prevented from getting through all his teaching material for the lesson. However, instead, he takes a deep breath and wonders aloud with the class about being puzzled as to why he doesn't seem to be able to support them all to get through the lesson material. He presents as curious and open to hearing their views, inviting them to reflect together about this difficult dynamic. He makes a few suggestions and is open to theirs. He communicates loud and clear that he wants to understand: "Help me to understand ..."

So as education staff, we will need

- Opportunity during our training to reflect on our own states, sensations and feelings, to better understand ourselves, what energises us, what deflates us or makes us defensive …

- Opportunity during our training to reflect on our own stressors and, most importantly, what calms us.

- Opportunity for all educators in every role in our schools to reflect on how we can tell when we are stressed or moving into feeling overwhelmed, so that we can use our brakes and switch gear in time to enable ourselves to continue with reflective practice.

- Opportunity to have ongoing support with continuing to develop reflective practice.

There are some positive indications that progress is being made in raising awareness in this area. Have a look at the work of Phillip Riley, a senior lecturer in school leadership and mentoring in the Faculty of Education, Monash University, that I outlined on p.47. Riley is working on the connections between staff's own attachment style and the pupils whom they teach.

Experienced teachers know the power of these emotions in the classroom but they are usually overlooked in teacher education courses, which place more emphasis on learning and cognitive processes. This is a mistake, because without an understanding of the raw emotion involved in teaching, and adequate training in how to look after one's self and the students during moments of intensity, teachers are placed into intensely emotional environments ill-equipped to deal with the strong emotions when they inevitably arise.   (Riley 2010, p.3)

This is an area that needs further exploration. And as I'm hoping you're saying to yourself by now, *self-awareness is the stepping stone to self-control*: and if that's true for pupils it's also true for us as adults. This also has implications for staff care: if we want our staff to engage in this open, reflective way, then they are going to need to experience this same approach from senior managers within their schools. As we'll see in more detail in Chapter 17, caring for those who support vulnerable and troubled pupils increases their care-giving capacity.

Dan writes: Yes, the kind of discipline for our pupils that we are speaking about requires *self-discipline* among the educational staff who interact with the pupils and with each other. This suggests the need for a more comprehensive view of both discipline, and the nature of the community that we call a school.

VI   THE BIGGER PICTURE

Finally, we need to acknowledge that at times, our relationship with our pupil, no matter how safe, reciprocal, playful, accepting, curious and empathic it is, will still not eliminate a pupil's significant behavioural problems. When that's the case, it's often still wise not to look for a specific consequence that we hope will manage the behaviour. Often granting or removing privileges has little effect on repetitive, almost compulsive, behavioural problems. Much better, we believe, is looking at the bigger picture. Here are some of the factors which will enable us to think about, understand and provide a day-to-day, effective context that assists our pupil in behaving in a manner that is best for both the pupil, the other pupils and the staff.

a)   Developmental age versus chronological age

The developmental age of the pupil may well be significantly below her chronological age, and our expectations may be too high. Sometimes when a pupil's academic performance is on track, we assume that her social, emotional and psychological development is similarly on track. Often however, troubled pupils have comprehensive developmental problems in the social/emotional areas that are not so obvious. The fact that these skill levels may vary from day to day or class to class make them even harder to assess accurately. Significant, ongoing, behavioural problems may well represent expectations that do not match the pupil's consistent functioning levels.

b)   Structure

Troubled pupils often require a high level of routine, predictability, and clear activities in sequence if they are to function in a more stable manner. Too often they are exposed to too many choices, variations in routine, changes in educators, and over-stimulating activities. Clear and comprehensive structure often provides them with a sense of safety and organisation that they are not able to attain on their own.

c)   Supervision

Often troubled pupils need someone beside them who they know and trust if they are able to remain on task, delay gratification, and work for more distant goals. They then are able to rely on the mind, motivation, and safety of the adult to experience for themselves the degree of integrated functioning that's necessary to manage the school day. For both structure and supervision to be effective, they need to be experienced by the pupil as a gift, not a punishment. They are provided because your pupil needs them to be successful, not because he is being punished for misbehaviour. Let's look at how these suggestions might look in the interaction between an educator, Ms. Stevens, and 14 year old, John.

John hadn't finished his assignment, then yelled that he was not going to do it, and then to really top it off, he yelled in front of the class that Ms. Stevens was a jerk and if she kept pushing him around she'd pay for it. Ms. Stevens told John to remain after class when the other students left.

MS. STEVENS *You really seem angry with me, John. What's going on?*

JOHN *You keep pushing me around. I'm tired of it.*

MS. STEVENS *If I were pushing you around I could see why you'd be tired of it! How so, John? How am I pushing you around?*

JOHN *Just let it go. I didn't do my assignment - so what? You don't care anyway.*

MS. STEVENS *I'm sorry, John, if you think that I don't care about you and how things turn out for you. If you think that I'm here to push you around to make my life easier and to take home my money, I can see why you're not going to go along with that.*

JOHN *You're like all the rest of them. You don't know anything about me and you don't really want to either. You just want me to smile and do whatever I'm told.*

MS. STEVENS *If you're right about that, John, you ought to give me a hard*

time! But what if you're not right? What if I do want your
life to work out for you? To be successful based on what
you want, not what I want?

JOHN   *Like I'm going to believe that!*

MS. STEVENS   *Because I'm a teacher and all teachers are the same?*
Great, thanks for that! And I'm sure that you'd feel great
if I said that you were the same as every other 14 year old
male with dark skin who is still learning English. And if
I said that because of that surface understanding of you, I
knew that you were lazy, not too bright, and were likely to
be on benefits when you get older. You'd be outraged
if I assumed those things about you - and with good
reason. I want to know who you are, John, and I don't
judge you by your skin or where you live or your parents'
income. So would you meet me there - don't judge me by
the color of my skin, my age, or the size of my flat. I'll get
to know you and you'll get to know me, how about that?

JOHN   *Why should I bother?*

MS. STEVENS   *You have to decide that, but if you do get to know me, you*
might want to let me teach you some things that I learned
over the years that might help you to get the life that you
want. I don't know what that is - the life you want. But I
want to know and I want to earn your trust about that.

JOHN   *Then let me do what I want and don't push what you think is*
important down my throat.

MS. STEVENS   *Again, meet me half way! If I think that having you learn*
about what happened in England 40 years or so ago around

minority rights will help you to have a better sense of where you are now, where you can go in the future, and what you might have to do again if you start to lose any of those rights - then I think that you might give me some credit for knowing something about what might be good for you to know in the days ahead.

JOHN   *And how is that half-way? Seems like it's all your way!*

MS. STEVENS   *It's a beginning. Now tell me what you want to learn! Tell me what you don't know and what you think would help you in your life if you knew it better.*

JOHN   *I want to know why my dad can't get a job and why we have to live here anyway. I want to know what I'm missing in my country - England is not my country.*

MS. STEVENS   (Staring into his eyes for quite some time) *Thank you, John, for showing me a bit of what is unique about you. How about we talk tomorrow about how I can help you to learn those things. And how what I asked you to learn might help with that too. I think that you are one clever 14 year old who has a lot to learn to build a life here or anywhere else you chose to live. I want to help with that. Will you let me?*

JOHN   *I guess, if you mean it.*

MS. STEVENS   *I mean it. But before we stop, there is something else that I'd like to you to meet me half way about.*

JOHN   *What now?*

MS. STEVENS   *I'm not a jerk and I'd like you to agree not to call me that in front of the class or when we're alone and not to threaten*

> *me. I will agree that when you are angry with me and you*
> *tell me directly about it, I will listen openly to your view and*
> *give you my honest response. I will listen.*
>
> JOHN   *OK. I'm sorry about what I said.*
>
> MS. STEVENS   *Thanks for that, John. And thanks for meeting me half way.*

We believe that such a dialogue is something that is reasonable to work for if we can remember some of the principles mentioned throughout this book. Remaining open and engaged, staying within the attitude of PACE, can often move the most angry and defensive pupils into a more open and engaged stance themselves. Discipline issues can be addressed within that context. In this dialogue, the 'consequence' for John's verbal defiance and threat emerged naturally within the context of Ms. Stevens meeting him half way. The consequence that she asked for - he would agree to not verbally attack her in that way again - she received, along with an unasked for, seemingly heart-felt, *"I'm sorry."* In the context of that dialogue, most likely that simple 'consequence' would have been much more effective than a large, specific, negative, consequence. Within a reciprocal relationship where mutual respect emerges, issues of discipline tend to be much smaller and more quickly resolved. The relationship calls for that from both pupil and member of staff.

Such dialogues will not always be successful and sometimes greater focus, structure, and supervision around very challenging behaviours may well be needed. But with such dialogues, such efforts are less likely to be needed and when they are needed, the relationship that existed before the disruption is more easily repaired.

To conclude: we understand that discipline can never be considered alone, or it will become a larger problem than it needs to be. When discipline simply means 'behavioural management' *without* a context of safety created by a strong, reciprocal relationship, along with efforts to understand the meanings of the behaviour, it tends to be an arduous process that brings little satisfaction to educational staff and often little success in the actual change for the better of the behaviours that we are trying to manage. Our pupils will resist our efforts to control their behaviour much more than they will resist entering a meaningful relationship with a good and caring adult. In such a relationship, discipline is much more successful.

Louise writes: Many of our pupils have already experienced an overdose of control, power and authority at the hands of adults, often from many family members - those who were meant to keep them safe and secure. Now is the time for these troubled and vulnerable pupils to have the opportunity to be on the receiving end of sensitive attuned care and support in our schools.

When the adult understands the nature of the big asks required of this particular pupil in this particular situation, the greater the trust and respect between them will grow. 'How' we relate to our pupils is therefore in question when the matter of discipline is raised. In short, we are here to support pupils to be all they were intended to be first time around, nothing less. To enable them to be able to move towards what we could call a 'learned security', so that they can live healthy and appropriate lives and be connected in to their communities, belonging and contributing to the best of their abilities. This is what 'discipline' is really about. Let's not lose sight of its true function.

Chapter 17

Persevere

Without vision, hope has nothing to attach itself to, and without hope, we all accept the world for what it is, rather than what it could be.

(Taransaud 2011, p.59)

Dan writes:

When our pupils have given up on ever being a 'regular kid' they will be watching us closely - have they succeeded in causing us to give up too? In the past they have found what little sense of safety they've ever had in the certainty of knowing that they will never change. This chapter is about carrying on when we seem to be failing in our efforts to make a difference in the lives of our troubled pupils. It's about how we can find ways to keep going when others, including our pupils, seem to have given up. We'll be looking at why we never can truly justify giving up hope in a pupil, as well as why it is so hard continuing to actively care for our pupils when they do not seem to care in return. Louise and I would like to acknowledge how hard this is - continuing, when we have a sense that our efforts might not matter - while also saying that it may truly matter, though we can't be certain for months or years to come. As educators we may be the only adults in our troubled pupil's life who have the ability to have a significant impact on his future development. If only we have the passion and energy, along with the persistence and determination to do so.

Our troubled pupils' view is that they are hopeless. They are worthless. There is no meaning in making an effort to become 'normal', since they hold no belief that normality is an option for them. Their world is safe and predictable when they see the disgust in the eyes of other children and adults who are looking at them, just as they expected to. They know that they are in control of the thoughts of others when they hear contempt in the voices of those who are talking to them, or talking about them, just as they thought they would. Not that they enjoy this, not that it brings them happiness. Those emotions are seldom experienced by children who live without hope. When they see disgust or hear contempt, they are more likely to feel rage or to feel nothing at all. Rage is about the only emotion that they trust. They split off other emotions from their consciousness. Feeling nothing is better than feeling anything but rage.

Louise writes: Dan, this is so hard for us as education staff to understand, and yet we must. Most of us are optimistic people. It requires a high level of optimism to teach, to expect, to carry on hoping. To relate to pupils who have this kind of experience is hard. Really hard. Everything can seem like an upward struggle. What you are describing is so alien to so many people involved in education.

I guess what you're saying is hopelessness is our pupils' starting point. No wonder we feel hopeless ourselves at times. I know that a lot of what you're describing is unconscious, and I think we need to remind ourselves of this. As we've said earlier, if we believe that our pupils are consciously 'out to get us' so to speak, or that they are very much 'in control', this may only serve to escalate our own defensive desire to take control and exercise our authority. As we've been describing, all too often this only makes the situation much worse.

It's also interesting that you describe how these pupils experience an element of safety by keeping things familiar. Here we are, as education staff, really wanting to make a difference, to support our pupils to move into healthier ways of being and relating; and yet the very thing they need frightens them. As education staff, we think that what we're offering - kindness, patience, care and support, is so positive and easy to receive; and yet this is so far from the truth. As we've both mentioned throughout this book, one of the biggest 'asks' for our pupils is to trust the motives and intentions of the grown-up.

What a task we have before us. To journey together with our pupils into unchartered territory, navigating a landscape that seems perilous to them, yet isn't.

Dan writes: Yes, it's a big task, and most of us really do want to reach our pupils. So we read some books, hear an inspiring speaker, refresh ourselves over a summer holiday and approach this 'challenging' pupil with the open and engaged attitude that we've been talking about. And we do it the next day and the next. Maybe even the next month and the next. And our efforts seem to be bearing no fruit. Is it us? So we re-read the books, and speak with senior management to attempt to re-kindle our empathy for this child's very hard history. And we continue onward. And we repeat and repeat again all of the ways of engagement, all of the acceptance, curiosity, and empathy that we can find.

And - we experience little if any change in this child. And we begin to doubt. And our doubts this time don't focus on our mistakes or our missed opportunities or our insufficient interventions. Now our doubts go toward the child. Maybe it is 'too late' to help him. Maybe he actually was a 'bad seed' to begin with. Maybe he was damaged beyond repair. Maybe he's not trying hard enough. Maybe he needs more of the old fashioned discipline that we witnessed or practised ourselves in years past. Maybe it's time for some 'tough love'. And when he doesn't respond to that - well, yes, he is hopeless. He has convinced us that his view of himself is the right one. Our view of him was wishful thinking. We were wrong. Maybe our minds and hearts should focus on someone else who would appreciate us and benefit from our efforts. Yes, now we also lack hope.

To persevere is the first response that is needed if we are to move a pupil from his only known safety, which consists of worthlessness and hopelessness, into a new world characterised by a sense of security, self-worth, and hope. To persevere must also be our second response and our third … hope must survive in our minds and hearts if it ever is to take root in his mind and heart. We must protect it, nourish it, and continuously find reasons to carry on.

Louise writes: Hope means … having ambition, anticipation, assumptions, belief, confidence, desires, dreams, expectancy, faith, longing … something I find helpful in my work and that gives me hope is the word **yet**.

☆   *"Sian is not able to maintain eye contact - **yet**."*
☆   *"Bob is not able to sit and focus for very long - **yet**."*
☆   *"Adele is not able to ask for help - **yet**."*

This applies to all of us. Our innate predisposition - and that of our troubled pupils - seems to be towards life, no matter what the mental, emotional or physical damage.

I think it's important here to remind ourselves of the perseverance it must have taken for our troubled pupils to have survived everything they've experienced. Many deserve medals for having got this far. When we read through their histories, many really shouldn't be alive, never mind sitting at desks in our classrooms doing GCSEs; and yet they are. Their testimonies are incredible. They are still here. It is this inbuilt determination and drive towards life that we must hold onto as well, in order to stay committed for the long haul. Our pupils need advocates. They need people who will keep going, even when the going gets tough. I've often found that when things get really tough, there's often a breakthrough just round the next corner. The 'growing pains' are evident, and they make us sit up and notice. The growing pains are paving the way to something new.

Dan writes: I have a story to tell. I am a psychologist who has provided psychological treatment to many children and young people and their families over the years. Often the parents and I witnessed and participated in the movement of many of these children into a position of hope, where they developed new ways of perceiving, acting, communicating and being engaged with others, especially their parents. The joy that emerged from being with those families was unforgettable. At the same time, I recall many times where the parents and I were close to despair. The children or young people seemed to neither want nor respond to anything that we had to offer. I recall times when sobbing parents would call to say that their teenage son or daughter had run away again. Times when they sent the young person away because of the violence, theft, or drugs that he brought into their home. Neither their parents nor their other children were safe. Times when the police took the young person away to be placed in a secure unit. The parents and I had failed to help the child move into a new life. And the months or even years went by.

However, one story has occurred a number of times. I receive a call from the parents after having had no contact with them for a number of years and the conversation goes something like this:

PARENT   *Jason came home last night. We had not seen him in eight*
              years. He brought along his partner and his infant son.

DAN   *What wonderful news! You had been so afraid that he did*

not make it and you would never see him again. Where had
he been?

PARENT   *He said that he did not want to tell us some of the places*
that he had been and some of the experiences that he had.
But he told us that he got a job, went to night school, got a
diploma and a better job, met Karen, and the two of them
had this wonderful son ten months ago.

DAN   *Why didn't he come back before this?*

PARENT   *He said that he wanted to prove to himself and to us that he*
was a different person than the person we told to leave eight
years ago because of his drugs.

DAN   *Why do you think that he was able to change his life*
around?

PARENT   *He said that he eventually changed because we never gave*
up on him.

DAN   *Because you never gave up on him?*

PARENT   *Yes. So I reminded him that we had told him that he had to*
leave our home. And you know what he said?

DAN   *What?*

PARENT   *He said that he knew that we did not want to.*

While stories like this are not always the outcome for these very troubled young people, we have heard them often enough for us to appreciate that we never can know what impact we are having with a child, and we can never predict how he will develop in the future. We never have reason to give up hope.

Why perseverance is so challenging

To persevere is hard, and to persevere for months or even years is harder still. Neuropsychologists and others who have studied the structure and functioning of the brain have some insights into the reasons why it is so hard (Hughes & Baylin, 2012a), as we mentioned in Chapter 8. Caring for a child, as a parent, teacher, counsellor, or mentor involves the activation of five brain systems which represent the integrated functioning of many different regions of the brain. These systems are:

I   APPROACH

This system involves regions in the brain that involve the neurotransmitter, oxytocin, which activates *the desire to be with* the young person. It is most intensely activated when a parent is holding and caressing an infant, but it also occurs when partners, or parents and children are cuddling or even relating in a relaxed, attuned, manner. It is active when the child also desires to be near the adult.

- *In the school context*: it involves experiencing the desire to be with a pupil and remain engaged with him.

II   REWARD

This system describes *the experience of pleasure that comes from ongoing engagement* with a child and is activated by the release of dopamine when these engagements are enjoyed by the child as well. There is much less pleasure in the interaction when the child does not enjoy it - the reciprocal enjoyment is what keeps it going.

- *In the school context*: it involves the pleasure that comes from successful, ongoing, interaction with a pupil.

III   CHILD-READING

This system involves the *active interest in getting to know a child* through the activation of parts of the brain involving intuition, empathy, and the ability to give meaning to non-verbal expressions of the other person. It is a subset of a larger system directed toward other people and is most active when combined with the activation of the other systems. Also, like the other systems, it remains active when the other (in this case the child) is also interested in getting to know the adult.

- *In the school context*: it involves the ongoing interest in getting to know a pupil through non-verbal and verbal communication and joint activities.

IV   MEANING-MAKING

This system refers to our strong neurological tendency *to seek meaning in our activities*. When the above three systems are active, we have a strong desire to seek positive meaning in our interactions - to see their value. However, this system gets weak when the child sees no value in interacting with the adult.

- *In the school context*: this involves the mental activity of giving meaning to the interactions that we have with the pupil, including the value and worth of these interactions.

V   EXECUTIVE

This is the most integrated system and is the slowest system to mature, not being fully mature until young adulthood. This system enables the parent or other adult to *engage in caring for the child when they do not feel like doing so*. It enables us to continue to act in appropriate ways with the child when our approach, reward, child-reading, and meaning-making systems are weak. This system can function for an extended time even when there is no reciprocal response from the child.

- *In the school context*: this involves the ability to see the big picture, to give the pupil what he needs even when we don't feel like doing so. This includes the ability to integrate the other systems and to continue to provide care for the child when the other systems are no longer working consistently.

When teachers and support staff are successfully providing good care, all five systems are working well in an integrated manner. However, the first four systems are increasingly influenced over time by how the pupil responds to their use.

If we approach the pupil and he doesn't approach us in return, over time, it becomes increasingly hard to approach him. When we experience reward in being with a pupil, but he doesn't experience a similar sense of pleasure and joy in being with us, over time we tend to experience less and less reward. When we notice a pupil and try to make sense of his actions, but he doesn't notice us and isn't interested in who we are, over time, our interest in him tends to weaken. When we give positive meaning to an interaction with a pupil and he gives negative meaning to the same interaction, it becomes increasingly hard to continue to see the interaction positively.

The need for reciprocity

Why have the first four systems evolved in a manner to function best when there is a reciprocal response? Most likely, as social mammals, our relationships are more successful when both individuals in a relationship benefit from it. If it is a win-win relationship it is likely to be much more lasting. Why waste time and energy - as well as oxytocin and dopamine - when the relationship is not successful for both people and is therefore unstable?

When those four systems are not working well, but the executive system is, we are able to continue to do our job in providing for our pupil's care. But our 'doing our job' is insufficient to enable him to discover qualities in himself that are enjoyable, interesting, and have positive value and meaning. I have called this state 'blocked care', familiar to many people trying to provide care over a prolonged period.

It might make it easier to understand the importance of these five systems if you consider your relationship with your partner. Reciprocity is a given for the success and continuity of the relationship. Imagine if your partner showed little interest in being near you, did not seem to enjoy his interactions with you, was not interested in your life, and seemed to experience little positive meaning in your activities together. You might be able to maintain the relationship for a period of time based on your commitment (the executive system) but it would be very difficult to do so for an extended period of time. Without reciprocity, your relationship with your partner would end or you would both have deactivated your first four systems and therefore would both being 'going through the motions' without any significant affection and joy.

Louise writes:

Let me introduce you to Katy, an amazing Key Adult who has persevered with a very troubled pupil, Stuart, for over 18 months. In weekly support sessions Katy has talked about rewarding moments and has seen real shifts in this pupil's presentation over time. However, despite all this there is something going on right now that has really got to her and affected her so, so deeply. Right now, she feels like a failure. She feels as if she's not making any difference whatsoever. She doesn't really feel anything anymore.

What had happened to Katy? She told me how she had actually considered resigning, as maybe Stuart needed someone better than her. She shared that even thinking about leaving made her feel bad and didn't bring the relief she thought it would, as she said it would be like letting Stuart and his family down. Katy communicated deep despair. She communicated feeling trapped in overwhelmingly painful feelings that seemed too much for her.

She told me that it would help if someone in the school really understood. She felt that staff looked down upon her, even communicating disgust when her pupil got into difficult situations. Rather than feeling supported, Katy felt alienated in the very place that had the potential to make such a difference both to her and to Stuart. She longed for one, empathic senior manager to get alongside her, to give her some quality time and to take her seriously. Instead, she experienced other members of staff as too busy and stressed themselves to even notice her - never mind pay her any attention. We talked about how real this was for her and that to kick start her relational, caring system again, that she would need some real time, attention and care from someone in the school - as well as from me.

Dan writes: This is a really pertinent example, Louise, exactly the kind of situation where people understandably give up, give in, and the cycle of rejection of the child is perpetuated. So let's focus on how to persevere when the pupil is not responding to our caregiving behaviours, and we are not experiencing a reciprocal relationship?

Persevering in the absence of reciprocity

I   FINDING CARE AND SUPPORT FOR YOURSELF

Most importantly we need to turn to, rely on, and deeply value the care that we receive from others who understand our efforts and our increasing discouragement. Whether they be our colleagues, mentors, partner, or good friends and family, we need to be able to turn to others with whom we *do* experience a deeply meaningful reciprocal relationship. Their understanding and empathy will give us the emotional support which will help us to continue to be open and engaged with our pupil though he doesn't seem to be responding. At a brain level, what will happen is that our meaningful reciprocal relationships with others will strengthen and support all five systems, even when our pupil isn't responding.

II   LEARNING YOUR PUPIL

We need to continue to search for and discover the unique strengths and vulnerabilities that lie under our pupil's challenging behaviours. When we can find them, we will experience delight in his strengths and have empathy for his vulnerabilities, and we'll be able to communicate these experiences clearly. In our brains, when we discover his hidden strengths, we will find additional reasons to continue to try to activate our pupil's potentials through our relationships with him.

III   ACCEPTING YOUR PUPIL

We accept our pupil where he is, while persistently asking him to take one small step forward at our side. When he does not take that step one day, we accept that he is doing the best that he can and we wait with him.

IV   ACCEPTING OURSELVES

We do the best that we can, while knowing that we are not perfect, and realising that we will not make an obvious impact on every pupil we try to accompany.

V   WAITING

We patiently await for the periodic surprises regarding a child we thought we may not have been influencing, who shows up one day, month, or year later, to give expression to the successes that he has attained along his hard journey.

Louise writes: These are really helpful guidelines. I particularly like no. 5, waiting, reminding us that these golden moments will come! An adoptive parent of one pupil I worked with proudly told me how moved he had been when, after three years of his child engaging in her annual hypervigilant scans of the summer festival field (even though he had always been with her), how she had taken his hand the following year and skipped into the centre to engage with all the activities! I felt a tear well up. Moments such as these are worth everything.

The importance of 'we' when we're working with troubled pupils in school

So there will be times when you may:

- want to give up
- feel we are not making any difference
- not be able to think clearly or logically
- feel we are going mad!
- be left with very intense feelings
- feel overwhelmed

It is so critical that you don't engage in support work on your own: you need to ensure you are connected to other staff members. At the very least you need a line manager within your school with whom you can check in with regularly. In effect, you need your own Key Adult to keep you 'in mind'!

In addition, it's really helpful to build relationships with other Key Adults working both in your school and in nearby schools. Some progressive local authorities are now realising how important it is to facilitate support groups and continual training/ supervision for those working with our most vulnerable pupils. Remember too that most adopters and foster carers attend support groups and are part of cyber networks and organisations. We need support in this work as well. It's important you don't get isolated within the school system, or that you flag this up with a line manager if you notice it happening. Notice that feeling reluctant to get support is often a really good sign that you need it - it doesn't mean you're a failure in anyway. This work is hard. We can be at risk emotionally, mentally and physically if we are not connected, in some way. Other people will be your lifeline, your anchor, your safe base and your haven in the midst of the storms that will inevitably come and go.

Many education support staff describe to me days that are so full up with directed activity that there is no time for reflective space, never mind time to check in with another colleague. I would urge all Senior managers out in schools to treat this as a serious concern. Our staff's own mental health is seriously being put at risk if time isn't protected for reflection and for passing on matters of concern. We have a duty of care to our staff.

If we look after our staff well, this will not only promote good mental health for them but will significantly affect the vulnerable pupils in their care for better. We must take this seriously.

Our pupils are going to need masses of repetition in order to build new neural connections or new pathways in their brains. So let's not tire of doing what we believe in! We're going to need to develop and embrace all the patience we can, find and make use of all the support we can, in order to be able to persevere. This journey will be full of ups and downs, steps that seem to move forward and steps that seems to move backwards. Brace yourself for a rollercoaster ride! The rewarding moments will be just as intense as the hopeless ones. It's worth holding on. Our pupils need:

● countless experiences of us remaining and still being present - regardless of the number of times they reject us

- countless experiences of us stepping in to translate for them, even if we feel we have done so already
- countless experiences of us wondering aloud and commentating even when it looks like the new message is not going in
- countless experiences of us reassuring them that we are coming back, even though we always do
- countless experiences of us staying connected despite being shocked by some of what they come out with or what they do

Finally, in relation to Dan's lovely example of a dialogue he has had with adoptive parents *(above),* working as I do amongst many troubled pupils in school, I too have seen hopelessness transformed. I have witnessed many pupils, who had previously been 'written off' by those in authority, make a complete turnaround, in the care of someone in school who chose to believe in them. These pupils notice everything, not just what we say but how we are and what we do. One older pupil who is now doing really well at college despite being permanently excluded at the age of five due to her extreme, disturbed behaviour told her Key Adult:

> *"I know I can trust you and that you care about me. You have always stuck around and you have never broken your promises."*

It's through comments like this that our own hope can be restored. And so we return to our relationship with our troubled, vulnerable pupil, ready and willing to be there with him for another day, another step, another challenge.

We wish you all the best as you journey on!

Dispelling the myths!

You become. It takes a long time. That's why it doesn't often happen to people who break easily, or have sharp edges, or who have to be carefully kept.

(*From* The Velveteen Rabbit, Williams, M.,
1922, Doubleday and Co. Inc.)

Louise writes: Out on my visits in schools I am reminded of how our value and belief systems affect our everyday practice. Some of these value and belief systems are not necessarily our own personal ones but are inherent in the school culture both from within the school, and from external bodies. There are some commonly held values and beliefs around that might adversely affect the pupils we are focusing on in this book.

So Dan and I would like to take this opportunity to gently challenge everyone to re-visit why we say what we say and do what we do, when thinking about the system of school. Together, we want to dispel some myths that have been around for quite some time. It's about time for all of us to update our thinking so that we have everything we need for the next part of our journey within education.

Here is a summary of the key points.

MYTH 1

We just need better teachers!

Not true! Anyone, regardless of experience or skill in teaching will be challenged in work supporting traumatised pupils. What are we doing creating fear in an already stressed system, by pointing the finger and criticising those around us? We don't need to sack teachers! We need teachers to have the staff care that they need, which should include clinical supervision. Many schools are now asking trained therapists to facilitate reflective spaces so staff can consider how to work with troubled pupils. This is good practice. We need to provide school staff with updated thinking that is underpinned by the latest neuroscientific research. We need to give staff permission to be flexible and creative - allowing and encouraging them to set up individual development programmes for vulnerable pupils.

Dan writes: I hear you saying, Louise, that we might challenge this myth by replying: *"What we actually need is better support and resources to bring out the best in our teachers!"*

MYTH 2

We mustn't create dependencies with pupils

Louise writes: With these particular pupils we *do* need to create *relative* dependency. Many of these children and adolescents have become pseudo-independent - completely by-passing the important developmental stage of dependency. In order to be healthy, we all need to be able to move between dependence and independence at different times, in different situations, and with the most appropriate people. To survive (and thrive) at school, pupils need to be able to be both dependent and independent. You can only learn dependency if someone gets alongside you and supports you to do this. No-one can learn healthy dependency alone.

Dan writes: The developmental research is very clear (Sroufe et al 2005). Children who successfully rely on the primary adults in their lives as children are, as adults, the most able to maintain a healthy balance between self-reliance and reliance on others. Children who rely on themselves too often and too soon are, as adults, inconsistent in their ability to rely on themselves.

MYTH 3

We mustn't comfort the pupil with touch

Louise writes: Yes, we must. Many of our troubled pupils have touch deficit, having been neglected, and/or having been touched inappropriately.

We need to introduce them to the use of safe and healthy touch. In the school context, this may be a hug, a hand on a shoulder, a tap mid-back, holding hands, sitting on your lap. Be transparent and write up what you are doing, and why, in your support plan. Be accountable. Know your boundaries and the boundaries of the pupil. Be mindful of not triggering trauma memories. If you do see evidence that this is happening, seek specialist support to guide your interventions, but please, please, don't give up. The pupil is merely letting you know that he is not ready to receive safe, healthy, appropriate touch *yet*. Respect your pupil's signals and together you will find a way to bring safe touch into your relationship.

Dan writes: I would simply like to echo what Louise has said: yes, we must.

MYTH 4

Pupils must look at us when we are speaking to them!

Louise writes: Traditionally we have viewed eye-contact from a pupil as appropriate when we (the education staff) have been talking. When we were at school ourselves it was commonplace to hear staff demanding eye contact. However, we now know the impact of this seemingly simple request upon some pupils. Such directness can be too intrusive for someone who has been traumatised. So let's not demand eye contact. Eye contact does need to be gently encouraged by a Key Adult over time once a genuine relationship has been developed, but only within positive interactions. Forcing eye contact may traumatise the already vulnerable pupil.

MYTH 5

Louise writes: Again, a very traditional belief that was heard on so many occasions when we were children ourselves, so no wonder we pass this on. However, instead, we need to gently and firmly hold the boundaries for our pupils so that they are enabled to engage in healthy and appropriate ways, providing challenges to encourage them to reflect on and adapt their perception of themselves, other people, and the world around them. But no-one has the right to tell others how to think, feel or what to believe, whatever their age. And everyone has a right to be heard. All human beings are worthy of being acknowledged and revered. Human life is valuable.

The adult knows best. Children should be seen and not heard!

Dan writes: When we limit our directives to behaviours and accept the pupil's thoughts, feelings, and beliefs, he is more likely to accept our directives about his behaviour.

MYTH 6

Louise writes: Sadly, and however much we might wish it were the case, everything is *not* all immediately OK once a child is adopted. It will take the pupil's body, heart and mind years to catch up with the reality of the 'here and now'. This doesn't happen overnight.

If a pupil is adopted, everything should be OK by now

Dan writes: And when the 'catching up' process is slow, please don't blame the adoptive parents. Many pupils, in the most loving adoptive homes, still take months and years before they can manage well without being overwhelmed by the horrible events of their past.

MYTH 7

Louise writes: Why these pupils do what they do is often so much more complex than a mere misdemeanour. Would a 'good ticking off' really achieve

Some of these pupils just need a good ticking off

that much? A good ticking off will induce further shame. In fact, this can often make things much, much worse! The level of shame in a traumatised pupil is usually very high already and so something like this can often tip them into toxic shame. Toxic shame results in further distressed and disturbed behaviour.

Dan writes: Also, when a vulnerable pupil has a history of maltreatment, a 'good ticking off' will be mild compared to what he's already experienced. If we try to motivate him to change his behaviour through fear and shame, we'll have to give him experiences similar to the original maltreatment. Do we really want to go down that road?

MYTH 8

Louise writes: The past is not an excuse for bad behaviour. The past provides us adults with a framework in which to *make sense of the behaviour* that we now observe in the present. If we can make sense of it, we will

The past is an excuse for bad behaviour

then have all the clues we need in order to plan the most effective interventions to move our pupils on into healthy adaption and recovery within the school context.

Dan writes: Yes, the past is not an excuse for bad behaviour, but it is often the reason why it is happening. A reason becomes an excuse only if it removes accountability for misbehaviour. The pupil is still accountable. But through knowing the reason, we can find the best way to address what is happening.

MYTH 9

Louise writes: On the contrary: time out will awaken very strong, powerful feelings in a pupil who has experienced relational trauma and loss. Time out is a form of 'relational withdrawal', so of course it would be traumatic

> 'Time out' will teach these pupils what is acceptable in this school

for a troubled, vulnerable pupil, who is likely to have strong responses to whatever feels like abandonment. We strongly recommend that this technique is *not* used with these particular pupils. At times of distress we need to be very close, not distant. 'Time in' is our recommended alternative.

MYTH 10

Louise writes: Exclusion will reinforce the internal message the pupil has already received that he is worthless, and that he doesn't belong. His sense of rejection will be reinforced most powerfully. Exclusion should only be used

> Exclusion will teach the pupil that we are not putting up with this kind of behaviour

on extremely rare occasions, as the absolute last port of call - once every support intervention has been exhausted. This is not what is happening in our schools at the moment, and we all need to have the courage to recognise and name this. There are no quick fixes and so it's essential that we don't exclude because the school doesn't want to put in the additional time needed. Let's be transparent. We should only exclude when we know that we have followed appropriate professional recommendations thoroughly; then we will be acting out of professional integrity.

MYTH 11

Louise writes: Even though we may *feel* this is what he's doing, this really isn't the main cause of concern for a pupil who has been traumatised. Believe me, our

> *He is out to ruin my teaching!*

teaching is the last thing on his mind. What lies beneath? What's going on? What is his genuine motive or intention for what he's doing? Could it be that he is terrified, and that he's communicating that? Many pupils I work with are often in a state of alarm and terror. One pupil I know desperately tried every kind of behaviour going to attempt to let the professionals know how distressed she was feeling. It took her three years before they realised she was in a very frightening situation at home. She had tried her best to express - *"Help, get me out of here!"* Eventually, the staff raised her SOS distress signal with social services, but that precious waiting time cost her significantly.

Dan writes: If and when a primary motive of the pupil is to make the teacher's life difficult, the first question would need to be, why would a pupil do that? If that is the pupil's motive, most likely she developed it because she believes that her teacher's motives in giving limits, expectations, and consequences are to ruin her life. In her mind, her teacher was mean to her first. Reacting with rage or withdrawing from our relationship with her will only convince her that she is right. We need to remember her attack is not personal, stay calm and help her manage her need to attack.

MYTH 12

Louise writes: Let's not collude with the pupil's unconscious drive to create rejection. Sometimes, without even being aware, we can

> *If he doesn't want to be here he can go somewhere else!*

say things or do things that create collusion with the pupil's distressed, faulty thinking. None of us would want to do this if we realised that it would just make things worse. This collusion can be extremely damaging for an already severely wounded pupil.

Dan writes: I would add that if our pupil does not want to be here, we need to design a programme for him to help him want to be here.

Louise writes: Yes, the responsibility for this lies with us - not the pupil! We sometimes need to remind ourselves that we are employed because of the pupils - not the other way round!

MYTH 13

Louise writes: Disrespect in the school context can be very threatening for a teacher. Probably we've all had the experience of a pupil disregarding us, talking down to us, swearing at us or being physically aggressive towards us, and all these things can be extremely difficult to deal with. However, we all need to remember that we are working with pupils. Let's not give them more power than they need to have. Remember they are *learning* about respect. Many have had little or no experience of anyone valuing, honouring or respecting them, so is it really so shocking that they can't give the same consideration to others - yet? Respect is the breeding ground for respect. So they will need many, many opportunities to learn respect. We may also have to point out what respect looks like; they might miss examples of it going on around them as they are so preoccupied with being on guard and anticipating threats.

> *I'm not having someone disrespect me*

Dan writes: Also, let's give thought to what we mean by 'disrespect'. Too often when we don't like a pupil's behaviour, we simply label it as 'disrespect': then we don't have to give thought to other possible reasons for his behaviour, as well as to what we may have done ourselves that contributed to it. We need to remember that when students disrespect authority, most likely it is based on their inablity to *trust* authority. We must build their trust, and then they are likely to show more respect.

However, we must not forget that teachers facing such disrespect - for whatever the reason - often proves extremely difficult, hour by hour, day by day. Teachers need the active understanding and support of their colleagues and senior leadership if they are to be able to continue to remain open and engaged with pupils who are showing such provocative behaviours.

MYTH 14

He shouldn't be here. He belongs in a residential

Louise writes: When we ourselves have moved into feeling overwhelmed, we can sometimes believe that moving the pupil on is the only and best option. However, despite how we feel, the benefits of remaining in the current school are considerable. I believe it's possible to include all pupils, as long as there are support staff, access to good staff care and a relevant understanding from which to work.

Dan writes: Well-meaning educators often recommend residential out of a belief that it really will help a pupil more than they are able to. However, in my many years' experience with residential settings, way too often I have seen pupils **not** benefit from having been removed from their home and community and placed there. Residential programmes do not have magic, but they do have to work with pupils now struggling with yet more losses, rejection, and failure.

MYTH 15

These pupils are manipulative and know exactly what they are doing

Louise writes: No, the behaviours we experience may 'feel' manipulative, but most of the time these pupils are reacting out of a very primitive part of the brain where there is no reflective function. We all notice that they don't show much evidence of reflective capacity at other times, so why would that capacity suddenly come online at times of distress? Many of our vulnerable pupils are not self-aware enough to even be in a place to control themselves - never mind reflect on why they do what they do.

Dan writes: I would add that even if and when a pupil is being manipulative, the core question is why. Most likely his manipulation is a survival skill - he has no experience with adults who notice his needs and requests and put his needs first. The only way to survive was to manipulate adults to give him what he needed. None of us need to manipulate if we feel safe enough to ask directly and have confidence that our request will be met with warmth and respect. Our vulnerable pupil most likely doesn't trust that his educators will be any different from the adults he knew in the past. Our work is to show him that we are different.

Louise writes: Yes, this reminds us how hard it is for these pupils to trust the grown ups. As the adults supporting them, we need to be constantly coming up with strategies that support the development of this trust. Dan and I have been exploring this 'ask' throughout our book.

MYTH 16

Louise writes: Well, sometimes pupils do do this intentionally - even securely attached pupils. However, troubled pupils may be doing so as a way of communicating distress. So we would argue that *we cannot assume that this is necessarily intentional behaviour* on the part of the pupil. We would argue that there is often something else being communicated. Just because our lessons are at the forefront of our own minds doesn't meant that they are at the forefront of a vulnerable pupil's mind. They are all too often struggling and preoccupied with other more dominant matters, such as their lack of safety, security and stability.

Much of the rage and anger that we see is fuelled by fear and shame: we're often distracted away from the root of the problem by the presenting behaviours. Let's become more curious as to why a pupil might be doing what they do. Our curiosity will lead us on a journey that will open up opportunities for change. Judgment closes down possibilities.

> *These pupils are out to disrupt my lessons*

MYTH 17

Louise writes: Really? Surely they need to learn that adults can be gentle, strong and kind this time round? Wouldn't we want to be certain that we were behaving

> *They need to learn that I'm the boss!*

like this? Our pupils need to learn that adults can be present, attentive, attuned and responsive to pupils' needs, especially if their needs have been previously overlooked and compromised. Our vulnerable pupils have often been abused and neglected, and so they need a very different message. They have usually had more than their fair share of power being used and misused over them by adults. They need a very different experience: an experience of warmth and compassion, not more power and control. Let's remember what's lacking: it will guide us in how to relate well to troubled pupils. They will remember novel experiences, not repeats of the same: so this time around, let's give them a healthy experience to remember.

Dan writes: Yes, they need to learn that the best relationships of any sort are based on reciprocal influences and interest, not power and control. Speaking openly with each other and listening to the other's perspective is the best way to make an impact on pupils.

MYTH 18

Louise writes: As school is such a large system, policies are necessary. There are so many pupils to oversee and whole school policies can prove very helpful in ensuring consistent practice. However, there do need to be some exceptions,

> *They need to follow the behaviour policy. There can be no exceptions*

as there will always be a few who do not fit within the main. Not all of us are text book cases. We are human beings, and with humanity comes difference and diversity. Many of the pupils we are focusing on in this book are *not* ready to follow our whole school behaviour policies - *yet*. They don't have the capacity for this - *yet*. They need individual development plans created as a match to their emotional and social ages, with their development history taken into account. We need to honour difference if we are to be truly inclusive. Inclusivity implies allowing for and making exceptions for difference. We cannot promise 'the same', but we can make a promise that pupils will receive what they need.

MYTH 19

Louise writes: By stating that consequences must always follow actions we are implying that the cause and effect part of our pupils' brains is online and functioning very well. How can they make the most of

> *They need to realise the consequences of their actions. That's where rewards and sanctions come in*

all our external controls when part of their brains lie under-developed and not even switched on yet? We are going to have to make the connections on their behalf for a while longer, before they can do this unaided. A lot of repetition is needed. *Our interventions need to be primarily relational, not behaviourist.*

Dan writes: Only a small area in the part of the brain that focuses on social and emotional learning is devoted to learning through rewards and punishments. The larger area is devoted to sharing experience with other people, empathy, and understanding the mind of another person. When we are able to utilise these other regions of our pre-frontal cortex - and so develop deeply safe, meaningful, and reciprocal relationships with our pupils, then the consequences that we give them in response to their behaviours will be much more effective.

MYTH 20

Louise writes: When we feel overwhelmed ourselves, many of us don't see any problem with communicating this loud and clear to the pupils in our care. Over the years we've been encouraged to communicate clearly, as we were told that others would then back down on understanding our points of view, if we communicated them clearly enough. Oh my! We don't fight fire with fire! We fight fire with water! (Rob Long, 2013) If we do vent our rage in this way, we'll increase the level of terror in our vulnerable pupil. Where there is terror, there is going to be disturbance. We mustn't lose control, raise our voices or become hysterical. We need to be careful not to collude with the pupil's unconscious patterns, despite our own feelings being very powerful and at times overwhelming. If this is how you are feeling, this is probably a sign that you need support. Don't give up until you get some!

> *I will show the pupil how angry I am with him. Then he will get it*

MYTH 21

Louise writes: By using individual support programmes and interventions the class will start to learn the invaluable lesson that we are all different. The earlier they discover this, the better! We all have different strengths and vulnerabilities. We all have different family situations and experiences. We all have different responses, based on our internal working models. If our school has signed up to being inclusive, then this is what we have to be. We are all equal but we are not the same. Let's not scorn or avoid difference and diversity - let's celebrate them. What a different place our communities would be, if we truly worked on this within education!

> *One pupil being treated differently will have a negative impact on the class*

Dan writes: Yes, let's give children credit for knowing that each pupil is different and each one deserves a programme that has been developed for the uniqueness of that pupil. Siblings at home know that. They may fuss about it at times, but they trust the motives of their parents to do what is best for each child in the family. The same can be true at school. When pupils know and trust the motives of their educators to address the unique needs of the vulnerable pupils, they will feel safer in the knowledge that their unique needs will be met too.

Appendix

Individual development plan

NAME _____	CLASS _____
PUPIL TEAM	
FUN ACTIVITIES ENJOYED IN AND OUTSIDE OF SCHOOL	
AFFIRMATION PLAN	
BUILDING RESILIENCE 1:1 TIME	
IDENTIFIED STRESS TRIGGERS	
STRESS PRESENTATION	

SENSORY BREAKS BEING USED	
FREQUENCY OF SENSORY BREAKS	
FREQUENCY OF SAFESPACE	
WHOLE STAFF RESPONSIBILITIES	
KA SPECIFIC RESPONSIBILITIES	
OVERWHELM PLAN	
TEAM REFLECTIONS	

FACTFILE

for vulnerable pupil: _____

_____

CONFIDENTIAL

(only to be read on a need to know basis by the small educational team around the pupil (Key Adult, Class Teacher, SENCO/INCO, Head Of Year/ Headteacher). Please store in confidential filing cabinet)

Do not leave out

Relational traumas and losses experienced:

*
*
*

Main Triggers known:

*
*
*

Strategies known to bring pupil back to calm/being regulated

*
*
*

The information above will be passed on each year within this school unless informed otherwise.

Parent/Carer: _____

Date: _____

Parent/Carer: _____

Date: _____

Social Worker: _____

Date: _____

Attachment Lead Teacher: _____

Date: _____

HOME/SCHOOL PARTNERSHIP WEE

Name of child/young person

_____

Year: _____

Areas of strengths this past week:

*
*
*

Areas of vulnerability this past week:

*
*
*

Any identified stress triggers:

*
*
*

What supported this child/young person back to being grounded/calm or more focused again:

*
*
*

Any possible stress triggers this coming week?

*
*
*

Signed : _____

Date: _____

Home/Scho

References

Batmanghelidjh, C. (2006) *Shattered Lives* Jessica Kingsley Publishers: London & Philadelphia

Batmanghelidjh, C. (2009) Terrorised and terrorising teenagers - the search for attachment and hope *in, Teenagers and Attachment: Helping adolescents engage with life and learning* edited by A. Perry 2009 Worth Publishing: London

Bhreathnach, E. (2012) *Sensory Processing, Attachment and the Learning Process: A sensory-attachment intervention perspective* http://sensoryattachmentintervention.com/Home.aspx

Bombèr, L. (2007) *Inside I'm Hurting: Practical strategies for supporting children with attachment difficulties in school* Worth Publishing: London

Bombèr, L. (2011) *What About Me? Inclusive strategies to support pupils with attachment difficulties make it through the school day* Worth Publishing: London

Booth, P. & Jernberg, A. (2009) *Theraplay: Helping parents and children build better relationships through attachment based play* Jossey Bass: US

Bowlby, J. (1980) *Attachment and Loss, Vol 3: Loss: Sadness and depression* Hogarth Press: London

Bretherton, I. & Munholland, K. A. Internal working models in attachment relationships *in, Handbook of Attachment Theory, Research & Clinical Applications* edited by J. Cassidy and P. R. Shaver 1999 The Guilford Press: New York

Cozolino, L. (2009) *The Neuroscience of Human Relationships: Attachment and the developing social brain* W.W. Norton: New York

Department for Children, Schools and Families (2009) *The Role and Responsibilities of the Designated Teacher for Looked After Children: Statutory guidance for school governing bodies* DCSF Publications: Nottingham

Dunn, J. (1988) *The beginnings of social understanding* Basil Blackwell: Oxford

Forbes, H. T. & Post, B. B. (2006) *Beyond Consequences, Logic and Control: A love-based approach to helping children with severe behaviours* Beyond Consequences Institute, LLC, Orlando, FL

Geddes, H. (2006) *Attachment in the Classroom: The links between children's early experience, emotional well-being and performance in school* Worth Publishing: London

Gerhardt, S. (2004) *Why Love Matters: How affection shapes a baby's brain* Brunner Routledge: Sussex

Gerhardt, S. (2010) *The Selfish Society: How we all forgot to love one another and made money instead* Simon & Schuster UK Ltd: London

Gilligan, R. (2009) *Promoting Resilience: Supporting children and young people who are in care, adopted or in need* (2nd Rvd Edn) BAAF: London

Golding, K. & Hughes, D. (2012) *Creating Loving Attachments: Parenting with PACE to nurture confidence and security in the troubled child* Jessica Kingsley Publishers: London & Philadelphia

Gott, S. (2011) *Teach to Inspire Better Behaviour* Speechmark Publishing: Bicester, Oxon

Gruwell, E. & The Freedom Writers (1999) *The Freedom Writers Diary: How a teacher and 150 teens used writing to change themselves and the world around them* Broadway Books: New York

Harris, B. (2008) Befriending the two headed monster:personal, social & emotional development in schools in challenging times *British Journal of Guidance & Counselling,* 36(4): 367-383

Harris, B. (2010) Reclaiming the radical legacy of Gestalt in contemporary educational practice *British Gestalt Journal* 19(1): 19-25

Howe, D. (2005) *Child Abuse and Neglect: Attachment, Development and Intervention* Palgrave Macmillan: Basingstoke

Howe, D. (2011) *Child Abuse and Neglect Conference* University of East Anglia: Norwich 22/1/2011

Hughes, D. (2006) *Building the Bonds of Attachment* 2nd Ed. Jason Aronson: Northvale, NJ

Hughes, D. (2009) *Attachment-Focused Parenting* W.W.Norton: New York

Hughes, D. (2011) *Attachment-Focused Family Therapy Workbook* W.W.Norton: New York

Hughes, D. & Baylin, J. (2012a) *Brain-based Parenting: The neuroscience of caregiving for healthy attachment* W.W. Norton: New York

Hughes, D. (2012b) *It Was That One Moment: Dan Hughes' poetry and reflections on a life of making relationships with children and young people* Worth Publishing: London

Kaufman, G. (1996) *The Psychology of Shame* Springer Publishing: California

Levine, P. (1996) *Waking the Tiger: Healing trauma* North Atlantic Books: California

Lewicki, R. J. (2003) *Essentials of Negotiation* McGraw Hill: New York

Luke, N., & Banerjee, R. (2012, September) Socio emotional outcomes for maltreated children: The role of empathy and social understanding *in, N. Luke & R. Banerjee (Chairs), Social and developmental processes in vulnerable populations of children and young people. Symposium conducted at the meeting of the British Psychological Society Developmental Section* Strathclyde University: Glasgow

Luke, N., & Banerjee, R. (2012) Maltreated children's social understanding and empathy: a preliminary exploration of foster carers' perspectives. *Journal of Child and Family Studies* 21(2): 237-246

Luke, N., & Banerjee, R. (2013) Differentiated associations between childhood maltreatment experiences and social understanding: a meta-analysis and systematic review *Developmental Review* 33(1): 1-28

Panksepp, J. & Biven, L. (2012) *The Archaeology of Mind: Neuro-evolutionary origins of human emotions* W.W.Norton: New York

Perry, A. (Ed.) (2009) *Teenagers and Attachment: Helping adolescents engage with life and learning* Worth Publishing: London

Pollak, S. D. & Tolley-Schell, S. A. (2003) Selective attention to facial expression in physically abused children *Journal of Abnormal Psychology.* 112, 323-338

Porges, S. (2011) *The Polyvagal Theory: Neurophysiological foundations of emotions, attachment, communication and self-regulation* W.W.Norton: New York

Riley, P. (2010) *Attachment Theory and the Teacher-Student Relationship: A practical guide for teachers, teacher-educators and school leaders* Taylor & Francis: London

Robinson, K. (2010) *The Element: How finding passion changes everything* Penguin Books: London

Rygaard, N. P. (2010) Designing the Fair Start Project - a free e-learning and organizational development program for orphanages and foster families in quality care giving *Clinical Neuropsychiatry* (2010)7,6,181-187

Schofield, G. et al (2012) *Looked After Children and Offending: Reducing Risk and Promoting Resilience* University of East Anglia: Norwich, & TACT Fostering and Adoption

Schore, A. N. (1994) *Affect Regulation and the Origin of the Self: The neurobiology of emotional development* Lawrence Erlbaum Associates: New York

Shemmings D. & Shemmings Y. (2011) *Understanding Disorganized Attachment: Theory and practice for working with adults and children* Jessica Kingsley Publishers: London & Philadelphia

Siegel, D. (1999) *The Developing Mind* Guilford Press: New York

Siegel, D. (2012) *The Developing Mind: Second Edition* Guilford Press: New York

Sroufe, L.A., Egeland, B., Carlson, E.A. & Collins, W.A. (2005) *The Development of the Person* Guilford: New York

Szalavitz, M. & Perry, B. D. (2010) *Born For Love: Why empathy is essential - and endangered* Harper Collins Publishers: New York

Tangney, J. & Dearing, R. (2002) *Shame and Guilt* Guilford Press: New York

Taransaud, D. (2011) *You think I'm Evil: Practical strategies for working with aggressive and rebellious adolescents* Worth Publishing: London

Taylor, C. (2010) *Caring for Children and Teenagers with Attachment Difficulties* Jessica Kingsley Publishers: London

Tough, P. (2012) *How Children Succeed: Grit, curiosity, and the hidden power of character* Mariner Books: Wilmington, MA

Tronick, E. (2007) *The Neurobehavioral and Social-Emotional Development of Infants and Children* W.W. Norton: New York

Van der Kolk, B. (1996) *Traumatic Stress: The effects of overwhelming experience on mind, body, and society* Guildford Press: New York

Wilkinson, R. & Pickett, K. (2010) *The Spirit Level: Why equality is better for everyone* Penguin Books Ltd: London

Young Minds (2012) *Improving the Mental Health of Looked After Young People: An exploration of mental health stigma*

Index